Ontology and Perversion

Futures of the Archive: Theory, Criticism, Crisis

Series Editors: Arthur Bradley and Simon Swift

What will be the future of critical theory's past? This series offers a set of radical interdisciplinary interventions which explore how the history of critical theory can contribute to an understanding of the contemporary. By returning to classic critical debates in philosophy, politics, aesthetics, religion and more, the volumes in this series seek to provide a new insight into the crises of our present moment: capitalism, revolution, biopolitics, human rights, the anthropocene. In this way, Futures of the Archive shows that the past – and in particular critical theory's own past – is not a dead letter, but an archive to which we still belong and which continues to shape our present and future.

Titles in the Series

The Labour of Subjectivity: Foucault on Biopolitics, Economy, Critique, by Andrea Rossi

The Aesthetics of Violence: Art, Fiction, Drama and Film, by Robert Appelbaum

Ontology and Perversion: Deleuze, Agamben, Lacan, by Boštjan Nedoh

Ontology and Perversion

Deleuze, Agamben, Lacan

Boštjan Nedoh

ROWMAN &
LITTLEFIELD
INTERNATIONAL

London • New York

Published by Rowman & Littlefield International, Ltd.
6 Tinworth Street, London SE11 5AL
www.rowmaninternational.com

Rowman & Littlefield International, Ltd. is an affiliate of
Rowman & Littlefield
4501 Forbes Boulevard, Suite 200, Lanham, Maryland 20706, USA
With additional offices in Boulder, New York, Toronto (Canada), and London (UK)
www.rowman.com

British Library Cataloguing in Publication Information
A catalogue record for this book is available from the British Library

ISBN: HB 978-1-78660-551-1

Library of Congress Cataloging-in-Publication Data

Names: Nedoh, Boštjan , author.
Title: Ontology and perversion : Deleuze, Agamben, Lacan /Boštjan Nedoh.
Description: Lanham : Rowman & Littlefield International, 2019. | Series: Futures of the archive : theory, criticism, crisis | Includes bibliographical references and index.
Identifiers: LCCN 2019005530| ISBN 9781786605511 (cloth) | ISBN 9781786605528 (electronic)
Subjects: LCSH: Ontology. | Deviant behavior. | Theater--Philosophy. | Deleuze, Gilles, 1925-1995. | Agamben, Giorgio, 1942- | Lacan, Jacques, 1901-1981.
Classification: LCC BD331 .N345 2019 | DDC 110--dc23
LC record available at https://lccn.loc.gov/2019005530

For Jerneja

Contents

Acknowledgements

The research in this book is a result of the research programme P6-0014 'Conditions and Problems of Contemporary Philosophy' and the research project J6-9392 'The Problem of Objectivity and Fiction in Contemporary Philosophy' which are funded by the Slovenian Research Agency.

Some parts of this book were originally published elsewhere: portions of chapter 5 and chapter 6 were originally published as 'Messianism between Religion and Post-Religion: On Giorgio Agamben's "New Politics"', *Journal for Cultural Research* 19, no. 4 (2015): 337–51, published online 8 May 2015, https://www.tandfonline.com/doi/abs/10.1080/14797585.2015.1033842; portions of chapter 7 were originally published as parts of the chapter 'Biopolitics Before Foucault: On Benjamin's Critique of Bare Life and Agamben's Theological Genealogy of the Apparatus', in *Routledge Handbook of Biopolitics*, ed. Sergei Prozorov and Simona Rentea (London: Routledge, 2016), 66–77; portions of chapter 8 were published as 'Alive or Undead? Biopolitics between Esposito's Vitalism and Lacanian Psychoanalysis', *Paragraph: A Journal of Modern Critical Thought* 39, no. 1 (2016): 65–81; and portions of chapter 10 were published as 'Does the Body without Organs Have Any Sex at All? Lacan and Deleuze on Perversion and Sexual Difference', in *Lacan and Deleuze: A Disjunctive Synthesis*, ed. Boštjan Nedoh and Andreja Zevnik (Edinburgh: Edinburgh University Press, 2017), 44–55.

On this particular occasion, I would like to express my sincere gratitude to several persons for their invaluable support of my work without which this book would never have come to the light of day. First, I would like to thank my former supervisor, my dear friend and colleague at the Institute of Philosophy Peter Klepec, who has continuously supported my career and encouraged me in many difficult moments while also assisting me with invaluable comments on the early draft of this monograph. In the same context, I would also like to thank Rado Riha, the head of the Institute of Philosophy, and Oto Luthar, the director of the Research Centre of the Slovenian Academy of Sciences and Arts, for the best possible working conditions and the friendly environment I have at the institute.

My sincere thanks also go to other colleagues and friends who supported me in many different ways (the order is random and I sincerely apologise to those not listed, but it would be impossible to list you all): Lorenzo Chiesa, Adrian Johnston, Alenka Zupančič, Mladen Dolar, Giovanni Bettini, Marco Piasentier, Davide Tarizzo, Simona Rentea, Sergei Prozorov, Martin Coward, Japhy Wilson, Mick Dillon, Scott Wilson, Gorazd Kovačič, Amelia Kreigher, Jana Šimenc, Martin Pogačar, Borut Telban, Marina Lukšič-Hacin, Aleš Bučar-Ručman, Samo Tomšič, Rok Benčin, Tadej Troha, Aleš Bunta, Lea Kuhar, Matej Ažman, Ciril Oberstar, Sabina Autor, and many others.

Distinct thanks go to my best friend Andreja Zevnik for her personal support and friendly collaboration on many different projects and for many inspiring, productive, and even polemical conversations we had in the past fifteen years!

Very special thanks go to my dear friend and colleague Arthur Bradley, the co-editor of the *Futures of the Archive* book series (with Simon Swift, to whom I'm also grateful), who not only assisted me with invaluable suggestions and encouraged me in the process of writing this book but also expressed his strongest support of my entire work throughout these years. I'm deeply indebted to him.

Special thanks also go to Sarah Campbell, Frankie Mace, Emily Eastridge, and Rebecca Anastasi of Rowman & Littlefield International and to the whole editorial and production team that made this book possible.

I would like to sincerely thank my family: my parents Bojan and Nives Nedoh, my brother Martin Nedoh, my late grandpas Albin Nedoh and Ivan Mahnič, my grandmas Ana Nedoh and Roža Mahnič, and my parents-in-law Vili and Marija Brumen.

Lastly and most importantly, I cannot express enough my gratitude to my son Oskar Nedoh and to my wife Jerneja Brumen for their patience and unconditional support of everything I'm doing. You are my greatest joy!

Preface

This book is not about perversion in general and far less about perversion as a mere sexual or cultural phenomenon; its purpose is not to present any kind of 'overview' of how perversion was perceived within the wider context of intellectual history either. To the contrary, this book is primarily about the role and place perversion has in some parts of contemporary philosophy and psychoanalysis, and above all it seeks to discuss the implications that perversion had and continues to have on these intellectual enterprises. More specifically, this book addresses the impact that perversion may have on what one could call 'critical ontologies' in contemporary philosophy and psychoanalysis. With this expression, I'm thinking of some philosophical and psychoanalytical attempts, developed in the second half of the twentieth century, to advance a critique of classical ontology and metaphysics. Such attempts can arguably be traced via three main figures or signatures from the intellectual history of the second half of twentieth-century intellectual history and through their respective theoretical projects: (1) Gilles Deleuze's philosophical project of transcendental empiricism and the ontology of immanence; (2) Giorgio Agamben's critique of metaphysics and genealogy of political and economic theology; and (3) Jacques Lacan's psychoanalytic critique of classical ontology. Yet unlike the main current in contemporary analytic philosophy, which tries to completely dismiss ontology as such, these three critical approaches to ontology do not end up simply refusing ontology but rather advance alternative ways of thinking ontology anew. Furthermore, although these three theoretical projects can be subsumed under the common framework of 'critical ontologies', this by no means implies their overall homogeneity. On the contrary, as this book will try to demonstrate, there are many crucial differences that can be delineated, especially between, on the one hand, Deleuze's and Agamben's vitalist critique of classical metaphysics, and, on the other, Lacan's structuralist or poststructuralist critique of ontology. And although perversion is certainly not the exclusive object of interest for these three theoretical giants, it cannot be dismissed as a marginal issue either. This book will try to show how perversion can function precisely as one of the most plausible keys for understanding the difference between these two critical approaches to ontology.

To sum up briefly, we can put the argument of this book as follows: presuming that culture and politics rely upon certain ontological presuppositions that are shaped in both implicit and explicit social norms and conventions—what Hegel had called *sittliche Substanz*—perversions usually appear as something that violates these norms which are supposed to regulate the functioning of social substance. In slightly different words, perversions are usually considered precisely as those phenomena which should be denied access to the realm of social being. Take, for instance, the phenomenon of exhibitionism which at the most superficial level consists in unveiling the most intimate parts of the body: if exhibitionism is 'problematic' from the point of view of hegemonic conservative cultural discourse, it is thus precisely because the exhibitionist tries to orient the gaze of the Other (that is, of the culture) to the point where, according to social norms, the gaze should be removed. However, this book will try not to simply 'return the gaze' back on the phenomena of perversions—this strategy has already been enacted by many authors in contemporary continental thought—but will instead try to estimate the consequences of this return enacted by Deleuze, Agamben, and Lacan. In other words, the present book attempts to highlight the impact this return of the gaze on perversion has for the aforementioned critical approaches to ontology. Its goal is therefore to fill a specific theoretical gap, which concerns the peculiar relationship between ontology and perversion: What can be said about the being that dresses in fur or wears high heels? What is the ontological status of social substance once it becomes staged in a theatre of masks, fetishes, when it simulates all the time, thus misleading the audience in its judgement of reality? What is true and what false; what does exist and what does not?

Deleuze and Lacan articulated their respective positions in relation to this question in a kind of 'esoteric' debate[1] in which perversion, indeed, plays anything but a marginal role. In contrast with predominant conceptions of the relation between these two thinkers, their respective understandings of perversion and ontology differ much less than is usually assumed. Yet they still differ. To anticipate briefly the basic thesis of this book, the difference between Lacan's and Deleuze's respective takes on perversion is epitomised already in the homophony of the word 'perversion' in French, which also means, as Lacan put it, *père-version*—*"a call to the father"*[2] or even, literally, a version of the father (*père*). If Deleuze, in his notorious anti-paternal and anti-Oedipal approach, understood masochism as a transfer of symbolic power to the mother, Lacan answered this gesture by claiming that perversion is actually *père-version*, that is, a 'turning to the father' or a version of the father, so as the woman *qua* mother is just another name-of-the-father. This difference might seem trivial or marginal, but it ultimately condenses the very difference this book will try to argue for: the difference between a vitalist ontology *without* the Other (Deleuze, Agamben) and a psychoanalytic sexuated ontology *with* the barred Other (Lacan), that is, the symbolic Other which is, however, essentially characterised by the lack of the one (first) signifier that constitutes the point of ontological negativity that is immanent to the symbolic as such.

***

This book is structured along three axes which correspond to the three main figures who will be discussed. Although from a historical perspective one might assume that the Freudian account of perversion was the first and was only afterwards (critically) appropriated by philosophy (Deleuze and Agamben), this actually holds only in part. In fact, while Lacan can be seen as a continuation of Freud, Deleuze's discussion of masochism sets Sade and Masoch well before Freud, who is brought into play only at the end of the essay 'Coldness and Cruelty'. This is one of the reasons why this book is divided into four main parts: in this manner, it will provide both an analysis of the position that perversion takes in three philosophical projects, those of Deleuze, Agamben, and Lacan respectively, while at the same time these three accounts of perversion will be put in constant dialogue with each other, which will allow us to emphasise the similarities and differences between them. After an introductory part (chapter 1) which offers a condensed trajectory of the book and exposes the main argument, part II will focus on the articulation and the role perversion has in Deleuze's ontological project of transcendental empiricism and the ontology of immanence. Specifically, chapter 2 explores Deleuze's figure of the simulacrum and the way the latter is employed as a means for the critical renewal of classical metaphysics which Deleuze, following Nietzsche, coins as a gesture of 'overturning Platonism'. Being not simply one copy among others, but a peculiar uncanny copy which suspends the metaphysical division between essence and appearance and the selection of pretenders, the simulacrum is the main figure of the divergent difference which constitutes the core of Deleuze's category of the univocity of being. Chapter 3 then estimates, following Alain Badiou's suggestion, to what extent and how precisely the figure of Masoch can be regarded as a 'case-for-thought' or 'the-name-of-being'. In fact, Masoch's writings on masochism open up the space for an articulation which sees masochism as divergent from the sadism to which it was attached for a long time. In other words, what Masoch performs is the operation of the detachment of masochism from sadism, thus creating the divergent difference which Deleuze attributes to the figure of the simulacrum. Chapter 4 then completes this picture by focusing on Deleuze's revision of masochism in *A Thousand Plateaus*. This revision takes a hostile stance towards pleasure which is now seen not as compatible with desire but as an external intruder to the 'field of immanence' or 'plan of consistency'. Additionally, it will be argued that this view actually corresponds to the reversal of the Freudian relation between fore-pleasure and end-pleasure, so that the former takes the position of the latter: the imperative of the Tao masochist, in contrast to Masoch, is to violently oppose the moment of end-pleasure by way of constantly delaying it to infinity.

Part III then moves on to discuss perversion in Agamben's book *Stanzas* (1977) and his critique of what he calls the 'metaphysics of signification'. Additionally, it is argued that the place of perversion in Agamben's early critique of the metaphysics of signification also has deep implications for his later *Homo Sacer* project. Chapter 5 provides first the context of Agamben's 'esoteric' criticism of Derrida's deconstruction, which he associates in a second step with the Freudian conception of psychoanalysis as a technique for the translation of the unconscious latent content into a manifest word. Agamben accompanies this conception by means of the ancient difference between the enigmatic speech of the Sphinx and the Oedipal deciphering of that enigma. While this Oedipal or psychoanalytical deciphering is seen by Agamben as the metaphysical operation *par excellence,* because it introduces a relation between the latent level of the unconscious content and the level of the manifest word, the speech of the Sphinx is associated precisely with the perverse fetishist's disavowal, which appropriates the unconscious content without bringing it into consciousness, or without truly appropriating it by the subject. Relatedly, chapter 6 focuses on how Agamben's early praise of perversion is mirrored in his later conception of messianic time, where Agamben doesn't refer to perversion at all. It is shown that not only is Agamben's own definition of messianic time as 'the time that remains' before the end of time in complete accordance with the 'freezing' of the image in the constitution of the fetish but also that, following this argument, perversion represents the very short circuit for Agamben's understanding of the messianic event. In fact, the fetishistic structure of messianic time means that the messianic event in which religion overcomes itself is extended to infinity, so that this self-overcoming cannot ever be actually accomplished. In chapter 7, the book deals with the position perversion takes in Agamben's *Homo Sacer* project. A detailed analysis of some crucial passages from Agamben's *Homo Sacer: Sovereign Power and Bare Life,* where he declares Sade's pamphlet 'Make More of an Effort, Frenchmen, If You Want to Be Republicans' to be 'the first and perhaps most radical biopolitical manifesto of modernity',[3] reveals Agamben's indebtedness to Deleuze's insights into the dynamic and exceptional character of Sadean institutions (as opposed to the law). However, the parallels do not stop here because Deleuze and Agamben's shared reference to Sabbatai Zevi's messianic movement from the seventeenth century also reads Zevi as a figure who opposes the sadistic biopolitical state of exception.

Finally, part IV completes the circle by outlining significant differences between the ways Deleuze and Agamben position perversion and especially masochism and the way Freudian and Lacanian psychoanalysis likewise deals with this clinical structure. While to some extent one could argue there are many similarities between psychoanalytic (Freud,

Lacan) and vitalist (Deleuze, Agamben) understandings of perversion, there are also some important differences. If psychoanalysis may agree that in some sense perversion can also be regarded as non-Oedipal, which is the way Deleuze and Agamben read the concept, psychoanalysis nevertheless introduces the third dimension which Miller grasps with his distinction between pre-Oedipal and pre-linguistic level. As chapter 8 argues, the Freudian drive, though pre-Oedipal, is not pre-linguistic because it is shaped by the hole of primal repression (the repression of the first signifier which, as Alenka Zupančič argued many times, was never conscious and exists only as constitutively lacking). The 'hole' of primal repression is not simply a repressed content but tantamount to an ontological negativity set up by the gap of the unconscious. By focusing on the repressed content instead of on the gap itself, perversion disavows this gap by way of transcendentalising it, that is, by way of a direct identification with the object *a* or enjoyment. This point is shown in detail in chapter 9 in relation to Christianity and the baroque perversion which Lacan discusses in his Seminar XX, while chapter 10 further develops the dissociation of the death drive from the superego, arguing, contrary to Miller's thesis, that perversion is in fact not the norm of the drive but is rather associated with the logic of the superego. In short, the drive is indifferent to *jouissance* and, following Alenka Zupančič, is only the materialisation of the ontological negativity established by the gap of the unconscious, whereas the only instance in which the sadistic manner imposes the imperative of satisfaction or *jouissance* is in fact the superego. Finally, the conclusion sums up the main arguments of the book.

NOTES

1. For the very ambiguous relation between Lacan and Deleuze and for how it was mirrored in their respective theoretical frameworks, see Peter Klepec, 'For Another Lacan–Deleuze Encounter', in *Lacan and Deleuze: A Disjunctive Synthesis*, ed. Boštjan Nedoh and Andreja Zevnik (Edinburgh: Edinburgh University Press, 2017), 13–31.
2. Jacques-Alain Miller, 'On Perversion', in *Reading Seminars I and II: Lacan's Return to Freud*, ed. Richard Feldstein, Bruce Fink, and Maire Jaanus (New York: State University of New York Press, 1996), 308.
3. Giorgio Agamben, *Homo Sacer: Sovereign Power and Bare Life*, trans. Daniel Heller-Roazen (Stanford: Stanford University Press, 1998), 134.

Part I

Introductory:
Perversion as a Theatre of Being

ONE

Perversions and Critical Ontologies

Ontologysing Perversion, Perverting Ontology in Deleuze, Agamben, and Lacan

I

Although perversion has been the subject of different philosophical accounts[1] for several decades now, it was treated by scholars mainly as a sexual or cultural phenomenon or as the means for social criticism at best. Both cultural and gender studies had often defended perversion against its most common understanding, according to which it is all about deviant and pathological sexual practices, that is, about clinical phenomena which deserve serious treatment. Moreover, where sadism and masochism are concerned, the request for healing derived from the assumed intolerable connection between pain and pleasure, which is supported by the deployment of multiple kinds of nonsexual instruments. The suspicious expression 'sadomasochism' which is still today widely used not only in ordinary everyday parlance but also in different theoretical analyses of perversion immediately evokes a certain kind of displeasure: How is it possible to enjoy pain? How is it possible that the victim seeks his or her own hangman, whereby this relationship between the victim and his or her hangman represents a kind of substitution for the sexual relationship?

However, the mere evocation of the problematic term 'sadomasochism' conceived as a kind of ideal synthesis of sadism and masochism entails another, much more important perspective: it reveals the origins of both attitudes because they originate in the literatures of Donatien Alphonse François Marquis de Sade and Leopold von Sacher-Masoch.

We are dealing here with two famous writers. In this respect, the birthplace of perversion is rather literature than the clinic or psychoanalysis. And yet as Deleuze writes in his famous essay 'Coldness and Cruelty', both Sade and Masoch are 'outstanding examples of the efficiency of literature'[2] insofar as each of the two presents 'unparalleled configurations of symptoms and signs'.[3] The 'efficiency of literature' therefore concerns less the transformation of literature itself than the change it introduces into the clinical understanding of perversion as the unity and ideal compatibility between sadism and masochism. According to Deleuze, sadism and masochism 'have been used to denote two basic perversions'[4] instead of one and only perversion in the singular which would consist in the unjustified term 'sadomasochism'. Not surprisingly, the whole account of Deleuze's essay is nothing but the deconstruction of the myth of sadomasochism understood as an ideal unity of both fundamental perversions. As he writes, 'Yet there is between sadism and masochism an irreducible dissymetry'.[5]

So far scholarship has paid little attention to the way Deleuze addresses the problem of the assumed sadomasochism. His approach can be observed already at the level of the Hegelian expressions that he uses in order to describe the problem: 'The theme of the unity of sadism and masochism and the concept of a sadomasochistic entity have done great harm to Masoch. He has suffered not only from unjust neglect but also from an unfair assumption of complementarity and *dialectical unity* with Sade'.[6] The anti-Hegelian tonality comes to the fore already at the terminological level. Yet Deleuze does not stop here. In fact, moving from these premises, he immediately proceeds by putting forward an essentially *anti-dialectical* epistemological statement of his essay, which consists primarily from 'questioning the very concept of an entity known as sadomasochism': 'In place of a dialectic which all too readily perceives the link between opposites, we should aim for a critical and clinical appraisal able to reveal *the truly differential mechanisms* as well as the artistic originalities'.[7]

As we see, Deleuze approaches Masoch and masochism quite with the same terms as he will substantially elaborate in his masterpiece of the next year *Difference and Repetition*: Masoch attracts Deleuze's interest precisely insofar as he invented a differential mechanism, that is, the mechanism of *divergent difference* which enabled him to detach himself from Sade, hence splitting up the presupposed sadomasochistic unity of the opposites.

Already these preliminary observations enable us to advance the following hypothesis: by searching for differential mechanisms, according to which Masoch diverges from Sade, Deleuze is not just simply applying one of his main ontological concepts, that is, the concept of difference, to the realm of perversion; in so doing, he also fully integrates the issue of perversion into his ontological project. From this perspective, perversion not only represents a subject for social criticism as it was for long understood but has itself direct implications for ontology in general, and particularly for social ontology. More specifically, according to Deleuze, masochism, insofar as it succeeds in diverging from sadism, implies its own kind of being or social ontological position rather than being simply excluded from being itself. If sadism has often been considered as a prototype of transgression, masochism can be thus considered as specifically subversive both with respect to sadism and to the social ontology the latter implies. In any case, for Deleuze, both fundamental perversions are important insofar as they introduce a kind of overturning or reversal into the ontological coordinates of classical ontology and metaphysics which Deleuze ultimately identifies with the Platonic division between the world of essence *and* the world of appearances.[8]

II

Deleuze published his essay 'Coldness and Cruelty' in 1967, a year before the publication of *Difference and Repetition* (1968) and two years before the appearance of *The Logic of Sense* (1969). If not simultaneously, the least we can say is that he wrote three of his most influential works in the same period and in the same intellectual milieu. Adding these historical notes to what we already said, we might say that Deleuze's interest in Masoch and Sade is inextricably connected with his ontological project which had been advanced according to 'how Nietzsche defined the task of his philosophy or, more generally, the task of the philosophy of the future': 'to reverse Platonism'.[9] What does it mean 'to reverse Platonism' and, subsequently, how does Deleuze's account with masochism fit into this project? To begin with, let's focus briefly on Deleuze's understanding of the aforementioned 'reversal'. Deleuze was well aware of the problem of the excessively abstract nature of this very task insofar as we could define 'philosophy at the limit as any attempt, regardless of its source, to reverse Platonism',[10] as Michel Foucault put it in his famous 1970s commentary on Deleuze's *Difference and Repetition* and *The Logic of Sense*.

In order to clarify how he understood the task of reversing Platonism, Deleuze emphasises that to achieve this reversal it does not suffice to contest directly the distinction between the world of essence and the world of appearances—the pair which constitutes the core of Plato's dialectic and his theory of Ideas; rather, the reversal of Platonism can be accomplished only by revealing and highlighting the motivation that lies behind Plato's dialectics: '"to reverse Platonism" must mean to bring this motivation out into the light of the day, to "track it down"'.[11] According to Deleuze, the motivation that generates Plato's dialectical procedure is 'a will to select and to choose'—this is why Plato's dialectics is based on the 'method of division': 'It is a question of "making a difference", of distinguishing the "thing" itself from its images, the original from the copy, the model from the simulacrum'.[12]

At first glance, the method of division generates two interrelated yet heterogeneous series: the thing itself—original—model; image—copy—simulacrum. Yet Deleuze's closer inspection reveals a specific divergence and inequality between elements ('But are all these expressions equivalent?'[13]): the short circuit appears between the copies and the simulacra insofar as the former are considered to be *true* whilst the latter are meant to be *false*. But the Platonic procedure does not stop here because, as Deleuze further argues, the 'purpose of division then is not at all to divide a genus into species, but, more profoundly, to select lineages: to distinguish pretenders; to distinguish the pure from the impure, the authentic from the inauthentic'.[14] This is why, Deleuze continues, 'the Platonic dialectic is neither a dialectic of contradiction nor of contrariety, but a dialectic of rivalry (*amphisbetesis*), a dialectic of rivals and suitors. The essence of division does not appear in its breadth, in the determination of the species of a genus, but in its depth, in the selection of the lineage. It is to screen the claims (*pretensions*) and to distinguish the true pretender from the false one'.[15] From this perspective, the selection of true pretenders which are allowed to participate in the Idea and therefore can obtain the status of being thus introduces a new series which in the history of philosophy is better known as *representation*.[16] The true copies derive from the model and function as its reproductive resemblance, while the model itself is also constituted by the myth. The relation between copies and the model is thus an internal relation of resemblance. This is why copies are considered as true and are therefore allowed to participate in the Idea. The simulacrum, in turn, is not just 'a copy of a copy' insofar as its relation to the model is only external. It does not participate in the lineage given by the myth which stands at the basis of the model. Hence, the simulacrum only externally imitates the model and this is why it is considered to be a false pretender. And insofar as it is a false pretender imitating the model, it implies nothing but the 'perversion' or subversion of the model, leading to its very dis-function. As Deleuze puts it, 'simulacra are like false pretenders, built upon a dissimilarity, implying an essential perversion or a deviation'.[17] This is why they are dismissed as false pretenders who should be expelled from the world of essence and subjected to overall repression. Deleuze continues: 'It is a question of assuring the triumph of the copies over simulacra, of repressing simulacra, keeping them completely submerged, preventing them from climbing to the surface, and "insinuating themselves" everywhere'.[18]

As we can observe, the Platonic model of the One, that is, the model of the identity between being and thought, is essentially based upon the violent exclusion of simulacra. Not surprisingly, Foucault described this model precisely as 'a model, that exists so forcefully that in its presence the sham vanity of the false copy is immediately reduced to nonexistence'.[19] The Platonic division between the world of the essence and the world of appearances has thus the ultimate purpose of eliminating the latter. Consequently, the only difference that is allowed to exist within this model is the difference which is subordinated to identity. Not the difference as such, but only the difference between two identities. The true difference, which is epitomised in the existence of simulacra as diverging elements, is indeed repressed and expelled from the realm of being.

This is why Deleuze doesn't stop at the point of merely highlighting the motivation of the Platonic procedure of selection. This is rather only one side of the reversal of Platonism. The other side consists, so to speak, in assigning being or the right to exist to the simulacra as the elements of heterogeneity and irregularity. In other words, the complete definition of the reversal of Platonism consists, according to Deleuze, also in recognising a positive power of simulacra, hence in the affirmation of the simulacra as being rather than nonbeing:

> So 'to reverse Platonism' means to make the simulacra rise and to affirm their rights among icons and copies. The problem no longer has to do with the distinction Essence-Appearance or Model-Copy. This distinction operates completely within the world of representation. Rather, it has to do with undertaking the subversion of this world—the 'twilling of the idols'. The simulacrum is not a degraded copy. It harbors a positive power which denies *the original and the copy, the model and the reproduction.* At least two divergent series are internalised in the simulacrum—neither can be assigned as the original, neither as the copy. It is not even enough to invoke a model of the Other, for no model can resist the vertigo of the simulacrum. There is no longer any privileged point of view except that of the object common to all points of view. There is no possible hierarchy, no second, no third. . . . In the reversal of Platonism, resemblance is said of internalised difference, and identity of the Different as primary power. The same and the similar no longer have an essence except as *simulated,* that is as expressing the functioning of the simulacrum. There is no longer any possible selection. The non-hierarchised work is a condensation of coexistences and a simultaneity of events. It is a triumph of the false pretender. It simulates at once the father, the pretender, and the fiancé in a superimposition of masks.[20]

Following Deleuze, this affirmation of the simulacra implies nothing but the disintegration of the division between the world of the essence and the world of the appearances. Now the former two worlds mingle in a single plane of immanence whereby the multiplicity of beings (simulacra) exist in their mutual 'resonance' which is how Deleuze defines the univocity of being.[21] Finally, this is the moment where the metaphysical opposition between true and false, between truth and lie is not operative any more. Rather, it is the false that achieves the status of the true. And as

Foucault had commented, this is the truly theatrical moment of the philosophy of Deleuze in which simulacrum, casting, fiction, fantasy, fetish, event, and mask become the figures of a philosophy conceived as a theatrical ontology of the univocity of being: 'This is philosophy not as thought but as theater'.[22]

And what is more theatrical, what is more a play of masks, than precisely fetishism which was considered by Freud as a privileged model of perversion;[23] fetishism which consists, in its basic disposition, of covering or masking not something but rather nothing—a lack of penis in woman.[24] However, unlike Freud's much more critical approach to fetishism which was later on advanced by Lacan, Deleuze is interested in this matter precisely insofar as fetishism has a subversive potential in relation to the socio-ontological coordinates of modern society which revolved around the family structure and the figure of the father. In other words, for Deleuze, fetishistic disavowal is not merely an ideological mechanism of reproduction of existing social bonds (as it was, for instance, for Marx), apparently based upon a conventional sexuality, but rather opens up the subversion of this structure and consequently for a new socio-ontological field. Deleuze's wager constantly relies upon a positive power of fetish which is a power of idealisation. This is the power, just to recall, which has the ability to devaluate the symbolic function of the father and transfer symbolic power to the figure of the mother. As he put it, 'There is a disavowal of the mother by magnifying her ("symbolically the mother lacks nothing") and a corresponding disavowal of the father by degrading him ("the father is nothing," in other words he is deprived of all symbolic function)'.[25] Perhaps this sentence best epitomises Deleuze's rereading of Freud: fetish is here conceived not just as a 'memorial' of castration[26] but as a positive and affirmative power which, by accepting castration directly, devalues its regulatory function; and by identifying with castration, the pervert makes of it a condition of possibility for access to what was prohibited. This access to the prohibited corresponds to the 'rebirth' of a masochist as of someone radically 'new': 'new Man devoid of sexual love'.[27]

It is clear enough from this point that Deleuze understood perversion as such, and especially the phenomena of masochism, precisely in terms of a new social ontology which relies upon the exclusion of castration and the abolishment of sexual difference. And he was indeed aware about the meaning this conception in the context of Freudian and Lacanian psychoanalysis: insofar as castration introduces the relation between the subject and the symbolic Other, perversion is meant precisely to be the exodus out of or, better yet, beyond this order of symbolic differences which revolves around castration and repression. Incidentally, Deleuze also assumed, although in my view wrongly, that this exclusion of the Other in perversion derives from Lacanian theory itself. As he writes,

> Lacan and his school insist profoundly . . . on the way in which the *difference of sexes* is disavowed by the pervert, in the interest of an androgynous world of *doubles*; on the annulment of the Other inside perversion, on the position of a 'beyond the Other' (*un au-delà de l'Autre*) or of an 'otherwise Other' (*un Autre qu'autrui*), as if the Other disengaged in the eyes of the pervert his own *metaphor*; finally, they insist on perverse 'desubjectivation'—for it is certain that neither the victim nor the accomplice function as Others . . . it is because the structure-Other is missing, and is replaced by a completely different structure, that the real 'others' are no longer able to play the role of terms actualising the lost primary structure. Real 'others' can only play now, in the second structure, the role of body-victims (in the very particular sense that the pervert attributes to bodies), or the role of accomplices-doubles, and accomplices-elements (again, in the very particular sense of the pervert). The world of the pervert is a world without Others, and thus a world without the possible.[28]

Considering that the Other is commonly conceived in psychoanalysis as the order of representation, it becomes clear that Deleuze regards perversion precisely to the extent that it advances a criticism of this order of representation by pointing to the socio-ontological position beyond the Other. Indeed, one of the main goals of all the 'Appendixes' to *The Logic of Sense* is to outline this peculiar conjunction between perversion and the reversal of Platonism. In this perspective, the affirmation of perverse heterogeneity and irregularity is inextricably connected with the process of becoming which, by means of simulation, overturns all fixed identities. In fact, becoming is the process which unties every self-identity of being; it overcomes all boundaries of the Self by pointing to something non-self-identical, hence to something collective and common. In this sense, becoming is a privileged category of 'transcendental empiricism' defined as an ontology of the sensible[29] which addresses the being of aesthetical intensity as the driving force behind every metamorphosis. This is what makes Deleuzian ontology always already a political ontology. Not surprisingly, Deleuze recognised in Masoch the same figure as he recognised also in Kafka and Melville: 'the bearer of a *collective enunciation*, which no longer forms part of literary history and preserves the rights of a people to come, or of a human becoming'.[30]

III

Unlike Deleuze, who had constant recourse to perversion throughout the majority of his works, Giorgio Agamben is certainly not a thinker of perversion in this sense. In his entire work, references to perversion are rather sporadic and rare. Yet there are some fundamental arguments which not only enable us to consider Agamben within the same line of thought as Deleuze when perversion is concerned but also somehow oblige us to do so. In fact, on the one hand, there are many common topics that open up a comparison between the two thinkers,[31] while, on the other hand, one of these topics is precisely perversion. Moreover, the position perversion takes in Agamben's work is rather similar to that in Deleuze's. In Agamben, we encounter a reference to perversion, for instance, at one of the most important points in his early works, the point which somehow anticipates and determines his later political philosophy of the *Homo Sacer* project. As Kevin Attell has convincingly argued,[32] Agamben's *Homo Sacer* project, which begins by arguing for the identity between biopolitics and the structure of the metaphysics—they both rely upon the operation of '"politicisation" of bare life' through its inclusive exclusion into the political realm[33]—should be read against the background of his earlier critique, unfolded in his 1977 book *Stanzas*,[34] of the 'metaphysics of signification' [*metafisica del significare*] and of semiology as its modern form. According to Agamben, classical metaphysics from Plato onwards had the violent tendency to unify the two worlds we already discussed earlier: the world of the essence and the world of the appearances. Yet in Agamben's perspective this unification is enacted by repressing and forgetting of the originary difference which divides the two worlds. This is the difference which in modern linguistics takes the form of the bar which irreducibly divides signifier and signified. As he put it,

> From the point of view of signification, metaphysics is nothing but the forgetting of the originary difference between signifier and signified. Every semiology that fails to ask why the barrier that establishes the possibility of signifying should itself be resistant to signification, falsifies, with that omission, its own most authentic intention. In Saussure's formula, 'the linguistic unity is double', the accent has been placed now on the pole of the signifier, now on that of the signified, without ever putting into question the paradox, insuperable for Saussure, that had testified on behalf of his own formulation.[35]

The paradox here concerns precisely the bar as a condition of possibility of signification, the bar which divides the signifier from the signified. Quite surprisingly, within this constellation Agamben assigns to the Freudian fetishistic disavowal the privileged role of revealing or making manifest—in the sense Heidegger gave to the Ancient Greek expression *aletheia*—the bar or originary difference which both linguistic metaphors and the theory of the sign conceal. As he argues,

> The *Verleugnung* [disavowal] presents us with a process in which, by means of a symbol, man succeeds in appropriating an unconscious content without bringing it to consciousness. . . . In this gesture of the fetishist, who succeeds in appropriating his own hidden treasure without unearthing it, the ancient apotropaic wisdom of the Sphinx, which repels by receiving and receives by repelling, once again comes to life.

> And just as the analyst can perhaps learn something from the pervert as far as pleasure is concerned, so too perhaps Oedipus can learn something from the Sphinx about symbols.[36]

In this context, it is worthwhile to further stress that Agamben understands his own criticism as one fixed on the 'orthodox conception of symbolism, and not at the Lacanian interpretation of Freud'.[37] According to him, the 'orthodox' or 'Freudian conception of symbolism' consists basically of an 'Oedipal' translating or deciphering of the repressed unconscious word into the conscious word which thus implies an appropriation of the unconscious content by bringing it *whole* into consciousness, yet leaving the bar untouched:

> The Oedipal interpretation of the speech of the Sphinx as a 'coded speech' secretly governs the Freudian conception of the symbol. Psychoanalysis in fact presupposes the splitting of discourse into an obscure speech by means of improper terms, based on repression (which is that of the unconscious), and into a clear speech of proper terms (which is that of consciousness). The passage ('the translation') from one discourse to the other properly constitutes analysis. This necessarily presupposes a process of 'desymbolisation' and of progressive reduction of the symbolic: the 'drying of the Zuider Zee,' which according to Freud substantiates the psychoanalytic process, is, once concluded, the equivalent of a complete translation of unconscious symbolic language into conscious sign. The myth of Oedipus therefore dominates the horizon of analysis in a manner much more profound than its critiques heretofore thought.[38]

For Agamben, this, in turn, implies the fundamentally anti-Oedipal and anti-Freudian nature of perversion in general, and particularly of fetishism, for he is convinced that fetishistic disavowal is that peculiar procedure which enables the appropriation of the unconscious material yet maintaining it 'unearthed', thus exposing the bar which divides the unconscious and the conscious. However, as we will try to show in this book in more detail, Agamben in this way nonetheless misreads precisely the most fundamental discovery of Freud's which Lacan later took over: the unconscious conceived not as a secret treasure but as a fundamental gap (the bar, perhaps, but a specific bar) in which not only is there no treasure at all but which even constitutes the very *mechanism* which generates the distinction between latent and manifest level. Instead what the fetishist misperceives as a secret treasure of the unconscious is precisely the fantasmatic construct which covers the empty space of the gap of the unconscious. From Lacan's perspective, the aim of analysis is thus not the complete translation of the unconscious material into the conscious content but rather the deduction of the gap of the unconscious which corresponds to a missing, rather than secret, signifier—a signifier, as Alenka Zupančič had argued already several times,[39] that is lacking already from the very beginning and which was never conscious nor was ever hidden in the unconscious as an existing word. To anticipate a little, this point of difference between, on the one hand, Deleuze and Agamben's and, on the other hand, Lacan's reading of the Freudian concept of fetishistic disavowal and, more generally, of perversion will constitute the key which will enable us to distinguish between two approaches to perversion as social ontology: vitalist and psychoanalytic.

However, because I will discuss this more in detail toward the end of this 'introduction', let's first turn back to the arguments which enable us to put Agamben and Deleuze in the same context where perversion is concerned. In fact, we can say that Agamben's general attraction to perversion is reflected in more detail in his later *Homo Sacer* project. As we will soon see, in this context similarities as well as differences between his and Deleuze's account of perversion come even more to the fore. Namely, another point of connection between the two philosophers is the so-called Kantian pure form of law. Both Agamben and Deleuze recognised the distinctive character of this central concept of Kantian ethics with respect to a pre-modern or ancient ethical tradition. According to Deleuze, Kantian moral law reverses the ancient asymmetric relation between Good and law in which the latter was subordinated to the determination of the former: 'The classical conception of the law found its perfect expression in Plato and in that form gained universal acceptance throughout the Christian world. According to this conception, the law may be viewed either in the light of its underlying or in the light of its consequences. From the first point of view, the law itself is not a primary but only a secondary or delegated power dependent on a supreme principle which is the Good'.[40] In other words, in the pre-modern ethical tradition, the ethical substance of community was governed by the principle of the Good. Living in accordance with this principle meant having the moral virtue. The law, in turn, could only function as an external expression of the form of life otherwise determined by the principle of the Good. This is why the law in ancient Greece was conceived only in the practical or empirical context of the multiplicity of particular laws, not as the law as such.

As has already been well documented throughout the history of modern philosophy, the Kantian concepts of moral law and of categorical imperative overthrew this conception. There are particularly two features in the Kantian conception of the law that are especially important in order to grasp this overthrowing: with Kant, the law becomes primary and cannot be delegated from the principle of Good; rather, the Good becomes the law itself. However, the law determines Good only formally, that is, the only thing that Kantian moral law prescribes is its form of universal validity—it is in force regardless of the specific content. As Deleuze describes this Kantian invention in very detail,

> In the *Critique of Practical Reason* Kant gave a rigorous formulation of a radically new conception, in which the law is no longer regarded as dependent on the Good, but on the contrary, the Good itself is made to depend on the law. This means that the law no longer has its foundation in some higher principle from which it would derive its authority, but that it is self-grounded and valid solely by the virtue of its own form. For the first time we can now speak of THE LAW, regarded as an absolute, without further specification or reference to an object. Whereas the classical conception only dealt with *the laws* according to the various spheres of the Good or the various circumstances attending the Best, Kant can speak of the moral law, and of its application to what otherwise remains totally undetermined. The moral law is the representation of a pure form and is independent of content or object, spheres of activity or circumstances. The moral law is THE LAW, the form of the law and as such it cannot be grounded in a higher principle. In this sense Kant is one of the first to break away from the classical conception of the law and to give us a truly modern conception.[41]

Indeed, according to Deleuze, there are two ways of subverting this radically new Kantian conception of law conceived as an empty form devoid of any positive content or object: on the one hand, Sade's ironic approach to law which is consistent with his invention of the dynamic institution meant to radicalise the principle of law and, on the other hand, Masoch's humorous approach which is consistent with his invention of the contract as the formal basis of masochistic relationship. The latter is meant precisely to be the means for bringing the consequences of the law as empty form at its most extreme limits, if not beyond. Yet these two reactions are quite unsymmetrical if, as Lacan pointed out in his famous essay 'Kant with Sade', Sade is not quite the opposite with respect to the Kantian ethics of moral law and the categorical imperative. Instead the former reveals the 'truth' of the latter: '*Philosophy in the Bedroom* came eight years after the *Critique of Practical Reason*. If, after showing that the former is consistent with the latter, I can demonstrate that the former completes the latter, I shall be able to claim that it yields the truth of the *Critique*'.[42]

What Lacan was aiming at with this consistency of Sade with Kant is precisely the following: as Alenka Zupančič has stressed, from the formal aspect, Kantian 'diabolical evil' which 'would occur if we were to elevate opposition to the moral law to the level of the maxim' and which Kant considers empirically impossible with Sade not only becomes possible but also fully corresponds or becomes indistinguishable from Kant's own definition of supreme good or moral law as empty form. As he puts it,

> 'Diabolical evil' would occur if we were to elevate opposition to the moral law to the level of the maxim. In this case the maxim would be opposed to the moral law not just 'negatively' (as it is in the case of radical evil), but *directly*. This would imply, for instance, that we would be ready to act contrary to the moral law even if this meant acting

> contrary to our self-interest and our well-being. We would make it a principle to act against the moral law, and we would stick to this principle no matter what (that is, even if it meant our own death). . . . Nothing can itself oppose to the moral law *on principle*—that is, for non-pathological reasons—without itself becoming a moral law. . . . Following Kant—but at the same time going against Kant [with Lacan]—we thus propose to assert explicitly that *diabolical evil, the highest evil, is indistinguishable from the highest good, and that they are nothing other than the definitions of an accomplished (ethical) act*. In other words, at the level of the structure of the ethical act, the difference between good and evil does not exist. At this level, evil is formally indistinguishable from the good.[43]

In this respect, Sade's *Philosophy in the Bedroom* is, perhaps, the purest example of diabolical evil precisely in the sense that it elevates transgression to the level of principle—even at the price of one's own death. However, as far as the abovementioned statement of Lacan is concerned, it would be wrong to consider Sade (a 'truth' of Kant) as a simple and direct degradation or devaluation of Kantian ethics. Instead, and in accordance with Deleuze's claim that both Sade and Masoch are first of all great symptomatologists, Sade's *Philosophy in the Bedroom* should be regarded above all as a successful attempt *to raise up sadism as a pathological phenomenon to the level of the (philosophical) concept*. In other words, due to Sade's work, we are able *to think* sadism as pathology instead of simply turning the gaze away from it.

Incidentally, in Agamben's *Homo Sacer* we can trace quite similar arguments concerning the relationship between Kant and Sade, although Agamben does not mention Lacan at all. On the one hand, when considering the paradox of Kafka's law as an empty form which is 'in force without significance',[44] Agamben stresses that this conception of law actually originates precisely in Kant's *Critique of Practical Reason* where it appears for the first time in modernity: 'In Kant the pure form of law as "being in force without significance" appears for the first time in modernity'.[45]According to Agamben, in Kant as well as in Kafka, the empty form of law, that is, the law 'reduced to the zero point of its significance,'[46] implies the fundamental position of the subject in relation to the law. This is a position of abandonment. Because the law doesn't prescribe anything except its own formal universal validity, the subject conceived in terms of a biological body, which is by definition always already pathological in Kantian sense, can be only excluded from the form of law, yet this exclusion is a paradoxical way of his simultaneous inclusion. And as has been already well documented, Agamben draws here an analogy between this position of the subject in Kant's empty form of law and the corresponding position of *homo sacer* that people occupied in the concentration camps: 'It is truly astounding how Kant, almost two centuries ago and under the heading of a sublime "moral feeling", was able to describe the very condition that was to become familiar to the mass societies and great totalitarian states of our time. For life under a law that is in force without signifying resembles life in the state of exception'.[47] To sum up, for Agamben, the pure form of law, the law which is 'in force without significance', implies the very modern biopolitical relation between sovereign power and bare life in which the latter becomes the exclusive object of calculations of the former.

Furthermore, Agamben, still in *Homo Sacer*, also points out how Sade's *Philosophy in the Bedroom* not only is perfectly consistent with a Kantian ethics of law but, in so doing, also reveals the very biopolitical structure that the pure form of law establishes. Within a vast amount of scholarship of Agamben, this point of the relation between Sade and biopolitics has been so far rather underestimated if not overlooked. This is quite surprising insofar as Agamben declares Sade's famous manifesto 'Make More of an Effort, Frenchmen, If You Want to Be Republicans', read by libertine Dolmancé in the *Philosophy in the Bedroom*, to be 'the first and perhaps most radical biopolitical manifesto of modernity'.[48] According to Agamben, Sade was aware of the historical change set up by the French Revolution. This change concerned in the first place the endgame of medieval monarchies which paved the way for the transition of sovereign power from the medieval kings to the modern people as a new bearer of sovereignty. The body of the people thus replaced the body of the king. This shift implied the emergence of biopolitical modernity because, as Eric Santner has argued, the body of the people was split into two in the same way as was the former body of the king: a symbolic body and a sublime second body (or nation) which became the object of biopolitical power and began to be treated in the same way as was the former second or sublime body of the king.[49] However, from Agamben's point of view, within biopolitical modernity, the second body actually completely overlaps with the first symbolic body so that the political body of people exists only insofar as it is always already considered to be the biopolitical body of nation.

From this perspective, Sade's *Philosophy in the Bedroom* and *120 Days of Sodom* are of the highest importance precisely because they had brought to light the consequences of this transition of sovereignty from the medieval monarchies to the modern republics. As Agamben does not fail to add,

> Sade's modernity does not consist in having foreseen the unpolitical primacy of sexuality in our unpolitical age. On the contrary, Sade is as contemporary as he is because of his incomparable presentation of the absolutely political (that is, 'biopolitical') meaning of sexuality and physiological life itself. Like the concentration camps of our century, the totalitarian character of the organisation of life in Silling's castle—with its meticulous regulations that do not spare any aspect of physiological life (not even the digestive function, which is obsessively cod-

> ified and publicised)—has its root in the fact that what is proposed here for the first time is a normal and collective (and hence political) organisation of human life founded solely on bare life.[50]

What is more here is that Agamben, surprisingly or not, describes this demonstrative aspect in Sade's work or his staging of bare life in the postrevolutionary period of the republic precisely by paraphrasing the title ('Theatrum philosophicum') of Foucault's 1970 review of *Difference and Repetition* and *The Logic of Sense*, namely, '*theatrum politicum*': 'At the very moment in which the revolution makes birth—which is to say, bare life—into the foundation of sovereignty and rights, Sade stages (in his entire work, and in particular in *120 Days of Sodom*) the *theatrum politicum* as a theater of bare life, in which the very physiological life of bodies appears, through sexuality, as the pure political element'.[51]

As we can note, Agamben's reference to Sade is crucial because the work of the latter sheds light on the otherwise overshadowed position of bare life in the state of exception. Moreover, this point becomes even more convincing if supported by Deleuze's analysis of the concept of institution in Sade's work: the dynamic institution hostile to the law is precisely the institution of the state of exception, driven by its own immanent regulations, operating in the empty space or *anomos* of the law. This makes for an even more interesting further inquiry in the comparative reading of perversion in Deleuze and Agamben. In fact, just as Deleuze had tried to extract Masoch from the shadow of Sade by pointing out the differential character of masochism with regard to sadomasochistic unity, so does Agamben search for a messianic event which would liberate bare life from its position of abandonment in the state of exception. However, this similarity goes even beyond mere analogy because both Deleuze and Agamben's source on this point is the historical messianic movement of the Kabbalist Sabbatai Zevi (or Zwi) from the seventeenth century, which Masoch[52] recognised as nothing other than the predecessor of the political movements of national minorities within the Austro-Hungarian Empire in the nineteenth century that was the historical context of his writings.[53] More specifically, for Agamben, the messianic event consists above all in the abolishment of the form of law by way of its complete fulfilment, that is, by way of revealing the position of the abandonment of bare life within the form of law. Similarly, Deleuze foresaw a masochistic overturning of social structure revolving around paternal symbolic power and the pressure of the superego precisely by way of the full adoption of castration and punishment by the masochist. In short, what is here coming to the fore in both Agamben and Deleuze is their common effort to find a subjective alternative for or exodus from the socio-ontological structure dominated by the figure of the father/sovereign. As Deleuze writes, 'In the case of masochism the totality of the law is invested upon the mother, who expels the father from the symbolic realm'.[54]

IV

The question is now how does Freudian-Lacanian psychoanalysis position itself in relation to such a philosophical conception which sees perversion—or at least some particular kind of perversion—as a means of social criticism which points also to the renewal of classical metaphysics. Although this may seem surprising, psychoanalysis, at least at first glance, seems to share this line of thought underpinning Deleuze and Agamben's respective conceptions of perversion. Incidentally, in his 1966–1967 unpublished seminar *The Logic of Phantasy*, some concluding lectures of which just followed the publication of Deleuze's essay 'Coldness and Cruelty' (1967), Lacan explicitly addressed the latter in a unexpectedly positive way: 'Someone who is not a psychoanalyst, Mr. Deleuze to name him, presents a book by Sacher Masoch: *Présentation de Sacher Masoch*. He writes on masochism undoubtedly the best text that has ever been written! I mean the best text, compared to everything that has been written on the theme in psychoanalysis'.[55] This clearly indicates the general proximity between Lacan's and Deleuze's reading of perversion. Yet it would be misleading to take this observation of Lacan's for granted without further questioning the arguments supporting this statement. In fact, as I will soon show, there is a small yet fundamental difference which ultimately keeps apart Lacan's (or psychoanalytic) and Deleuze's (or philosophical) understandings of perversion. This difference concerns precisely the very questionable conclusion that Deleuze (and Agamben as well) takes from his (mis)reading of the Freudian concept of the death drive and its relation to perversion.

Hence, to begin with, we might start first by outlining the affinity between both conceptions and then proceed by pointing out the aforementioned crucial difference towards the end. According to Freud, polymorphous perversion is one of the basic characteristics of childish libidinal life which is then reflected in the 'sexual aberrations'[56] in the adult phase of sexuality. With the term 'polymorphous perversion' Freud indicates the phase of libidinal organisation in which partial drives (oral, anal, etc.) are not yet synthesised or normalised under the primacy of the so-called genital function. However, these 'deviations' of partial drives from their assumed general scope persist also after the genital function is established. According to Freud, this can be observed precisely in adult perverse behaviours which consist in deviations in respect of both sexual object (partner) and sexual aim (copulation). To put it bluntly, perversions are those non- or pre-copulative practices which engage nongenital zones of the body or otherwise nonsexual instruments, or the practices which slow down or even replace the act of copulation. As one can imagine when observing sexuality in the modern age, the most ordinary sexuality is quite full of non- or pre-genital 'additives' (from oral sex to fetishism). This is why Freud ultimately acknowledged an inherently antagonistic, contradictory, and essentially perverse nature of sexuality as such, including bare heterosexual copulation: 'Thus from the point of view of psycho-analysis the exclusive sexual interest felt by men for women is also a problem that needs elucidating and is not a self-evident fact based upon an attraction that is ultimately of a chemical nature'.[57]

Following the assumed temporal differentiation between the period of the polymorphously perverse organisation of libidinal life in early childhood and the later synthetisation of the drives under the primacy of the genital norm, Jacques-Alain Miller has argued that, in Freud, perversion is somehow natural or primary with respect to the emergence of the so-called phallic function (synthetisation of the drives under the 'supremacy of the genital organs'[58]). As he has it,

> According to Freud, children are naturally polymorphously perverse. Thus for Freud, perversion is natural, that is, primary. Perversion is more primal than the norm, that norm being secondary or even cultural for Freud—though not for Lacan. In psychoanalysis, there is a problematic of normalisation, of normative integration of multiple drives.[59]

Drawing on this insight, along with acknowledging the general persistence of perversion in the mature phase, Miller further explicates how Lacan's reading differs from this conception of Freud's. If the Freudian clinic might be regarded as the attempt of 'normalisation', having the task of integrating the partial drives or 'reminders' into the genital norm, the task of the Lacanian clinic is, on the contrary, to give 'permission for perversion'.[60] According to Miller, this difference derives from a different conception of the relation between the drive and castration in Lacan with respect to Freud because for the former the drive is framed by castration already from the very beginning.[61] That is, there is nothing 'natural' in the drive. Instead the drive is rather a '*montage*', as Lacan puts it in *Seminar XI*,[62] in the precise sense: it is not a free-floating energy as it might seem which should be shaped by the genital norm afterwards but circulates around the hole implied by castration, whereby the latter means the operation, according to which the subject establishes himself in the symbolic realm of the Other at the price of losing a part of his own being. This is the origin of the articulation of the subject *qua* 'lack of being'. What the subject unconsciously relates to in the Other is thus what he fantasmatically thinks to be the missing part of his own being, which is the object *a*. According to Lacan, the object *a* functions in a twofold manner: on the one hand, as the object produced by the circulation of the drives around the surfaces of the erogenous zones of the body (anatomical holes on the body surface) while, on the other hand, precisely insofar as the object structurally lacks, it represents the cause of the subject's desire which then metonymically slides from one empirical object to the other.

However, the important point that should be emphasised is that the aforementioned hole implied by castration corresponds to what Lacan in the later period coined as 'the non-existence of sexual relationship'. In short, this axiom of Lacan's epitomises the structural absence of any *ratio* or measure which would signify the relation between sexes. Following Miller, for Lacan, perversion takes this empty place of the inexistence of sexual relationship and as such tries to provide an 'innovation' with respect to this acknowledged structural absence of the primal signifier. Thus, he sums up this point as follows:

> Lacan shows that the primacy of genitals is a negative primacy, that is, that object *a* is connected to minus phi ($-\phi$), which translates the Freudian supremacy of the genitals, but takes into account castration. Lacan introduces the whole problematic of the connection between satisfaction and the signifier, and various definitions of the phallus as the symbol of the place of satisfaction or as the signifier of jouissance, which attempt to explain what Freud calls the synthesis of the partial drives under the primacy of the genitals. In Lacan's work, that synthesis translates as the connection between jouissance and the primacy of the phallus as signifier. Lacan tries to elaborate it logically. Freud recognises the perverse components of supposedly normal sexuality, and views them as reminders of primal perversion. If you take them as reminders of primal perversion, you have to define the aim of treatment as that of completing normalisation, of absorbing the residue. Lacan defines the aim of treatment differently: it is not to complete normalisation or absorb non-normalised residues, but to give permission for perversion, permission for object *a*.[63]

Yet the conclusion that Miller draws from his overall comprehension of perversion in Lacan can be somehow misleading. In fact, along the same lines he argues about the very perverse nature of the drive itself: 'But this makes no sense if we do not admit that the drive is by its very nature perverse, and that perversion is the norm of the drive'.[64] Considering the 'inexistence of sexual relationship', that is, the absence of any 'fixed sexual formula', perversion thus becomes the very norm of the drive which takes the empty place of the missing sexual relationship. In Miller's view, this would be somehow the moment corresponding to the subjective destitution (separation from the Other) at the end of analysis. This conception is apparently further supported by Lacan's own 'searching' for a 'new perversion' which would represent a kind of 'innovation' with respect to the acknowledged absence of sexual relationship. In this context, Dominiek Hoens went so far as to even propose the reading according to which the upper level of psychoanalytic discourse—as developed in Lacan's *Seminar XVII* on 'four discourses'—should be read in terms of the perverse fantasy ($a\lozenge\$$),[65] whereby the analyst would occupy the role of the instrument of the neurotic's enjoyment.

Although these readings may sound plausible, they become doubtful if not misleading as soon as one recalls Lacan's explicit denial of the equation between the drive and perversion in his *Seminar XI*.[66] Nonetheless, the rejection of this equation does not solve entirely a much more complex relation between perversion and the drive. In fact, it does not suffice to estimate whether the 'permission for perversion' anyhow implies the consideration of the drive as not yet framed by the symbolic Other, which is to say, the drive as something raw or primitive. And to be sure, Miller doesn't fail to sufficiently emphasise the difference which actually enables us to make some steps further, claiming that 'the pre-Oedipal drive is not pre-linguistic or raw', which is to say, that 'what Lacan called Other is already there in the drive'.[67] The difference at stake is thus one between the Oedipus complex and the Other. How, then, can the drive be regarded at the same time as pre-Oedipal yet not unshaped by the Other? The answer to this fundamental question comes out from Lacan's rather peculiar articulation of the Other: the latter is not just merely the order of signifying differences but also includes an '*ontological negativity*'[68] as its own (negative) condition of possibility. The 'ontological negativity' at stake here consists in what Freud put forward as the hypothesis of primal repression (*Urverdrängung*) which involves 'the necessary fall of the first signifier',[69] that is, the primal repression of the first signifier which *fixes* the drive:

> We have reason to assume that there is a primal repression, a first phase of repression, which consists in the psychical (ideational) representative of the drive [*die psychische (Vorstellungs-) Repräsentanz des Tribes*] being denied entrance into the conscious. With this a *fixation* is established; the representative in question persists unaltered from then onwards and the drive remains attached to it.[70]

Although I will have recourse to this point a few more times throughout this book, it is nevertheless worth tackling at least the issue at stake. In fact, here the greatest attention needs to be paid to this crucial formulation in Freud's psychoanalysis: unlike the standard understanding, Freud here clearly says that what is repressed is not the drive itself but rather its '(ideational) representative [*(Vorstellungs-) Repräsentanz*]' or signifier. In this sense, primal repression by no means concerns directly the drive itself but rather its representative or signifier as the 'subject's marker of this representation'.[71] Furthermore, the real character of primal repression consists in the fact that this primal repressed representative is not at all something that would first be conscious and would be repressed only afterwards. Rather, as Alenka Zupančič has already stressed several times, this representative appears already for the first time as already repressed. As she puts it,

> The 'primary repressed' marker or representative of the drive is something that has never been conscious, and has never been part of any

> subjective experience, but constitutes its ground. The logic of repression by association is the logic of what Freud calls the repression proper, whereas the primal repression is precisely not a repression in this sense. In it the causality usually associated with the unconscious is turned upside down: it is not that we repress a signifier because of a traumatic experience related to it, it is rather because this signifier is repressed that we can experience something as traumatic (and not simply as painful, frustrating etc.) and repress it.[72]

Moving from these premises, the singularity of the topology of the unconscious as articulated by Lacan soon becomes clear. This topology, in fact, revolves around the hole of primal repression (the primary repressed signifier) resulting in a twofold structure: on the one side, the subject as that which one signifier represents for another signifier while, on the other side, the drive as the 'headless subject' which circulates around the very same hole. Lacan does not fail to make this clear:

> This articulation leads us to make of the manifestation of the drive the mode of a headless subject, for everything is articulated in it in terms of tension, and has no relation to the subject other than one of common topology. I have been able to articulate the unconscious for you as being situated in the gaps that the distribution of the signifying investments sets up in the subject, and which figure in the algorithm in the form of a lozenge [◊], which I place at the centre of any relation of the unconscious between reality and the subject. Well! It is in so far as something in the apparatus of the body is structured in the same way, it is because of the topological unity of the gaps in play, that the drive assumes its role in the functioning of the unconscious.[73]

The 'common topology' shared by the subject and the drive (as 'headless subject', which is to say, the not-yet-subjectivised subject) already implies the presence of the Other in the drive: because the Other actually includes the hole of the primally repressed as its own condition of existence, this implies the very 'contamination' of the erogenous zones of the body (anatomical holes) with the phallus and castration from the very beginning. In other words, the primal repressed (or phallic) signifier (symbolically) marks these zones as a support of *jouissance*—by way of the image of the penis lacking in the image of woman.[74] This is the main reason why the drive in psychoanalytic theory cannot be considered as something 'raw' but rather as something always already 'cooked', as Miller has put it. The Oedipus complex, in turn, appears to be only secondary with respect to this fundamental hole of primally repressed signifier, secondary in the precise sense of being fundamentally a reaction to or consequence of this originary disposition.

In my view, this is the main reason why Lacan also admitted the failure to invent a 'new perversion' in psychoanalysis: 'You have heard me more than once saying that psychoanalysis did not even succeed in inventing a new perversion. That is sad'.[75] In such a context, the missing question concerns precisely the reason why psychoanalysis failed in this project. As this book will try to argue, it is so, perhaps, because what psychoanalysis discovered in the 'new perversion' was 'not at all innovative',[76] as Miller does not fail to add. In short, the point is that, if Deleuze, on the one hand, insisted in his anti-Oedipal fashion that, in masochism, the symbolic power is invested upon the Mother by means of the fetishistic disavowal of her castration, while this gesture simultaneously implies the devaluation of the figure of the father, from Lacan's point of view, this is possible only at the price that Mother *qua* Woman functions as a version of the father. Lacan is more than clear on this point: 'Woman [*La femme*] as the version of the Father couldn't configure herself otherwise than as *Father-version* [*Père-version*]'.[77] Finally, this is why Lacan had ultimately acknowledged that perversion as a clinical structure is not the most subversive but rather the most supportive gesture as far as the function of the father is concerned: 'Perversion [*père-version*] being the sole guarantee of his function of father, which is the function of the symptom, as I have written it'.[78]

V

Summing up the two approaches to the relation between perversion and ontology, we might say the following: on the one hand, Deleuze and Agamben advance an understanding of perversion as a social structure 'beyond the Other' adding to this 'beyond' a full ontological value (this is especially the case with Deleuze). This entails precisely a new type of subjectivity which founds itself upon a strict separation between pleasure and sexuality or, in psychoanalytic terms, between *jouissance* and the Other. The figure which best epitomises this disposition of perversion as 'beyond the Other' is obviously Deleuze's masochist as a 'new man, devoid of sexual love'. The Deleuzian comprehension of perversion as social ontology is thus encompassed by the idea of ontology without the Other.

Although the Lacanian conception of perversion shows its proximity with Deleuze, it nevertheless differs from the latter to the extent that it cannot be regarded as identical. Unlike Deleuze, Lacan considered perversion as a social structure which is essentially not without the Other. However, as previously mentioned, Lacan defined the Other as a structure which revolves around the 'ontological negativity' which is as such an integral part of the Other. The Other is thus the *locus*, an empty place established by the primally repressed signifier. Alenka Zupančič nicely grasped this crucial aspect of Lacan's approach to ontology with the term 'with-without',[79] which is to say, the Other (as barred) is defined as 'with-without' the first or primally repressed signifier. Taking into account that this expression actually represents another way of articulating Lacan's definition of the unconscious, defined not simply as a latent content that should be 'unearthed' in the course of the analysis but as a gap which amounts to 'neither being, nor non-being, but the unrealised',[80] we can see how this conception opens up a *third dimension of being* which goes beyond the being/nonbeing opposition. In this context, it becomes clear why in psychoanalytic theory it is impossible to think perversion, even at the level of 'pure drive', without this third dimension of being.

NOTES

1. Besides Deleuze and Agamben, it is important to mention their predecessors and contemporaries: Bataille, Klossowski, Foucault, and Žižek at the least.
2. Gilles Deleuze, 'Coldness and Cruelty', in *Masochism: Coldness and Cruelty and Venus in Furs,* trans. Jean McNeil, ed. Gilles Deleuze and Leopold von Sacher-Masoch (New York: Zone Books, 1991), 15.
3. Ibid., 16.
4. Ibid., 15.
5. Ibid., 68.
6. Ibid., 13; my emphasis.
7. Ibid., 14; my emphasis.
8. Gilles Deleuze, *The Logic of Sense,* trans. Mark Lester with Charles Stivale (London: The Athlone Press, 1990), 253.
9. Ibid.
10. Michel Foucault, 'Theatrum Philosophicum', in *Aesthetics, Method, and Epistemology* (Essential Works of Foucault 1954–1984, Volume Two), trans. Robert Hurely and others, ed. James D. Faubion (New York: The New Press, 1998), 343.
11. Deleuze, *The Logic of Sense,* 253. In this overview of the role simulacrum plays in Deleuzian 'reversal of Platonism' I'm much relying on the two masterpiece contributions dealing with the issue at stake: Nathan Widder, 'The Rights of Simulacra: Deleuze and the Univocity of Being', *Continental Philosophy Review* 34, no. 4 (2001): 437–53; Daniel W. Smith, 'The Concept of the Simulacrum: Deleuze and the Overturning of Platonism', *Continental Philosophy Review* 38, no. 1–2 (2005): 89–123.
12. Deleuze, *The Logic of Sense,* 253.
13. Ibid.
14. Ibid., 254.
15. Ibid.
16. 'Platonism thus founds the entire domain that philosophy will later recognise as its own: the domain of representation filled by copies-icons, and defined not by an extrinsic relation to an object, but by an intrinsic relation to the model or foundation' (ibid., 259).
17. Ibid., 256.
18. Ibid., 257.
19. Foucault, 'Theatrum Philosophicum', 345.
20. Deleuze, *The Logic of Sense,* 262.
21. 'The univocity of Being does not mean that there is one and the same Being; on the contrary, beings are multiple and different, they are always produced by a disjunctive synthesis, and they themselves are disjoined and divergent, *membra disjuncta.* The univocity of Being signifies that Being is Voice that it is said, and that it is said in one and the same "sense" of everything about which it is said. . . . Univocity means that it is the same thing which occurs and is said. . . . Univocity means the identity of the noematic attribute and that which is expressed linguistically—event and sense' (ibid., 179, 180).
22. Foucault, 'Theatrum Philosophicum', 367.

23. Sigmund Freud, 'Three Essays on the Theory of Sexuality', in *The Standard Edition of the Complete Psychological Works of Sigmund Freud, Vol. VII*, ed. James Strachey (London: Vintage, 2001), 153.

24. 'Fetish is a substitute for the woman's (the mother's) penis that the little boy once believed in and—for reasons familiar to us—does not want to give up' (Sigmund Freud, 'Fetishism', in *The Standard Edition of the Complete Psychological Works of Sigmund Freud, Vol. XXI*, ed. James Strachey [London: Vintage, 2001], 153).

25. Deleuze, 'Coldness and Cruelty', 64.

26. 'The horror of castration has set up a memorial to itself in the creation of this substitute' (Freud, 'Fetishism', 154).

27. Deleuze, 'Coldness and Cruelty', 128.

28. Deleuze, *The Logic of Sense*, 319–20. For the overall complex yet productive relation between Deleuze and the Lacanian school (especially with Serge Leclaire), see the recent book by Guillaume Collett, *The Psychoanalysis of Sense: Deleuze and the Lacanian School* (Edinburgh: Edinburgh University Press, 2016).

29. As Deleuze writes in *Difference and Repetition*, 'Empiricism truly becomes transcendental, and aesthetics an apodictic discipline, only when we apprehend directly in the sensible that which can only be sensed, the very being *of* the sensible: difference, potential difference and difference in intensity as the reason behind qualitative diversity' (Gilles Deleuze, *Difference and Repetition*, trans. Paul Patton [New York: Columbia University Press, 1994], 56–57).

30. Gilles Deleuze, *Essays Critical and Clinical*, trans. Daniel W. Smith and Michael A. Greco (Minneapolis and London: University of Minnesota Press, 1997), 90.

31. For instance, Bartleby, Kafka, literature, Foucault, Kantian form of law, critique of metaphysics, etc. In general, a systematic analysis of the relationship between Deleuze's and Agamben's respective philosophical projects still remains to be done. The present book covers only a small part of this relationship. One of the rare existing contributions in this context is included in William Watkin's book *Agamben and Indifference: A Critical Overview* (London and New York: Rowman & Littlefield International, 2014), chaps. 7 and 8, 137–78.

32. See Kevin Attell, 'An Esoteric Dossier: Agamben and Derrida Read Saussure', *ELH* 76, no. 4 (2009): 821–46. A revised and extended version of this article was later included in Attell's book which explores the 'esoteric' relationship between Derrida and Agamben and especially the way Agamben's philosophy of language and the critique of semiology go beyond Derrida's deconstruction. See Kevin Attell, *Giorgio Agamben: Beyond the Threshold of Deconstruction* (New York: Fordham University Press, 2015).

33. Giorgio Agamben, *Homo Sacer: Sovereign Power and Bare Life*, trans. Daniel Heller-Roazen (Stanford, CA: Stanford University Press, 1998), 8. For the sake of clarity, it is worthwhile citing the whole passage in which Agamben, by drawing the analogy between the relationship of inclusive exclusion of voice in language as described in the famous passage of Aristotle's *Politics* (1253a, 10–18) and the inclusive exclusion of bare life into *polis*, points out the very metaphysical nature of Western (bio)politics: 'The question "In what way does the living being have language?" corresponds exactly to the question "In what way does bare life dwell in the *polis*?" The living being has *logos* by taking away and conserving its own voice in it, even as it dwells in the *polis* by letting its own bare life be excluded, as an exception, within it. Politics therefore appears as the truly fundamental structure of Western metaphysics insofar as it occupies the threshold on which the relation between the living being and the *logos* is realised. In the "politicisation" of bare life—the metaphysical task *par excellence*—the humanity of living man is decided. In assuming this task, modernity does nothing other than declare its own faithfulness to the essential structure of the metaphysical tradition' (ibid.).

34. See Giorgio Agamben, *Stanzas: Word and Phantasm in Western Culture*, trans. Ronald L. Martinez (Minneapolis and London: University of Minnesota Press, 1993).

35. Ibid., 137.

36. Ibid., 147.
37. Ibid., 150n9.
38. Ibid., 145.
39. Alenka Zupančič, 'On Repetition', *Sats — Nordic Journal of Philosophy* 8, no. 1 (2007): 39.
40. Deleuze, 'Coldness and Cruelty', 81.
41. Ibid., 82–83.
42. Jacques Lacan, 'Kant with Sade', in *Écrits: The First Complete Edition in English,* trans. Bruce Fink (London and New York: W. W. Norton and Co., 2006), 646.
43. Alenka Zupančič, *Ethics of the Real: Kant and Lacan* (New York and London: Verso, 2000), 90, 92.
44. This is the English translation of Gershom Scholem's expression *Geltung ohne Bedeutung* with which he described 'the status of law in Kafka's novel [The Trail]' (Agamben, *Homo Sacer*, 51).
45. Ibid.
46. Ibid.
47. Ibid., 52.
48. Ibid., 134.
49. See Eric L. Santner, *The Royal Remains: The People's Two Bodies and the Endgames of Sovereignty* (Chicago: University of Chicago Press, 2011), 3–86.
50. Agamben, *Homo Sacer*, 135.
51. Ibid., 134.
52. Leopold von Sacher-Masoch, *Jewish Life: Tales from Nineteenth-Century Europe,* trans. Virginia L. Lewis (Riverside, CA: Ariadne Press, 2002).
53. See Agamben, *Homo Sacer*, 57; Deleuze, 'Coldness and Cruelty', 98–99.
54. Deleuze, 'Coldness and Cruelty', 90.
55. Jacques Lacan, *The Logic of Phantasy, 1966–67* (unpublished seminar, trans. Cormac Gallagher from unedited French manuscripts), lecture from 19 April 1967, available at http://www.lacaninireland.com (translation modified).
56. Freud, 'Three Essays', 135–72.
57. Ibid., 146. Although this is already a commonplace in psychoanalytic theory, it is nevertheless worth mentioning the recent book which I will substantially refer to later on and which to the best of my knowledge offers the most systematic examination of the inherently *contradictory* nature of sexuality in psychoanalytic theory: Alenka Zupančič, *What* Is *Sex?* (Cambridge, MA: MIT Press, 2017).
58. Jacques-Alain Miller, 'On Perversion', in *Reading Seminars I and II: Lacan's Return to Freud,* ed. Richard Feldstein, Bruce Fink, and Maire Jannus (New York: State University of New York Press, 1996), 314.
59. Ibid., 313.
60. Ibid., 314.
61. As I will try to show later in this book, this can be said for Freud too. In fact, Lacan's reading is set up against the background of Freud's theory of repression from a later period. Especially Freud's hypothesis about the 'primal repression' enables us to reread anew his conception of the drive and polymorphous perversion from the 'Three Essays' which appear far from being natural.
62. 'Let me say that if there is anything resembling a drive it is a *montage*' (Jacques Lacan, *The Seminar of Jacques Lacan, Book XI: The Four Fundamental Concepts of Psychoanalysis* [hereafter abbreviated as *Seminar XI*], trans. Alan Sheridan [London and New York: W. W. Norton and Company, 1998], 169).
63. Miller, 'On Perversion', 314.
64. Ibid., 313.
65. Dominiek Hoens, 'Toward a New Perversion: Psychoanalysis', in *Jacques Lacan and the Other Side of Psychoanalysis: Reflections on Seminar XVII*, ed. Justin Clemens and Russell Grigg (Durham, NC, and London: Duke University Press, 2006), 88–102.
66. 'I stress that the drive is not perversion. What constitutes the enigmatic character of Freud's presentation derives precisely from the fact that he wishes to give us a

radical structure—in which the subject is not yet placed. On the contrary, what defines perversion is precisely the way in which the subject is placed in it' (Lacan, *Seminar XI*, 181–82).

67. Miller, 'On Perversion', 315.

68. Zupančič, *What* Is *Sex?*, 16.

69. Lacan, *Seminar XI*, 251.

70. Sigmund Freud, 'Repression', in *The Standard Edition of the Complete Psychological Works of Sigmund Freud, Vol. XIV*, ed. James Strachey (London: Vintage, 2001), 148 (translation modified).

71. Zupančič, 'On Repetition', 39.

72. Ibid.

73. Lacan, *Seminar XI*, 181 (translation modified).

74. As Lacan puts it, 'It is thus that the erectile organ—not as itself, or even as an image, but as a part that is missing in the desired image—comes to symbolise the place of jouissance' (Jacques Lacan, 'The Subversion of the Subject and the Dialectic of Desire in the Freudian Unconscious', in *Écrits: The First Complete Edition in English*, trans. Bruce Fink [London and New York: W. W. Norton and Co., 2006], 697). See on this also Samo Tomšič, *The Capitalist Unconscious: Marx and Lacan* (London and New York: Verso, 2015), chapter 'The Organ and the Animal'.

75. Cited in Hoens, 'Toward a New Perversion: Psychoanalysis', 98.

76. Miller, 'On Perversion', 314.

77. Jacques Lacan, 'Préface à *L'éveil du printemps*', *Ornicar?* 39 (1986): 7.

78. Jacques Lacan, 'Seminar of 21 January 1975', in *Feminine Sexuality: Jacques Lacan and the* école freudienne, trans. Jacqueline Rose, ed. Juliet Mitchell and Jacqueline Rose (London and New York: W. W. Norton and Co., 1985), 167.

79. Zupančič, *What* Is *Sex?*, 48.

80. Lacan, *Seminar XI*, 30.

Part II

Perversion between Deleuze's Transcendental Empiricism and the Ontology of Immanence: *Theatrum Philosophicum*

TWO

Deleuze's Transcendental Empiricism

Simulacrum, Divergence, and the Ontology of Difference

I

Let's begin once again with a chronological note. Between 1967 and 1969, Deleuze published three of his major works which can be regarded as the kernel of his early philosophy (namely, the period prior to his collaboration with Félix Guattari). In 1967, the essay 'Presentation of Sacher-Masoch: Coldness and Cruelty' appeared and quickly achieved the status of a canonical text. This essay appeared in the context of the mass popularity and influence of Lacan's lectures, delivered at the École normal supérieure in Paris, and paved the way for rethinking perversion on the basis of an 'irreducible dissymmetry' between sadism and masochism and between the literatures of Sade and Masoch respectively. It immediately met with a wide response, so that Lacan himself recognised its significance just a few months after its publication.[1] In the next two years, Deleuze published another two masterpieces: *Difference and Repetition* in 1968 and *The Logic of Sense* a year later. These two books represent in all respects the core of Deleuze's early ontological project which the well-known philosopher of immanence gave a peculiar name: 'transcendental empiricism or science of the sensible'.[2] In his 1970 review of these two masterpieces 'of exceptional merit and importance', Michel Foucault notably announced the bright prospects for Deleuze's philosophy: 'and perhaps one day, this century will be known as Deleuzian'.[3]

To be sure, this chronological sequence of publications doesn't imply any philosophical or conceptual necessity. The three works at stake are all ultimately independent and autonomous wholes and could eventually have been published in an inverted sequence or even in more distant chronological periods. Yet even though the publication sequence may be contingent, this does not preclude us from analysing their mutual conceptual connections, which is nowadays perhaps even more attractive due to our temporal distance. So in spite of the conceptual autonomy of these three works which prevents us from considering any of them as a kind of precondition for the other, it is nonetheless worthwhile to tackle the question of the conceptual proximity, at the least between, on the one hand, Deleuze's essay on Masoch and, on the other hand, his early ontological project of transcendental empiricism. The fact that Deleuze himself didn't provide any systematic analysis of this connection—in both *Difference and Repetition* and *The Logic of Sense* he just roughly refers to sadism and masochism—together with the fact that this connection also remains somehow neglected so far within the vast scholarship of Deleuze's work, should not discourage us from searching deeply in this direction. This search, however, does not at all imply any supremacy of the topic of perversion with respect to other figures in Deleuze's early ontology; yet nor does it imply either that the figures of perversion should be underestimated within Deleuze's ontological project of transcendental empiricism. Roughly speaking, sadism and masochism are indeed just two among many other figures of Deleuze's ontology, yet they represent perhaps the best possible ground to estimate the difference between Deleuze's critical approach to ontology and Lacan's.

From this point of view, we can put forward the hypothesis that there indeed exists a more determinate conceptual connection between the sadism-masochism relation, on the one hand, and propositions about the univocity of being, on the other. More specifically, considering Badiou's description of Deleuze's ontological procedure, this part will try to estimate to what extent Masoch is not only a 'case-of-thought' (indeed, one among others), but also that he is, as Badiou has argued, a name of the univocity of being.[4] In order to verify this thesis, it's necessary to focus again on the main emphasis of Deleuze's 'reversal of Platonism' which can be seen, as Daniel Smith argues, 'at the same time . . . as a rejuvenated Platonism or even a completed Platonism',[5] rather than a vulgar anti-Platonism. Here is, again, the decisive passage from *The Logic of Sense*:

> So 'to reverse Platonism' means to make the simulacra rise and to affirm their rights among icons and copies. The problem no longer has to do with the distinction Essence-Appearance or Model-Copy. This distinction operates completely within the world of representation. Rather, it has to do with undertaking the subversion of this world—the 'twilling of the idols'. The simulacrum is not a degraded copy. It harbors a positive power which denies *the original and the copy, the model and the reproduction*. At least two divergent series are internalised in the simulacrum—neither can be assigned as the original, neither as the copy. It is not even enough to invoke a model of the Other, for no model can resist the vertigo of the simulacrum. There is no longer any

> privileged point of view except that of the object common to all points of view. There is no possible hierarchy, no second, no third. . . . In the reversal of Platonism, resemblance is said of internalised difference, and identity of the Different as primary power. The same and the similar no longer have an essence except as *simulated,* that is as expressing the functioning of the simulacrum. There is no longer any possible selection. The non-hierarchised work is a condensation of coexistences and a simultaneity of events. It is a triumph of the false pretender. It simulates at once the father, the pretender, and the fiancé in a superimposition of masks.[6]

The main question one can pose against the background of this passage concerns precisely the peculiar relation between simulacrum, negation, and difference. What kind of negation does the simulacrum operate and what does it negate in order to establish itself as the agent of divergent difference? The answer to this fundamental question, which provides the key for understanding why Deleuze considered Masoch's literature as an 'invention' that entails the differential between sadism and masochism, is possible and has some sense only to the extent that we recognise in it a certain fundamental gesture of Deleuze's project of transcendental empiricism.

II

So to begin with, we should focus first on the concept of difference, which is one of the cornerstones of Deleuze's project of transcendental empiricism. Importantly, this project was set up by Deleuze as a follow-up to his singular criticism of the philosophies of representation. It this context, it's worthwhile to start with Levi R. Bryant,[7] who pointed out—in one of the keenest interpretations of the account and meaning of Deleuze's idea of transcendental empiricism—a specific feature which is widespread among the majority of interpretations of Deleuze's early work. This feature, or, better yet, cliché, entails the assumption that Deleuze's project is intended to direct itself against the representationalism which is allegedly the key feature of transcendental philosophy in general and particularly of post-Kantian German idealism. The purpose of such an emphasis of Bryant is indeed not to argue Deleuze is in some secret way a philosopher of representation so that the generally acknowledged anti-representational character of Deleuze's philosophy would be somehow misleading if not wrong. On the contrary, Deleuze certainly *is* the philosopher who struggles against representation with the philosophical weapons of transcendental empiricism and the ontology of immanence. However, as Bryant does not fail to add, Deleuze's struggle against representation is not only the consequence of some particular issue within representation itself but is also rather immanent to it. In other words, we don't fight the philosophy of representation from an external position; we fight the philosophy of representation because it ends up in a deadlock which this very same philosophy is unable to solve. And Deleuze's transcendental empiricism and ontology of immanence are meant to be the solutions to this very same problem which the philosophy of representation encounters. In Bryant's words, 'One does not adopt the position of transcendental empiricism because it is *against* representation. Rather, one adopts the position because something is wrong with the philosophy of representation *and* transcendental empiricism is able to solve this problem'.[8]

Moving on from this premise, it seems necessary to first dig deeper into this problem which the philosophy of representation articulates yet is unable to solve without the assistance of transcendental empiricism. Roughly speaking, this problem concerns the conditions of real rather than of possible experience. In other words, the conditions of real experience, as opposed to those of possible experience, amount to the givenness of the things that are given, that is to say, they explore those conditions by which things are given as immanent to the things themselves rather than in some external transcendental form. The conditions of possible experience, in turn, relate to the question of how we as human beings *can* or *could* experience things themselves, while the conditions of real experience relate to the question of the conditions which lie behind our *actual* experiences, conditions that necessarily have to be fulfilled when we *actually* experience things as given. In contrast to the transcendental philosophy of representation which had explained how things actually differ from each other at the basis of the external transcendental form (the Kantian transcendental unity of apperception), Deleuze searches for another concept of difference which would not be subjected to the determination of any external form which determines the identity of things. Differently put, Deleuze searches for a concept of difference which would be immanent rather than attesting to some transcendental apparatus which explains difference only after identity is determined.

In so doing, Deleuze challenges the very foundations of Western metaphysics and the philosophy of representation which found themselves upon the sharpest distinction between mind (concepts) and senses (appearances). More specifically, objects can be comprehended only indirectly, which is to say, only through their appearances. Yet this does not suffice. Appearances, in fact, have to appear within intuitions as forms of the sensible. This is why, for instance, Kant in the *Critique of Pure Reason* introduces two fundamental elements of transcendental aesthetics, that is, space and time as forms of intuition through which the object is given as appearance. Insofar as space and time are the conditions of possibility of possible experience, Kant insists that they are synthetic judgements a priori. Yet if space and time are the conditions of possibility for the intuition of appearances, this, in turn, also implies that the relation between the two (intuitions and appearances) is only external. At the most extreme point, we come across the conclusion about the primacy of intuitions over appearances. As Kant writes regarding the relation between objects and space as pure intuition, 'One can never represent that there is no space, although one can very well think that there are no objects to be encountered in it'.[9] This clearly indicates the supremacy of intuitions over appearances, which finally appear to be separated from one another. However, from Kant's perspective, this does not suffice for the comprehension of the appearances. What does suffice is, in turn, 'a synthesis of concepts *and* intuitions',[10] as Bryant argues, which Kant himself called a transcendental unity of apperception. Roughly speaking, if the things are given as different between themselves, this difference can be determined only within the transcendental unity of apperception conceived as a synthesis of concept and intuitions. Kant does not fail to add that without this transcendental form of comprehension, objects would appear to be only a 'rhapsody of intuitions'.[11] In short, experience is possible only insofar as the appearances are given within a transcendental schematism, which is to say, within the synthesis of concepts and intuitions. This is the way Kant determines the conditions of possibility of experience as a criterion of the objective validity of our comprehension:

> The possibility of experience is therefore that which gives all of our cognitions *a priori* objective reality. Now experience rests on the synthetic unity of appearances, i.e., on a synthesis according to concepts of the object of appearances in general, without which it would not even be cognition but rather a rhapsody of perceptions, which would not fit together in any context in accordance with rules of a thoroughly connected (possible) consciousness, thus not into the transcendental and necessary unity of apperception.[12]

Kant, here, obviously prioritises concept over appearance. This further implies that the difference in given appearances can only be determined out of the primacy of the concept. Kant will loosen this schema only in his third critique (*Critique of the Power of Judgment*) by introducing a reflective power of judgement as opposed to the determined power of judgement. Very roughly, while the latter pertains to the structure of the transcendental schematism which relies upon the subsumption of the object under the concept (through the unity of apperception), the former thinks the object there where the concept is missing.[13] In any case, this is the point—of the determination of difference within the unity of apperception—where Deleuze intervenes with the concept of transcendental empiricism which is simultaneously also an attempt to overturn Platonism. For if difference can only appear within the transcendental synthesis of concept and intuition, that is, as the difference between two identities, this implies the subjection of the former to the latter. According to Bryant, this is the point of a peculiar conjunction of transcendental philosophy of representation (Kant) and empiricism (Locke, Hume). In fact, both transcendental philosophy and empiricism 'continue to maintain the primacy of the subject or mind to which givens are given in sensibility'.[14] By maintaining the primacy of the subject over object as it is given in the sensible, both transcendental philosophy and empiricism fail to explain precisely 'those differentials or rules out of which our intuition is produced'.[15] In other words, by maintaining the primacy of subject over object, transcendental philosophy and empiricism both assume the difference 'in kind' between concept and intuition, yet they both fail to explain how concept and intuition at all relate to each other, assuming their difference 'in kind'. This failure is most evident in the case of 'empirical concepts'. As Bryant writes, 'While the issue of empirical concepts is not normally seen as a problem for Kant, the question arises as to how it is possible for concepts and intuitions to be related to one another at all if the two differ in kind'.[16] The fact is that in transcendental philosophy the two can be related to one another only by the mediation of the (transcendental) third (unity of the apperception).

Deleuze contrasts this by proposing how to think this relation immanently, that is, without the mediation of the transcendental third. The transcendental empiricist's view is that, insofar as intuitions and concepts are *actually* in the relation, this relation can be only the relation 'in degree' yet not 'in kind'. This proposal of Deleuze's has far-reaching consequences because it undermines the very kernel of transcendental philosophy which consists in opposing the intelligible to the sensible. The task of transcendental empiricism is thus precisely to discover the 'intelligibility in the givens of experience itself'.[17] This is why Bryant proposes to conceive Deleuze's transcendental empiricism also in terms of 'hyper-rationalism'. As he writes,

> Insofar as differentials function as the productive rules for the qualitative givens of being, Deleuze's position is best thought of as a hyper-rationalism rather than an empiricism. In this way Deleuze undermines the opposition between the universal and the particular, concepts and intuitions, the sensible and the intelligible, or *noesis* and *aesthesis* by discovering intelligibility in the givens of experience itself. The opposition between the sensible and the intelligible is not even operative in Deleuze's ontology. As such, there can be no question or problem of the schematism for Deleuze insofar as there are not two terms requiring the mediation of a third term.[18]

As mentioned previously, for Deleuze, the difference between concepts and intuitions is only in degree, not in kind. This further enables him to think being not at the level of external determination, which is the case of transcendental philosophy, but at the level of the sensible itself. The purpose of transcendental empiricism is thus to affirm the being of the sensible itself insofar as it is not opposed but rather encompasses the dimension of intelligibility too. This is the point of Deleuze's most elementary definition of transcendental empiricism: 'Empiricism truly becomes transcendental, and aesthetics an apodictic discipline, only when we apprehend directly in the sensible that which can only be sensed, the very being *of* the sensible: difference, potential difference and difference in intensity as the reason behind qualitative diversity'.[19]

To come across the 'very being of the sensible'—this is the axiom of transcendental empiricism. Subject and object here don't differ any more in kind, only in degree. This is why Deleuze insisted that the *cogito* in transcendental empiricism is 'the dissolved self, the cracked I'.[20] The difference between subject and object is generated by the immanent differential and can be comprehended only at the level of intensity: if there is a qualitative difference between subject and object, this difference is only secondary and subordinated to the difference in the degree of intensity. However, the generative difference, which gives rise to qualitatively different givens, implies precisely a nonrelation between particular beings, while this nonrelation is maintained precisely by attesting to the ontological status (univocity of Being as One) of this multiplicity of beings. In other words, 'one has to think the nonrelation according to the One, which founds it by radically separating the terms involved. One has to steadfastly rest within the activity of separation, understood as a power of Being'.[21]

III

Alain Badiou acknowledges the decisive status of this point for Deleuze's ontology. According to Badiou, Deleuze in this way performs the passage from phenomenology and intentionality which presents 'thought . . . as dependent on an internalised relation: between consciousness and its object',[22] to the univocity of being. By dislodging the relationship between mind and intuition from externality to the inside, he breaks with a phenomenological and metaphysical hierarchy between mind and senses. The philosopher who, according to Badiou, had started this break was indeed Heidegger. However, although he set foot in the right direction, he nonetheless 'stops halfway' insofar as his ontological difference still maintains the relationship between beings within Being as One. As Badiou argues, Heidegger 'does not see (unlike Foucault) that the consequence of ontological unity is not a harmony or a communication between beings, not even an "interval in between" where the relation can be thought outside all substantial grounding, but rather the absolute nonrelation or the indifference of the terms involved to all forms of relation'.[23] This is why Badiou is right to further remark that, from Deleuze's point of view, Heidegger 'stops halfway' in accomplishing the 'disjunctive synthesis': on the one hand, he accomplished the disjunction between consciousness and the object thus overcoming intentionality, yet, on the other hand, he kept maintaining the relation between beings. According to Badiou, Deleuze is the philosopher who brought the disjunctive synthesis to its most radical accomplishment: terms or beings are generated through the difference as divergent, which is to say, beings are given through their difference from themselves, not between themselves which implies that they do not need any external comparison or relation to be determined. Difference as differentiating (as the agent of divergence of the terms) is thus the synonym for a nonrelation.

As Bryant had noted, we are only here able to properly grasp the problem of both empiricism and transcendental philosophy: they are both too 'empiricist' and '*not transcendental enough*'.[24] This means that they both still keep maintaining the primacy of external relations which implies the assumption of a predetermined identity that determines the difference between the two only afterwards. Deleuze makes this point explicit by making reference to Maïmon's criticism towards Kant:

> It is Salomon Maïmon who proposes a fundamental reformulation of the Critique and an overcoming of the Kantian duality between concept and intuition. Such a duality refers us back to the extrinsic criterion of constructability and leaves us with an external relation between the determinable (Kantian space as a pure given) and the determination (the concept in so far as it is thought).[25]

This simply means that empiricism, as well as transcendental philosophy, fails to think determination as such, that is, the immanent relation between the determination and the determinable conceived as a process of genesis. According to Deleuze, thinking this relation immanently is made possible only by the concept of difference *qua* difference:

> Difference is the state in which one can speak of determination *as such* [la *determination*]. The difference 'between' two things is only empirical, and the corresponding determinations [les *determinations*] are only extrinsic. However, instead of something distinguished from something else, imagine something which distinguishes itself—and yet that from which it distinguishes itself does not distinguish itself from it. Lightning, for example, distinguishes itself from the black sky but must also trail it behind, as though it were distinguishing itself from that which does not distinguish itself from it. It is as if the ground rose to the surface, without ceasing to be ground.[26]

Deleuze, here, clearly insists on searching for an intrinsic or immanent difference rather than an external or empirical one insofar as the latter can only be contingent and dependent on identity. What is at stake in Deleuze's transcendental empiricism is thus not the difference 'between' the two, which presupposes the relation; instead what is at stake is the difference as such, the difference in itself which only explains the diversity of the given. Hence, this difference is an inherently divergent difference because it makes each thing diverge or distinguish from itself rather than enabling things to converge to each other.[27]

Deleuze's accomplishment of the disjunctive synthesis has also far-reaching consequences for the conception of the relation between immanence and transcendence. For if, as Bryant pointed out, Deleuze's univocity of being presupposes the immanence of beings within the One, while at the same time implying the radicalisation of Kantian transcendental philosophy, this seems to lead us to a new concept of immanence which achieves the status of transcendence without, however, generating any relation between the two. In other words, immanence as One implies that there's no Two in the sense of the distinction between immanence and transcendence; however, immanence as One, precisely insofar as it prevents the existence of Two, achieves the status of a radical transcendence, a transcendence which radicalises Kantian 'imperfect' transcendence and corresponds to what Deleuze (together with Guattari) will later on articulate as 'nonthought within thought',[28] or as an obscured presupposition lying on the other side of being itself. As Philip Goodchild puts it, 'Deleuze's plane of immanence is also transcendent in the Kantian sense, being not only a presupposition about the nature of thought, but also a matter of being'.[29]

Conceiving immanence in such a way that it is simultaneously grasped as a presupposition of thinking as well as of the matter of being itself seems to reveal the ultimate meaning of Deleuze's expression of 'crowned anarchy', which he uses to describe univocal Being ('Univocal Being is at one and the same time nomadic distribution and crowned anarchy'[30]): the nonrelational immanence of beings which are in this respect nomadically distributed on the level of an an-archic surface of equality is preserved by the peculiar 'crown' called the One. In other words, through the containment of nonrelated beings within the One, the nonrelation (the absence of transcendence) is raised to the level of the highest or absolute transcendence. For Deleuze, the One of Being is thus also the One of Difference (as divergent). From this follows the conclusion which is the kernel of transcendental empiricism, which is to say, the univocity of being implies the equation between Being as One and Difference as divergent.

IV

Seen from this perspective, we are now in the position to better estimate the differential character of the simulacrum operating within the Platonic dialectic of rivalry. Deleuze's point of departure is here the misleading Aristotelian assumption that Plato's dialectic should be seen as a dialectic of specification and determination, rather than of selection and rivalry. According to Aristotle, there's an epistemological necessity to divide the genre onto the opposite species. On a more abstract level, this entails dividing identity into opposites. As Deleuze criticises the Aristotelian perspective on Plato's dialectic, this 'procedure not only lacks "reason" by itself, it lacks a reason in terms of which we could decide whether something falls into one species rather than another'.[31] In other words, the decision-making process for whether one element should be assigned to one rather than another species is arbitrary because of the lack of the concept as a mediating 'third'.

According to Deleuze, Plato, unlike Aristotle, does not even pretend to determine the opposite species within a certain genre. Or, better yet, Plato determines the species 'superficially and even ironically, the better to hide under this mask its true secret'.[32] As we have already discussed, the 'true secret' of Plato's dialectic is its hidden 'motivation' which Deleuze tries to bring out to the light of the day: '"to reverse Platonism" must mean to bring this motivation out into the light of the day, to "track it down"'.[33] According to Deleuze, the true motivation of Platonic dialectic is not that 'of dividing a determinate genus into definite species, but of dividing a confused species into pure lines of descent, or of selecting a pure line from the material which is not'.[34] In other words, Plato begins with 'an undifferentiated logical matter, an indifferent material, a mixture, an indefinite representing multiplicity which must be eliminated in order to bring to light the Idea which constitutes a pure line of descent'.[35] As Deleuze further argues, the difference is thus not between two species but is entirely within a single genus operating as a difference between the pure and the impure or between the authentic and the inauthentic. This is why the true method of Plato's procedure is a method of division or rivalry between true and false pretenders, which corresponds to the division between the essence and the appearance ('distinguishing between *things and their simulacra* within a pseudo-genus'[36]) with the ultimate goal of repressing the latter. Because, as Deleuze does not fail to add, 'according to the ancient custom of myth and epic, false claimants must die'.[37]

This is the ironic aspect of Plato's method of division: to introduce rivalry and struggle between pretenders not in order to determine the opposite species but rather to select between true and false pretenders and, finally, to let the latter die. On this point, Deleuze points out the singular origin which determines the participation of the Idea in the form of lineage: at the point of the absent 'third' (concept) which would mediate between two species, Plato introduces the myth as the criterion of determination, the myth which establishes the determination of the self-identity of the Idea as the ground: 'Justice alone is just, says Plato. . . . That justice alone should be just is not a simple analytic proposition. It is the designation of the Idea as the ground which possesses in the first place'.[38] Such a designation is, according to Deleuze, far from being innocent because it sets up the ground as an ontological measure, which then allows participation in the second place, third place, and so on: 'The function of the ground is then to allow participation, to give in second place'.[39] Yet, and this is a kind of sado-ironic aspect of Plato's procedure, the myth which gives ground does not in so doing establish the 'neutral' terrain on which the struggle between pretenders or claimants should unfold. On the contrary, by establishing the ground as the ontological measure at the basis of the 'lineage', the myth decides the struggle in advance. In fact, according to such an ontological measure, some pretenders are in advance disqualified as false pretenders which are not allowed to participate in the Idea.

Thus, in the long chain of entities which achieve participation, albeit distant,[40] in the Idea, there is a simulacrum as a false pretender, a pretender which introduces a short circuit into the procedure of division and participation. On this point, it's worthwhile to ask a simple yet fundamental question, namely, why the simulacrum is not considered simply as the last element in the chain of participation; that is, as the one who participates in the last place but is instead considered to be a false pretender which deserves exclusion from the line of participation in the Idea altogether. And relatedly, how one can even recognise the simulacrum as, for instance, different from the copy (a good resemblance) which is allowed to participate. Deleuze's answer is here quite simple: the simulacrum pretends to the All, which is to say, to the totality. For the simulacrum, unlike for copies, it's not a question of gaining participation in some particular place within the line of participation, and, in this sense, Deleuze is right to stress that the rights of simulacra are not the same as those of copies. What the simulacrum simulates is thus the series as a whole which goes from the ground as the Idea to the last copy. This is the way the simulacrum raises the ground of the Idea to the surface and, in this respect, also pretends that the Idea is the undivided One,[41] the One which does not found itself upon the exclusion of the Other.

V

Along this line of argument, we are finally able to comprehend more precisely the status of 'nonbeing' as the (non)place where Platonic dialectic dislodges simulacrum. As previously mentioned, the simulacrum does not pretend to take place in the line of lineage which would imply relating to the other participants in the Idea. Precisely insofar as it simulates the Idea itself, the simulacrum disorients the very procedure of division which cannot afford any more the selection of true pretenders. More than the simple negation of being which directly implies the relation, the simulacrum thus corresponds to the fold of being or to the nonbeing as Difference (literally: 'non-being is Difference: *heteron*, not *enantion*'[42]). Difference not as a relational difference between two identities but instead as a divergent or nonrelational difference. In other words, the simulacrum corresponds to the question ('?-being'[43]) which devaluates the hierarchy not only between the copy and the simulacrum but also between the Model-Idea and the copy, leading to the abolition of the division between the world of appearances and the world of essence on the general level. The simulacrum is thus the manifestation or expression of Difference which effectuates the divergence of the series and establishes a nonrelation between them. However, according to Deleuze, Difference can have such an effect precisely to the extent that it is always already considered to be One-All, that is, univocal Being as that which is said of Difference.[44]

In order to exemplify a little more how the simulacrum provokes a disorientation in the procedure of the division between true and false pretenders, let's take a brief look at an example given by Nathan Widder:

> According to this model a physical object, for example, is a copy of its Form, while simulacra such as shadows, reflections, mirages, and even artwork, are copies of the physical object. But the character of a 'good' simulation is precisely that it appears to be as real as the thing it copies, and this duplicity cannot be accounted for according to an order that defines the simulation as merely a copy twice removed.[45]

As we can see, Widder's example clearly points to the very peculiar mimesis of the simulacrum: its mimesis is so original that it puts into question the judgement between the true and the false. Roughly put, the simulacrum simulates the original in such a way that one cannot even distinguish between true and false, between the original, the copy, and the simulacrum. In this respect, the simulacrum (which is a Latin translation of Greek *Phantasm*) not surprisingly reminds us precisely to the Freudian figure of *Das Unheimlich* which points not to something mimetically similar but rather to the uncanny dimension of the double which has no resemblance but which has the capacity to undermine our most fixed symbolic and imaginary identities. In any case, as far as the simulacrum is concerned, Deleuze is thus right to stress its ultimate impact on the procedure of selection: 'There is no longer any possible selection'.

Thus, we can say that this is the main reason why the difference which the simulacrum expresses is not a metaphysical difference between two identities but is rather a divergent difference, a difference which makes things themselves not identical, but rather non-self-identical; things which diverge from themselves. Finally, in so doing, the simulacrum abolishes the shared ontological measure which underpins the method of division. However, it does not thereby introduce a relation of equality between beings but rather an equality of nonrelation, an absolute divergence and nonrelation which is, paradoxically enough, kept together precisely by the univocal Being or Being as One. As Badiou had efficiently summed up,

> If Being is said in one and the same sense of everything of which it is said, then beings are all identically simulacra and all affirm, by an inflection of intensity whose difference is purely formal or modal, the living power of the One. Once again, it is the disjunctive synthesis that is opposed to Plato: beings are merely disjointed, divergent simulacra

> that lack any internal relation between themselves or with any transcendent Idea whatsoever.[46]

As Badiou is right to emphasise, one of the most peculiar characteristics of Deleuze's theory of the univocity of Being or of Being as One is that it is essentially simulated or, better yet, that the simulation of simulacra fully affirms the Being as One. The diverging effect that is produced by the raising of simulacra on the surface thus devaluates the myth as the ground or ontological measure. By untying the metaphysical bond between myth and dialectic, Deleuze's transcendental empiricism thus operates the very demythologisation of Being.[47] The myth as the fixed ontological measure is, in fact, completely devaluated, while this devaluation implies also a replacement of the sedentary *nomos* of the ground—as Deleuze calls the law of distribution according to myth—with 'a nomad *nomos*' which is 'without property, enclosure or measure'.[48] In contrast to the sedentary *nomos* which regulates the putting on of copies on a fixed ground placed under according to their fixed identities, the nomadic or nomad *nomos* is here introduced by Deleuze as a new, paradoxical, ontological measure, which is, however, 'closer to the immeasurable state of things than to the first kind of measure'; as a new ontological hierarchy which is, however, 'closer to the hubris and anarchy of beings than to the first hierarchy'; as 'the monster which combines all the demons'.[49] As such, nomadic *nomos* represents the rule according to which beings are distributed within univocal and undivided Being: 'It is an errant and even "delirious" distribution, in which things are deployed across the entire extensity of a univocal and undistributed Being. It is not a matter of being which is distributed according to the requirements of representation, but of all things being divided up within being in the univocity of simple presence (the One—All)'.[50]

In drawing this chapter to a close, we can thus sum up our line of argument concerning the role of simulacrum and difference in Deleuze's transcendental empiricism as such:

1. Deleuze thinks the simulacrum as the expression of a Difference which is not a classic difference between two identities, but rather a diverging difference;
2. This divergent difference determines the existence of beings in their divergent modality, whereby beings diverge from each other hence they exist in their nonrelation;
3. What holds together a multiplicity of beings in their nonrelation is precisely Being as One, which is to say, Being as univocal where nonrelated beings all equally express the univocity;
4. What determines Being as univocal which then holds together the multiplicity of nonrelated beings within the One is precisely the equation between Being and Difference as divergent; in other words, the nonrelation between what happens and what is said

> expresses the Being of Difference as that which generates the non-relations and non-self-identity of things that are given.

It is now necessary to see how Deleuze's engagement with Masoch's masochism corresponds to these basic coordinates of his ontology of difference. In the next chapter I will estimate, following Badiou's suggestion, to what extent, and how precisely, Masoch can be regarded as a 'name of being' or a 'case-of-thought' in the context of Deleuze's early ontological project.

NOTES

1. 'He writes on masochism undoubtedly the best text that has ever been written! I mean the best text, compared to everything that has been written on the theme in psychoanalysis' (Jacques Lacan, *The Logic of Phantasy, 1966–67* [unpublished seminar, trans. Cormac Gallagher from unedited French manuscripts], lecture from 19 April 1967, available at http://www.lacaninireland.com).
2. Gilles Deleuze, *Difference and Repetition*, trans. Paul Patton (New York: Columbia University Press, 1994), 56.
3. Michel Foucault, 'Theatrum Philosophicum', in *Aesthetics, Method, and Epistemology* (Essential Works of Foucault 1954–1984, Volume Two), trans. Robert Hurely and others, ed. James D. Faubion (New York: The New Press, 1998), 343.
4. 'This means that in a considerable part of his work, Deleuze adopts a procedure that, starting from the constraint exercised by a particular case-of-thought—it does not matter whether this concerns Foucault or Sacher-Masoch—consists in trying out a name of Being and in constructing a protocol of thought (that is to be as automatic as possible) by which the pertinence of this name can be evaluated with respect to the essential property that one expects it to preserve (or even to reinforce within thought): namely, univocity' (Alain Badiou, *Deleuze: The Clamour of Being*, trans. Louise Burchill [Minneapolis and London: University of Minnesota Press, 2000], 27).
5. Daniel W. Smith, 'The Concept of the Simulacrum: Deleuze and the Overturning of Platonism', *Continental Philosophy Review* 38, no. 1–2 (2005): 89.
6. Gilles Deleuze, *The Logic of Sense*, trans. Mark Lester with Charles Stivale (London: The Athlone Press, 1990), 262.
7. See Levi R. Bryant, *Difference and Givenness: Deleuze's Transcendental Empiricism and the Ontology of Immanence* (Evanston, IL: Northwestern University Press, 2008).
8. Ibid., 4.
9. Immanuel Kant, *Critique of Pure Reason*, trans. Paul Guyer and Allen W. Wood (Cambridge: Cambridge University Press, 1998), 158.
10. Bryant, *Difference and Givenness*, 9.
11. Kant, *Critique of Pure Reason*, 282.
12. Ibid.
13. 'The power of judgement in general is the faculty for thinking of the particular as contained under the universal. If the universal (the rule, the principle, the law) is given, then the power of judgement, which subsumes the particular under it (even when, as a transcendental power of judgement, it provides the conditions a priori in accordance with which alone anything can be subsumed under that universal), is determining. If, however, only the particular is given, for which the universal is to be found, then the power of judgement is merely *reflecting*' (Immanuel Kant, *Critique of the Power of Judgment*, trans. Paul Guyer and Eric Matthews [Cambridge: Cambridge University Press, 2000], 66–67). Although it is a non-Anglophone reading, it is worthwhile mentioning here the original insight on this point provided by Rado Riha: reading the distinction between determining and reflecting power of judgement through a

Badiouian-Lacanian lens, he points out how the reflective power of judgement or the aesthetic judgement of taste actually introduces the third dimension beyond the opposition between particular and universal: singularity. At this basis, he further interprets the third critique as a 'second Copernican turn' of Kantian philosophy (see Rado Riha, *Kant in drugi kopernikanski obrat v filozofiji* [Kant and the Second Copernican Turn in Philosophy] [Ljubljana: ZRC Publisher, 2012]).

14. Bryant, *Difference and Givenness*, 11.
15. Ibid.
16. Ibid., 28.
17. Ibid., 11.
18. Ibid.
19. Deleuze, *Difference and Repetition*, 56–57.
20. Deleuze, *The Logic of Sense*, 141. Although it is not an Anglophone work, I must admit I'm much indebted in my understanding of this point of Deleuze's to Peter Klepec and his book *Vznik subjekta* [The Emergence of the Subject] (Ljubljana: ZRC Publisher, 2004), 51–60, while my overall reading of perversion in this book relies much on Klepec's other book *Dobičkonosne strasti: Kapitalizem in perverzija 1* [Profitable Passions: Capitalism and Perversion 1] (Ljubljana: Society for Theoretical Psychoanalysis, 2008).
21. Badiou, *Deleuze*, 21.
22. Ibid., 20.
23. Ibid., 22.
24. 'If Deleuze critiques these positions it is not because he is rejecting the notion of critique, of having to ground one's claims, but rather because these positions are not critical enough' (Bryant, *Difference and Givenness*, 18). 'Deleuze criticizes Kant for leaving concepts and intuitions external to one another . . . , just as he criticises Plato and essentialism for leaving copies and simulacra external to each other. . . . In other words, the fallacy that Kant, Plato, and essentialism are equally subject to is, for Deleuze, an empiricist fallacy. *Paradoxically, for Deleuze, these philosophies are not transcendental enough*' (ibid., 22).
25. Deleuze, *Difference and Repetition*, 173.
26. Ibid., 28.
27. 'Difference is not diversity. Diversity is given, but difference is that by which the given is given, that by which the given is given as diverse' (ibid., 222).
28. Gilles Deleuze and Félix Guattari, *What Is Philosophy?*, trans. Graham Burchell and Hugh Tomlinson (London: Verso, 1994), 59.
29. Philip Goodchild, 'Why Is Philosophy So Compromised with God?' in *Deleuze and Religion*, ed. Mary Bryden (London and New York: Routledge, 2000), 158. This point was put forwards also by Badiou with the difference that in Badiou the immanence is conceived in terms of the category of the virtual: 'Early in the spring of 1993, I raised the objection to Deleuze that the category of the virtual seemed to me to maintain a kind of transcendence, transposed, so to speak, "beneath" the simulacra of the world, in a sort of symmetrical relation to the "beyond" of classical transcendence. Additionally, I linked the maintaining of this inverted transcendence to the retention of the category of the All' (Badiou, *Deleuze*, 45).
30. Deleuze, *Difference and Repetition*, 37.
31. Ibid., 59.
32. Ibid.
33. Deleuze, *The Logic of Sense*, 253.
34. Deleuze, *Difference and Repetition*, 59–60.
35. Ibid., 60.
36. Ibid.
37. Ibid.
38. Ibid., 62.
39. Ibid.

40. For example, as in the case of the lineage deriving from the *Statesman*, 'In effect, once the question of the claimants is reached, the *Statesman* invokes the image of an ancient God who ruled the world and men: strictly speaking, only this God deserves the name of shepherd–King of mankind. None of the claimants is his equal, but there is a certain "care" of the human community which devolves to the statesman *par excellence*, since he is closest to the model of the archaic shepherd–God. The claimants find themselves in a sense measured according to an order of elective participation, and among the statesman's rivals we can distinguish (according to the ontological measure afforded by the myth) parents, servants, auxiliaries and, finally, charlatans and counterfeits' (ibid., 60–61).

41. According to Badiou, this conception of the One as undivided Being is the main feature of Deleuze's ontology: 'We can therefore first state that one must carefully identify a metaphysics of the One in the work of Deleuze. He himself indicates what its requisites are: "one single event for all events; a single and same *aliquid* for that which happens and that which is said; and a single and same being for the impossible, the possible and the real" [Deleuze, *The Logic of Sense*, 180; translation modified]. The real basis of the supposed democracy of desire lies, in fact, in the attaining of this "one single"' (Badiou, *Deleuze*, 10). For a criticism of this reading of Badiou's, see Clayton Crockett, *Deleuze Beyond Badiou: Ontology, Multiplicity, and Event* (New York: Columbia University Press, 2013), especially part I.

42. Deleuze, *Difference and Repetition*, 64.

43. Ibid.

44. 'With univocity, however, it is not the differences which are and must be: it is being which is Difference, in the sense that it is said of difference' (ibid., 39).

45. Nathan Widder, 'The Rights of Simulacra: Deleuze and the Univocity of Being', *Continental Philosophy Review* 34, no. 4 (2001): 448.

46. Badiou, *Deleuze*, 25–26.

47. 'Division demands such a foundation as the ground capable of making the difference. Conversely, the foundation demands division as the state of difference in that which must be grounded. Division is the true unity of dialectic and mythology, of the myth as foundation and of the logos as *logos tomeus*' (Deleuze, *Difference and Repetition*, 62).

48. Ibid., 36.

49. Ibid., 37.

50. Ibid., 36–37.

THREE

Masoch as a Name-of-Being

I

Following the outline of Deleuze's ontology of difference sketched in the previous chapter, we are now in a position to tackle the question of the conceptual proximity between the case of Masoch and the main concepts of Deleuze's ontology. As previously mentioned, within the vast field of Deleuzian scholarship one can notice an abundance of discussions referring to the essay on Masoch as well as those concerning Deleuze's early ontology of difference and transcendental empiricism. What is lacking, though, is precisely a more systematic consideration of the relation between the two. More specifically, what is missing is an analysis of how the differential difference expressed by the simulacrum operates at the level of the irreducible differential between sadism and masochism. Only by analysing this conceptual relation will it become possible to comprehend Badiou's claim that Masoch is the 'name-of-being' in Deleuze's ontology.

By adopting this perspective, the most plausible way to begin is to directly pose the question concerning the genesis of the difference between sadism and masochism. On this initial point, we should pay special attention to the fact that what is staged at the very beginning of Deleuze's essay on Masoch is precisely not the difference between sadism and masochism but rather their unjustified synthesis in the 'sadomasochistic unity', conceived as a symmetrical relation between both fundamental perversions. Deleuze's argument about why we should conceive Masoch's literature as an extraordinary clinical invention thus concerns the impact Masoch has on the presupposed sadomasochistic unity. For Deleuze, Masoch is a great clinician and even greater symptomatologist insofar as he undermines the sadomasochistic unity, according to which the masochist should take a position which is complementary to that of the sadist. Moreover, Masoch links this difference introduced into the sadomasochistic unity with his proper name. So when Deleuze writes that Sade and even more so Masoch 'are outstanding examples of the efficiency of literature',[1] it is thus because each of them undermines sadomasochistic unity: they both introduce an irreducible differential between the sadist and masochist position respectively, while also connecting these inventions with their own respective proper names. The gesture performed by both Sade and Masoch is thus twofold: first, they both regroup the symptoms anew at the basis of their dissociation from the previous grouping rather than from unification; and second, they suture these new groups of differential symptoms with the proper name:

> Illnesses are sometimes named after typical patients, but more often it is the doctor's name that is given to the disease (Roger's disease, Parkinson's disease, etc.). The principles behind this labelling deserve closer analysis. The doctor does not invent the illness, he dissociates symptoms that were previously grouped together, and links up others that were dissociated. In short he builds up a profoundly original clinical picture. . . . Great clinicians are the greatest doctors: when a doctor gives his name to an illness this is a major linguistic and semiological step, inasmuch as a proper name is linked to a given group of signs, that is, *a proper name is made to connote signs.*[2]

As Levi Bryant suggested, Deleuze's procedure is here quite homologous to his criticism of the primacy of the concept over the intuition, upon which the secret alliance between empiricism and transcendental philosophy is set up. The sadomasochistic unity of opposites has a similar status here to the myth in Platonic dialectic because it hinders the possibility that sadism and masochism could be thought outside of this very same unity. The first questions are thus, how is sadomasochistic unity set up and what is its main assumption as far as it implies the unification rather than dissociation of sadism and masochism? What constitutes the kernel of this unity is precisely the pleasure-pain complex which is, crucially, taken as self-identical in sadism and masochism. However, this self-identity of pain and pleasure in sadism and masochism is constructed at the price of their mutual abstraction, which entails the exclusion of the existential level of the real existence of sadistic and masochistic pain and pleasure. In other words, the self-identity of pain and pleasure is here set up as the identity within the concept at the price of neglecting the reality of intuition. The prioritisation of the concept over the intuition or of identity over difference thus leads us to postulate the following argument: the sadist is the one who seeks pleasure in inflicting pain on the other, while the masochist is the one who seeks pleasure in his own pain. Once the pain-pleasure pair is abstracted and taken as self-identical in both cases and separated from its concrete manifestations, masochism can thus only appear as an 'inverted sadism'. From the idea that the sadist is the one who beats and the masochist is the one who is beaten, one draws the seemingly inevitable conclusion about the complementarity of both positions so that the sadist is the one who beats the masochist. The assumed self-identity of the pain-pleasure pair (the essence, as Deleuze proposes) leads towards an unjustified conclusion about the complementarity of the subjects (sadist and masochist). As previously mentioned, such a conclusion becomes possible only if one neglects the existential level of the concrete manifestation of both perversions, which is to say, the concrete geneses of pain and pleasure in sadism and masochism. Deleuze is clear on this point: 'Sadism and masochism are confused when they are treated like abstract entities each in isolation from its specific universe. Once they have been cut off from their *Umwelt* and stripped of their flesh and blood, it seems natural that they should fit in with each other'.[3]

As far as sadomasochistic unity is concerned, the difference between sadism and masochism is thus set up as a difference between two self-identities within one and the same concept. Rather than a divergent difference which manifests a non-self-identity, the difference at stake in sadomasochistic unity is a unifying dialectical difference. This difference is made possible only by abstracting sadism and masochism from their respective concrete manifestations, from their respective worlds. Following Levi Bryant's suggestion, we can approach the problem of the unjustified assumption of the real existence of sadomasochistic unity through the form of a classical syllogism and the paradoxes it contains. As he pointed out, every syllogism can be analysed on three different levels, namely, on syntactic, semantic, or existential levels.[4] The syntactic level of a syllogism deals with its abstract formalisation, which withdraws from the concrete content to which the syllogism refers in order to extract the very form of thought with the help of mathematical signs. On the semantic level of the syllogism, we analyse the meaning of both subject and predicate as well as the meaning of their relation. Finally, as far as the existential level of the syllogism is concerned, we verify whether it corresponds to reality or not, that is, whether it is true or false from the perspective of existence.

Now take, for example, the case of a unicorn, as Bryant suggests, and suppose that the truthfulness of its existence is determined by the usage of the verb 'to be'. We can describe a unicorn, we can say what a unicorn 'is', yet this does not involve any judgement concerning its existence and once we think of it, we can only admit its falsity. Although we can provide several descriptions of what a unicorn 'is', we cannot say it also really exists. Hence, this means that we encounter the problem with such a syllogism not when we think the three levels separately, as independent from each other, but when we think the three levels in their summary validity. As Bryant argues,

> Problems quickly begin to emerge as soon as I make judgments such as 'Socrates is a human'. Why does this form of judgment lead to problems? Well, we might ask ourselves whether being-a-human and Socrates are one and the same thing. The answer seems to be no. We can say what a human is, and we can also, in part, say what Socrates is independent of his 'humanness'. Consequently, there seems to be a way in which predicative judgments involve two different forms of being: namely, the being of the predicate and the being of the subject.[5]

Isn't this precisely the case with masochism and of sadomasochistic unity? The form of the syllogism might be of some help here as well. Let us first approach the problem of masochism alone:

All humans seek pleasure.
Masochists seek pain.
Masochists are not human.

From the difference at the level of predicate, this syllogism unjustifiably leads to a conclusion about a difference at the level of subject. If the human psyche is determined by the pleasure principle, and if the masochist at manifest level is someone who seeks pain, then the syllogism concludes that the masochist does not belong to the totality of humans. In other words, as Bryant stresses, one quickly gets into trouble with a syllogism like this as soon as it verifies the existence of the subject on the same level as the existence of the predicate.

The problem with the syllogism comes even more to the fore in the case of sadomasochistic unity. If we adjust such a syllogism and replace the totality of humans with the unity of masochists and of sadists, the situation becomes even more problematic:

Sadists find pleasure in inflicting pain.
Masochists find pleasure in suffering pain.
The masochist is the one upon whom the sadist inflicts pain.

Such a reasoning is problematic precisely because it takes pain and pleasure as two self-identical givens, from which it then draws the conclusion about the necessary reciprocity and complementarity between the subjects (sadist and masochist). Roughly put, this kind of argument assumes that the pain and pleasure in sadism and masochism are of one and the same kind. Insofar as the sadist is the one who inflicts pain and the masochist the one who receives this *very same* pain, then sadomasochism *really exists* as an ideal unity of the opposites. What occurs in this kind of logical deduction is precisely the external subsumption of both subjects under the same abstract unity, which represses the existential level of the respective *differential geneses of sadism and masochism*. This is the point upon which Deleuze is steadfast:

> In the sphere of perversions, it is a mistake to confuse the formations, the concrete and specific manifestations, with an abstract 'grid', as

> though a common libidinal substance flowed now into one form, now into another. We are told that some individuals experienced pleasure both in inflicting pain and in suffering it. We are told furthermore that the person who enjoys inflicting pain experiences in his innermost being the link that exists between the pleasure and the pain. But the question is whether these 'facts' are not mere abstractions, whether the pleasure–pain link is being abstracted from the concrete formal conditions in which it arises. The pleasure–pain complex is regarded as a sort of neutral substance common to both sadism and masochism. The link is even further specified by being ascribed to a particular subject, and it is supposed to be experienced equally and identically by the sadistic and the masochistic subject, regardless of the concrete forms *from which it results* in each case.[6]

What Deleuze criticises where sadomasochistic unity is concerned is thus precisely the operation upon which this unity relies, namely *the transformation of analogy into homology*. From the fact that sadism and masochism are analogical, it is unjustified to consider them as homological or complementary. This transformation in fact excludes the differential geneses of sadism and masochism, and the differential manifestations of pain and pleasure in them, which are then replaced with the abstraction of this complex, thus generating the link between the two. What we encounter, here, is, once again, the privileging of the concept over dispersed sensations or, what is the same, the subsumption of the many (a 'rhapsody of intuitions') under the one (concept). In so doing, sadomasochistic unity neglects precisely the differential geneses or the differential realities of sadism and masochism. As Bryant explains with great clarity,

> Ultimately, material or empirical definitions find themselves unable to maintain the difference they strive to explain and are thus arbitrary and insufficient. More importantly, the reason they are unable to arrive at the being of the being they seek to comprehend is that they seek to locate this being in the material content (sense-data) of its manifestations. In the case of sadism and masochism, they take pleasure and pain as mere givens, as the defining or determining features of sadism and masochism, without determining the conditions under which this pain and pleasure in their particular manifestation is possible. As a result, such approaches are led to postulate a complementarity between sadism and masochism that betrays their reality.[7]

II

From these premises, we are now better able to understand Deleuze's interest in Masoch's literature: it is precisely due to Masoch's efficiency in expressing a completely divergent genesis of masochism with respect to the alleged sadomasochistic unity. As implied, the divergence or, more precisely, the divergent difference consists in resisting the temptation to abstract masochism and the pain-pleasure complex from the concrete context in which they originate. In other words, by attaching the pain-pleasure complex to the genesis of its emergence in masochism, Masoch puts into question the assumed self-identity of pain and pleasure respectively: Are they always one and the same thing? Indeed, the masochist finds pleasure in his own pain (or, more precisely, by means of the pain), and the sadist certainly enjoys inflicting pain to the other; however, due to the completely divergent geneses of pain and pleasure in sadism and masochism, the masochist will never find pleasure in the pain inflicted by the sadist, and the sadist will never really enjoy inflicting pain on the masochist.

Following Badiou, we can now clearly see why he suggested taking Masoch as a 'case-of-thought' in Deleuze's philosophy: the existential level of masochism puts in question the concept of sadomasochism conceived as the unity of two self-identical opposites. In so doing, Masoch expresses the divergent nature of masochism with respect to sadism insofar as it dissociates the self-identity of the pain-pleasure complex. From the point of view of sadomasochistic unity, we are sure pain is one and the same. We are also sure that pleasure is one and the same, but from the point of view of Masoch's masochism, this certitude is immediately suspended, put into question. Once we comprehend that pain and pleasure, due to their differential geneses, in masochism are not quite the same as those presupposed in sadomasochistic unity, we start questioning the very self-identity of pain and pleasure in general. Are the two really always one and the same?

From the perspective of transcendental philosophy which entails the primacy of the concept over intuition, masochism so conceived cannot but appear as unbearable. For if masochism diverges from the conceptual determination of sadomasochistic unity, it can only be dismissed as an unthinkable phenomenon or as a misleading intuition. Adopting the point of view of transcendental empiricism, however, one can comprehend masochism as an event-of-thought precisely for the very same reason because, for Deleuze, the thought always begins at the very short circuit between the concept and the intuition. From this perspective, masochism, rather than an irrational intuition, appears to be precisely a rational intuition, which is to say, an intuition which entails the dimension of thought precisely insofar as it puts in question the certitude of the concept. This procedure, in which thought is generated not by the subject but rather by an object which does not fit the concept, perhaps best reveals the nature of thought in Deleuze's transcendental empiricism and the ontology of immanence. In this philosophy, there's no subject who contemplates the object, but instead it is an object which engages the subject by way of an automatism which does not allow the subject any choice in thinking the object. Insofar as there is an object which triggers thought, it does so precisely to the extent that it appears to be something which the subject *cannot but think*. In this respect, Badiou was right in arguing that the case-of-thought in Deleuze's philosophy is somehow always a 'purified automaton',[8] which engages the subject automatically regardless of his will.

III

We are now in a position to analyse in more detail some basic features of Masoch's masochism which, according to Deleuze, constitute its divergent difference with respect to sadomasochistic unity and the alleged complicity between sadism and masochism. The first feature indeed concerns the 'simulation' at work in masochism. Where this feature is concerned, Deleuze does not fail to argue that masochism is essentially an 'art of fantasy'.[9] Moreover, according to Deleuze, by engaging psychic mechanisms of 'disavowal, suspense, waiting, fetishism and fantasy together',[10] masochism founds itself precisely upon the redoubling of reality, or, to use Foucault's expression again, it is essentially the 'power of the false'. Not surprisingly, following Deleuze, Sade's sadism is totally hostile to such artistic mechanisms which are inoperative within the much more dynamic constellation of sadistic plays. The portrait, for instance, which depicts Wanda von Sacher-Masoch with the whip up in the air, suspended in the moment immediately before the fall of the whip which will inflict pain on Severin, thus enables the constitution of the fantasy. Dreaming or fantasising about violent subordination to a woman torturer is an integral part of the reality of Masoch's masochism. Such a fantasy is essentially inoperative within sadistic constellations which entail, on the contrary, a specific rhythm of practical demonstrations which do not allow for any pauses or caesuras. Importantly, the pain in masochism is precisely not the goal of the masochist; for the masochist, pain is paradoxically the means for achieving a prohibited pleasure, a pleasure of which is very much close to Lacan's definition of surplus enjoyment in which the rejection of (direct/total) enjoyment starts functioning as the 'source' of (surplus) enjoyment. Moreover, the pain the masochist awaits can function as a means of pleasure precisely to the extent that it is inflicted by a 'cold' woman torturer who, from the masochist's point of view, in this way expresses material care. The moment of divergence between sadism and masochism within the alleged sadomasochistic unity thus emerges precisely at the point where masochism simulates and hence raises to the surface something that in sadism should be repressed at all costs.[11] This is why the masochist's desire for pain inflicted by a woman torturer is inoperative in sadism and vice versa, that is, the sadist's desire to inflict pain is incompatible with the pedagogical character of the masochist who must 'educate' his woman torturer. According to Deleuze, this is why the infamous jokes about the complicity of sadist and masochist are actually bad jokes. As he writes,

> The belief in this unity is to a large extent the result of misunderstandings and careless reasoning. It may seem obvious that the sadist and the masochist are destined to meet. The fact that the one enjoys inflicting while the other enjoys suffering pain seems to be such striking proof of their complementarity that it would be disappointing if the encounter did not take place. A popular joke tells of the meeting between a sadist and a masochist: the masochist says: 'Hurt me'. The sadist replies: 'No'. This is a particularly stupid joke, not only because it is unrealistic but because it foolishly claims competence to pass judgment on the world of perversions. It is unrealistic because a genuine sadist could never tolerate a masochist victim (one of the monks' victims in *Justine* explains: 'They wish to be certain their crimes cost tears; they would send away any girl who was to come here voluntarily'.) Neither would the masochist tolerate a truly sadistic torturer. He does of course require a special 'nature' in the woman torturer, but he needs to mold this nature, to educate and persuade it in accordance with his secret project, which would never be fulfilled with a sadistic woman.[12]

Of course, the divergent difference between sadism and masochism emerges at several different levels. However, there's perhaps one aspect which is crucial not only for the proper understanding of masochism but also for advocating its socio-ontological status. This aspect concerns the role of fetishism or, more precisely, of the fetishistic disavowal and the alleged abolishment of the Other in masochism and, as Deleuze put it, the rebirth of the masochist as a 'new man devoid of sexual love'.

According to Deleuze, fetishistic disavowal functions as a mechanism by which the masochist achieves the transference of symbolic power from the father to the mother. Yet the symbolic figures of the father and the mother respectively are not symmetrical. Or, better yet, precisely because they are in some sense symmetrical, insofar as the castration of the mother is disavowed ('symbolically the mother lacks nothing'[13]), they produce difference. Deleuze sets up this argument against the background of the classical Freudian conception of the figure of the father as that which introduces the symbolic law into the realm of the subject. According to Freud, symbolic law consists mainly in the prohibition of the incest, which is to say, it constrains access to the mother as the object of the child's satisfaction. Furthermore, this prohibition is regulated by the threat of castration (punishment) and the superego's injunction of guilt.

On the other end, Freud conceives the fetish in terms of the substitute for the mother's penis;[14] specifically, it functions as a mechanism which enables the subject to deal with the threat of castration. Yet precisely to the extent that the fetish is a kind of tool allowing the subject to defend himself against the threat of castration, it functions as a 'monument' to the latter. Importantly, for Freud the fetish is essentially determined by the process of its constitution, which also establishes the mother as phallic:

> One would expect that the organs or objects chosen as substitutes for the absent female phallus would be such as appear as symbols of the penis in other connections as well. This may happen often enough, but is certainly not a deciding factor. It seems rather that when the fetish is instituted some process occurs which reminds one of the stopping of memory in traumatic amnesia. As in this latter case, the subject's interest comes to a halt half-way, as it were; it is as though the last impression before the uncanny and traumatic one is retained as a fetish. Thus the foot or shoe owes its preference as a fetish—or a part of it—to the circumstance that the inquisitive boy peered at the woman's genitals from below, from her legs up; fur and velvet—as has long been suspected—are a fixation of the sight of the pubic hair, which should have been followed by the longed-for sight of the female member; pieces of underclothing, which are so often chosen as a fetish, crystallise the moment of undressing, the last moment in which the woman could still be regarded as phallic.[15]

To sum up, what establishes the mother/woman as phallic is precisely the process in which her undressing is virtually frozen by means of the fetish at the very last moment before the lack of penis is revealed. The fetish, here, implies the 'overestimation' of the woman and this overestimation plays a central role in the sexual relationships of adult life. However, Freud himself considered fetishism not only in terms of the overestimation of the object-person but also as a pre-copulative or nongenital phenomenon which is quite universal in the field of sexuality as such, being employed in different sexual relationships as a means to achieve copulation. This means that the fetishist's disavowal solely is certainly insufficient to determine masochism, which, according to Deleuze, aims at a position outside sexuality and sexual difference. Freud was well aware of this problem, hence he introduced a sharper sense of when the fetishism should be regarded as a perversion in a pathological sense of the term: according to him, fetishism becomes pathological in the situation when the fetish is not taken as the means to achieve the sexual aim of copulation but becomes in itself an aim, detached from a particular person:

> The situation only becomes pathological when the longing for the fetish passes beyond the point of being merely a necessary condition attached to the sexual object and actually *takes the place* of the normal aim, and, further, when the fetish becomes detached from a particular individual and becomes the *sole* sexual object.[16]

What constitutes the kernel of masochism is thus precisely the identification with the object-fetish which holds also for the castration. According to Deleuze, Masoch's masochist—and this is a humorous aspect of masochism—begins with castration and the fetish: he puts them at the very beginning of the process which then leads towards the achievement of the prohibited pleasure. However, in so doing, that is, in absolutising the whole realm of pre-copulative and nongenital sexual practices without ending up in the copulation—not surprisingly, the genitals are not at all mentioned in *Venus in Furs*—the masochist seemingly achieves the devaluation of castration and its symbolic regulative function. By identifying with castration, the masochist seemingly deterritorialises the pleasure from the territory of erogenous zones, while he also devaluates the superego's injunction and the fear of castration. For Deleuze, this is how the masochist finally liberates himself not only from the realm of the father but from the realm of sexual difference itself as well. In this way, Alenka Zupančič's critique of Foucault's misreading of Freud's theory of repression also applies to Deleuze's engagement with masochism: what is fundamentally at stake here is nothing but the task 'to *separate enjoyment from sexuality* as neatly as possible'.[17]

Most importantly, Deleuze even goes so far as to extend this line of argument to the theory of the drive. In chapter X, 'The Death Instinct', of his essay 'Coldness and Cruelty', he claims to provide a 'philosophical reflection' on Freud's 'Beyond the Pleasure Principle'[18] and suggests thinking 'the pleasure principle' as a 'transcendental' principle.[19] Although this claim might seem unambiguous at first glance, Deleuze does not fail to add a crucial specification as to what exactly the Kantian term 'transcendental' means in the 'pleasure principle'. It does not refer to the universality of the empirical 'pleasure-seeking' principle (this is, for Deleuze, only a secondary principle) which governs the human psyche; rather, it refers to the principle which subjects or links the human psyche to the power of the empirical pleasure principle. As he writes,

> Thus we say that the pleasure principle governs life universally and without exception. But there is another and quite distinct question, namely in virtue of what is a field governed by a principle; there must be a principle of another kind, a second-order principle, which accounts for a necessary compliance of the field with the empirical principle. It is this second-order principle that we call transcendental. Pleasure is a principle insofar as it governs our psychic life. But we must still ask what is the highest authority which subjects our psychic life to the dominance of this principle.[20]

Not surprisingly, Deleuze—at first glance in sharp opposition to the 'vitalist' prioritisation of 'life' over 'death'—further proposes to identify this 'transcendental' principle precisely with the 'beyond' the 'pleasure principle', namely, with the repetition or compulsion to repeat (or the death drive—Thanatos): 'Beyond Eros we encounter Thanatos'.[21] What links or subjects our psyche to Eros or the pleasure principle is thus Thanatos or repetition itself. Hence, as Alenka Zupančič stresses, Eros and Thanatos cannot be situated on the same level. While Eros is an empirical principle, Thanatos is not merely the opposite of Eros but rather points to a peculiar second-order transcendental principle which links psychic life to the former. Yet what precisely does repetition refer to here? Following Freud literally, Deleuze argues that it refers to the 'binding of excitation',[22] that is, to the surplus excitation which, according to Freud, originates in the repetition of the satisfaction of the (biological) need, and it is only due to this binding that the pleasure principle can be established as a governing principle.

As far as the pleasure principle is concerned, Deleuze maintains that perverts do not differ from others (neurotics). Regarding the masochist, he argues that he seeks pain in order to achieve pleasure: pain is not the ultimate scope of the masochistic libidinal disposition. The point where perversion properly speaking emerges is elsewhere, namely, at the point of desexualisation or the detachment of the drive from sexuality, which opens up for further resexualisation. In other words, desexualisation amounts exactly to the detachment of repetition (Thanatos) from pleasure (Eros) as if the two would change their roles:

> Beneath the sound and fury of sadism and masochism the terrible force of repetition is at work. What is altered here is the normal function of repetition in its relation to the pleasure principle: instead of repetition being experienced as a form of behaviour related to the pleasure already obtained or anticipated, instead of repetition being governed by the idea of experiencing or re-experiencing pleasure, repetition runs wild and becomes independent of all previous pleasure. It has itself become an idea or ideal. Pleasure is now a form of behaviour related to repetition, accompanying and following repetition, which has itself become an awesome, independent force. Pleasure and repetition have thus exchanged roles, as a consequence of the instantaneous leap, that is to say the twofold process of desexualisation and resexualisation.[23]

Most importantly, Deleuze does not fail to add that the resexualisation of the desexualised 'takes place instantaneously'.[24] Not only does he claim that the 'deeper the coldness of the desexualisation, the more powerful and extensive the process of perverse resexualisation' is,[25] but fundamentally that the split/place of separation between desexualisation and resexualisation is to be directly identified with the death drive itself as a generative force (independent repetition) of perverse affirmation: 'In between the two processes the Death Instinct seems to speak about.'[26] For Deleuze, Masoch's masochist is the figure that most efficiently expresses this split in which the death drive appears as a generative force generating a 'new man devoid of sexual love'. Moreover, this identification of the split or negativity with the generative force of the drive itself constitutes the kernel of what could be regarded as Deleuze's (vitalist) 'ontology of the drive', insofar as he does not fail to assign the ontological status of Being to the difference which originates in the repetition. In fact, as Zupančič convincingly argues in her comparative reading of the death drive in Deleuze and Lacan respectively, this becomes far clearer in Deleuze's discussion of the relation between the death drive, repetition, and difference, in both *Difference and Repetition* and *The Logic of Sense*.

As we have already seen in the previous chapter, the difference Deleuze is searching for is essentially a diverging or pure difference, which is to say, it emerges precisely as a non-self-identity of the object-simulacrum. Yet as such, it is determined by and dependent on the more originary and fundamental movement of repetition (Thanatos) which is by definition always the repetition of the same. Insofar as repetition always entails the repetition of the same (object), it produces the object as a simulacrum, that is, as a non-self-identical uncanny double, which implies the emergence of difference. Thus, we can say that this configuration 'posits repetition as an absolute beginning'.[27] There's nothing prior to repetition and everything, including difference, emerges out of the movement of repetition. However, this prioritisation of repetition over difference should not be understood in a transcendental sense, as if difference is only externally linked with repetition as its external by-product. On the contrary, difference is inextricably connected with the movement of repetition. More precisely, if repetition is conceived by Deleuze as a surplus of excitation which is beyond the pleasant satisfaction of biological need, it is because it expresses precisely the non-self-identity of pleasure itself: on the one hand, excitation is bound with the pleasure principle, while on the other hand, it does not fully correspond with it but rather exceeds it. In such a way, however, Deleuze conceives difference and the surplus of excitation as one and the same thing. As Alenka Zupančič argues, 'For Deleuze, however, the excess/surplus is *directly* the pure productive excess of negativity (crack, Difference) repeating itself in different disguises and with different signifiers and symbols. The original negativity directly *is* the "positive", "productive" movement or force ("drive")'.[28]

There is only one additional step necessary to bring us to the very ontologisation of the drive in Deleuze. Insofar as the repetition of the drive (as surplus of excitation) is already directly conceived as difference, such a difference always expresses the being of Difference (as One/univocity). As Zupančič continues,

> In what Deleuze will call 'realised ontology', all that remains is the Difference itself (pure difference, not a difference between this and that). This Difference is pure being *qua* being in its univocity. And it equals pure *movement*, just as the *fêlure*, the 'crack', is finally not so much a rift as a pure movement or force. This shift from *topological* to *dynamic* tropes is indeed crucial for Deleuze: the topological non-coincidence of being and appearing, their *rift*, is 'liquefied' into Being as a pure *movement* of Difference.[29]

From this vantage point, it is not hard to recognise the logic that underpins Deleuze's discussion of perversion and particularly of masochism. Precisely to the extent that the drive as the repetition or the excess of excitation is independent (separated from sexuality), while at the same time always already sealed with Difference as Being, it becomes neutralised, indifferent and thus transmittable. It can thus appear without constraints at the same time in sadism and in masochism, without necessitating its reversibility, which would pave the way to reading the concept of masochism as an inverted sadism. In other words, the desexualisation of the libido—which is the same as the separation of the drive from the realm of sexuality—is, for Deleuze, a necessary condition for the mutual independency of sadism and masochism. Insofar as both express their mutual independence and incompatibility, they also express their Difference: the nonrelationship between the masochist and the sadist is held together by their equal presence in univocal Being.

NOTES

1. Gilles Deleuze, 'Coldness and Cruelty', in *Masochism: Coldness and Cruelty and Venus in Furs*, trans. Jean McNeil, ed. Gilles Deleuze and Leopold von Sacher-Masoch (New York: Zone Books, 1991), 15.
2. Ibid., 15–16.
3. Ibid., 42.
4. Levi R. Bryant, *Difference and Givenness: Deleuze's Transcendental Empiricism and the Ontology of Immanence* (Evanston, IL: Northwestern University Press, 2008), 6.
5. Ibid., 7.
6. Deleuze, 'Coldness and Cruelty', 45–46.
7. Bryant, *Difference and Givenness*, 23.
8. Alain Badiou, *Deleuze: The Clamour of Being*, trans. Louise Burchill (Minneapolis and London: University of Minnesota Press, 2000), 11.
9. Deleuze, 'Coldness and Cruelty', 72.
10. Ibid.
11. This is why Deleuze ultimately puts more weight on Masoch when the disjunction of the sadomasochistic unity is concerned: 'Hence our suggestion that Masoch was perhaps an even greater clinician than Sade, in that he provided various elucidations and intuitions which help to break down the spurious sadomasochistic unity' (ibid., 40).
12. Ibid., 40–41.
13. Ibid., 64. As we shall see in the following chapters, this is the point where Lacan and Deleuze ultimately differ from one another. If for Deleuze there's a symbolic dissymmetry between the figure of the father and that of the mother, Lacan adds to this conception that the figure of the mother is not located outside of the symbolic order revolving around the figure of the father as Deleuze thought. On the contrary, as Lacan pointed out, the mother/woman is yet another name-of-the-father which implies that, as Alenka Zupančič recently argued, the symbolic 'power' of the mother is by no means less power than that of the father.
14. 'When now I announce that the fetish is a substitute for the penis, I shall certainly create disappointment; so I hasten to add that it is not a substitute for any chance penis, but for a particular and quite special penis that had been extremely important in early childhood but had later been lost. That is to say, it should normally have been given up, but the fetish is precisely designed to preserve it from extinction. To put it more plainly: fetish is a substitute for the woman's (the mother's) penis that the little boy once believed in and—for reasons familiar to us—does not want to give up' (Sigmund Freud, 'Fetishism', in *The Standard Edition of the Complete Psychological Works of Sigmund Freud, Vol. XXI*, ed. James Strachey [London: Vintage, 2001], 152–53).

15. Ibid., 155. For the sake of clarity, it is necessary to cite the complete formula of fetishism as defined by Freud: 'When now I announce that the fetish is a substitute for the penis, I shall certainly create disappointment; so I hasten to add that it is not a substitute for any chance penis, but for a particular and quite special penis that had been extremely important in early childhood but had later been lost. That is to say, it should normally have been given up, but the fetish is precisely designed to preserve it from extinction. To put it more plainly: fetish is a substitute for the woman's (the mother's) penis that the little boy once believed in and—for reasons familiar to us—does not want to give up' (ibid., 152–53).

16. Sigmund Freud, 'Three Essays on the Theory of Sexuality', in *The Standard Edition of the Complete Psychological Works of Sigmund Freud, Vol. VII*, ed. James Strachey (London: Vintage, 2001), 154.

17. Alenka Zupančič, *What* Is *Sex?* (Cambridge, MA: MIT Press, 2017), 15. I will provide arguments to explain why Deleuze actually misreads Freud on this occasion in the part on the psychoanalytic articulation of perversion.

18. Sigmund Freud, 'Beyond the Pleasure Principle', in *The Standard Edition of the Complete Psychological Works of Sigmund Freud, Vol. XVIII*, ed. James Strachey (London: Vintage, 2001), 7–64.

19. Deleuze, 'Coldness and Cruelty', 112.

20. Ibid.

21. Ibid., 114.

22. Ibid., 113.

23. Ibid., 120.

24. Ibid., 118.

25. Ibid., 117.

26. Ibid., 120.

27. Zupančič, *What* Is *Sex?*, 113.

28. Ibid., 118.

29. Ibid.

FOUR

From Masoch to Tao

The Revision of Masochism in Late Deleuze

I

I concluded the previous chapter by pointing out how Deleuze's reading of masochism as a socio-ontological difference relies upon an assumption of separation between pleasure and sexuality. Only to the extent that he posits this separation is he able to maintain the idea of a direct and immediately affirmative positivity of the Difference or negativity. In this chapter, I will continue this line of argument by highlighting how, in Deleuze's later philosophy, this idea is not simply overturned as is usually assumed but rather secretly maintained through its radicalisation. Moreover, this radicalisation not only concerns the fact that, after *Difference and Repetition* and *The Logic of Sense*, 'the concept of simulacrum is ultimately replaced by the concept of the assemblage',[1] as Daniel Smith had argued, but, most importantly, that the concepts of One, univocity, and pleasure are replaced with those of desire and of a multiplicity which is essentially without the One. However, as we shall soon see, the concepts of desire and multiplicity are not merely in opposition to those of the simulacrum, One, univocity, and pleasure but rather represent the very radicalisation or intensification of the latter. In fact, according to Éric Alliez's suggestion, the basic formula of multiplicity ('n – 1'[2]) that Deleuze and Guattari formulate at the very beginning of *A Thousand Plateaus* should be read in terms of the subtraction of multiplicity from the principle of the One. In other words, we get multiplicity by simply subtracting the One. And insofar as the concept of the One is here conceived as a metaphor for the function of the Father as defined by psychoanalysis, namely, the Father who governs the family triangle and territorialises pleasure around the erogenous zones of the body, Alliez further maintains that such a formula of multiplicity should be understood also as the subtraction of the function of the Father: 'n – father'.[3] We get multiplicity by simply subtracting the function of the Father. Yet by this subtraction, Deleuze does not simply contradict his previous position, I will argue, but rather tries to radicalise it, as if it were not sufficiently radical in itself. When speaking about the deterritorialisation of desire in Kafka, he is clear enough: 'The question of the father isn't how to become free in relation to him (an Oedipal question) but how to find a path there where he didn't find any'.[4] The separation of multiplicity from the Father thus echoes with the persistence of desire where the father betrayed his own desire (for instance, the betrayal of his Jewishness in his submission to the dominant order of the German language under the Austrian Empire of the early twentieth century, as in the case of Kafka's father himself).

The figure that most efficiently expresses this subtraction of the Father from multiplicity is obviously the figure of the *body without organs*.[5] It is around this figure that the shift from transcendental empiricism to the ontology of immanence mostly occurs. And considering the fact that Deleuze revises the figure of the masochist against the background of the *BwO* ('The masochist is looking for a type of BwO . . .'[6]), it is also the figure that enables us to see how he rethinks the concept of pleasure in this passage from the One to multiplicity, from pleasure to desire.

II

To recall very briefly, in the previous chapter we saw that Deleuze engages deeply with the concept of pleasure in 'Coldness and Cruelty', although he wrongly ends up in ontologising the movement of repetition or the death drive as a transcendental principle. He further maintains that the masochist is not at all different from other subjects as far as pleasure is concerned. The masochist is looking for pleasure, yet he is able to achieve it only through pain and suffering. This dynamic is shaped by a peculiar form of time in masochism which is characterised by 'waiting and suspense': 'Formally speaking, masochism is a state of waiting; the masochist experiences waiting in its pure form'.[7] Yet precisely because the aim of the masochist is pleasure, which he can achieve only through 'humiliation, expiation, punishment and guilt',[8] the form of waiting and suspense has to be composed of two simultaneous currents. As Deleuze continues,

> Pure waiting divides naturally into two simultaneous currents, the first representing what is awaited, something essentially tardy, always late and always postponed, the second representing something that is expected and on which depends the speeding up of the awaited object. It is inevitable that such a form, such a rhythmic division of time into two streams, should be 'filled' by the particular combination of pleasure

> and pain. For at the same time as pain fulfils what is expected, it becomes possible for pleasure to fulfil what is awaited. The masochist waits for pleasure as something that is bound to be late, and expects pain as the condition that will finally ensure (both physically and morally) the advent of pleasure. He therefore postpones pleasure in expectation of the pain which will make gratification possible.[9]

Although Deleuze never refers to it, this division between awaited pleasure and expected pain whereby the latter is the means to achieve the former clearly echoes the Freudian conceptual distinction between 'fore-pleasure' (*Vorlust*) and 'end-pleasure' from his 'Three Essays'.[10] Awaiting and postponing pleasure in Masoch's rituals corresponds to the excitation of the libido which Freud calls 'fore-pleasure' in the context of sexual or copulative dynamics. However, in what Freud calls 'normal' sexuality (assumed heterosexual copulation), the surplus of excitation is satisfied with the 'end-pleasure' or sexual copulative act which contains both the female orgasm and the male ejaculation. What makes the masochist a pervert in the Freudian sense is not that he endlessly maintains the moment of 'fore-pleasure' without ever passing to final (albeit partial) satisfaction; rather, what makes him a pervert is the fact that he achieves final satisfaction or 'end-pleasure' without engaging the genitals, by engaging partial or nongenital erogenous zones. In other words, at the level of 'Coldness and Cruelty', the masochist does achieve the moment of 'end-pleasure'; however, he achieves it only by way of accepting the pain he expects.

Despite the fact that the masochist plays here at the level of partial drive and repetition, there's still a division or conceptual difference between these two stages: on the one hand, a second-order transcendental principle or repetition which binds pleasure with a surplus of excitation, and, on the other hand, the missing level of sexuality from which the drive as repetition should be detached. Only to the extent that this transcendental principle, which binds pleasure with excitation, exists can pain function as a means for achieving pleasure. Waiting and suspense as temporal principles in masochism are thus not the opposite of the movement of repetition of the drive but, on the contrary, as close to the latter as possible. In this sense, masochistic painting, which depicts waiting at its purest state (in the form of a woman torturer who holds the whip but does not strike), is therefore precisely the best way of expressing the proximity of waiting to the depth of the death drive. As Deleuze clearly states,

> Masoch, on the contrary, has every reason to rely on art and the immobile and reflective quality of culture. In his view the plastic arts confer an eternal character on their subject because they suspend gestures and attitudes. The whip or the sword that never strikes, the fur that never discloses the flesh, the heel that is forever descending on the victim, are

> the expression, beyond all movement, of a profound state of waiting closer to the sources of life and death.[11]

The art of Masoch and the whole temporal form of waiting and suspense, insofar as it is inextricably connected with the repetition and the movement of the death drive, are thus the means of expressing the intensity of vital metamorphosis, which will produce 'a new man devoid of sexual love' at the end of this process of transformation. However, at the level of 'Coldness and Cruelty', Deleuze still employs pleasure as a means of expressing this metamorphosis and its vital intensities.

III

In stark contrast, the Deleuze of the later period completely revises this vision of masochism in line with his categorical rejection of the concept of pleasure, which he now considers to be a 'rotten idea'.[12] For instance, when writing again on Masoch in *Essays Critical and Clinical*, Deleuze now rereads the above passage from 'Coldness and Cruelty' and the opposition between pleasure and desire in a radically anti-dialectical way: now 'pleasure interrupts desire, so that the constitution of desire as a process must ward off pleasure, repress it to infinity. The woman-torturer sends a delayed wave of pain over the masochist, who makes use of it, obviously not as a source of pleasure, but as a flow to be followed in the constitution of an uninterrupted process of desire. What becomes essential is waiting and suspense as a plenitude, as a physical and spiritual intensity'.[13] In Freudian terms, what is at stake here is a kind of radical cut between fore-pleasure and end-pleasure within the dynamics of excitation. If, at the level of 'Coldness and Cruelty', one achieves pleasure by traversing the moment of pain (end-pleasure which satisfies previous excitation which is otherwise felt as unpleasant), a few decades later Deleuze maintains that the moment of end-pleasure has to be postponed endlessly so that the previous moment of excitation (desire) is extended to infinity and should never be interrupted. In other words, the dynamics of excitation (fore-pleasure) should be extended to infinity and should never be interrupted with the moment of pleasure proper (end-pleasure).

This rereading, which not only prioritises desire over pleasure but sees pleasure as a main threat to the positivity of desire, can be traced back to the discussion of the *BwO* in *A Thousand Plateaus* and to the reformulation of the (psychoanalytical) notion of desire that occurs there. If, according to Lacan, desire is inherently connected to the moment of negativity in the constitution of the human psyche, that is, to castration and the emergence of the object-cause of desire, then in Deleuze and Guattari's field of immanence, desire is transformed in such a way that '[it] lacks nothing and therefore cannot be linked to any external or transcendent criterion'.[14] In other words, for Deleuze and Guattari, desire is immanent to itself, is itself its own object and is not determined by any kind of external lack. As mentioned before, the operation that allows desire itself to become its own object or the field of immanence is the dissolution of the pseudo-link between desire and pleasure. The positivity of desire emerges precisely at the point of this dissolution insofar as the pleasure principle, from the outside, as an external or transcendent measure interrupts or, better, represses desire as a positive entity. What comes to the fore, here, is thus the immanence of desire as a process of vital intensity, a field of immanence without any lack, a *BwO* which replaces the transcendental principle of repetition and which sees pleasure now as an external intruder.[15]

According to this position, Deleuze and Guattari rearticulate the effect of the temporal suspense. Insofar as desire excludes pleasure as its own (anti-)dialectical opposite, desire itself becomes an infinite and continuous process which should by no means be interrupted because every interruption is nothing but the signal of the presence of some transcendental element acting from the outside upon the field of immanence. Waiting and suspense are thus no longer considered as the elements of the excitation of fore-pleasure, which are supposed to bring the subject to the pleasant satisfaction (end-pleasure) of the surplus of excitation. Rather, insofar as the end-pleasure, or simply pleasure, is now meant to be an external intruder which interrupts the immanence of desire, a desire which desires nothing but itself, the moment of fore-pleasure becomes the end in itself, which is now extended to the infinity. As far as the names-of-being or cases-of-thought are concerned, it is necessary to emphasise how on this point the replacement of Masoch with Tao and of the 'new man devoid of sexual love' with the *BwO* is enacted:

> A great Japanese compilation of Chinese Taoist treatises was made in A.D. 982–984. We see in it the formation of a circuit of intensities between female and male energy, with the woman playing the role of the innate or instinctive force (Yin) stolen by or transmitted to the man in such a way that the transmitted force of the man (Yang) in turn becomes innate, all the more innate: an augmentation of powers. The condition for this circulation and multiplication is that the man not ejaculate. It is not a question of experiencing desire as an internal lack, nor of delaying pleasure in order to produce a kind of externalisable surplus value, but instead of constituting an intensive body without organs, Tao, a field of immanence in which desire lacks nothing and therefore cannot be linked to any external or transcendental criterion.[16]

Deleuze and Guattari maintain precisely the endless extension of the moment of fore-pleasure without ever interrupting it with the emergence of that end-pleasure which would partially and temporarily interrupt the consistency of desire. What they argue for is 'coitus reservatus' as opposed to 'coitus interruptus'. The former is 'reservatus' in relation to the Lacanian notion of *jouissance* as always partial end-pleasure, determined by the phallus and castration. In this respect, the plane of immanence of desire is thought to be the plane without (external) limits, the latter being always already considered of a transcendental character. Although he is far from being an exclusive example, the masochist thus becomes the figure of *BwO* or the immanence of desire. And he relates to other *BwO*s as a part of the plan of consistency set up by the multiplicity of different *BwO*s or plateaus. If in Deleuze's early ontological project the multiplicity of different elements, produced by the movement of repetition, was held together by the indifference of the One or the univocity of Being, we can see how Deleuze and Guattari here replace the One with the notion of the plane of consistency or immanence. Not surprisingly, the main philosophical reference here is Spinoza which implies also a return of the notion of substance—the notion completely marginalised in Deleuze's early ontological project: 'There is a continuum of all of the attributes or genuses of intensity under a single substance, and a continuum of the intensities of a certain genus under a single type or attribute. A continuum of all substances in intensity and of all intensities in substance. The uninterrupted continuum of BwO. BwO, immanence, immanent limit. Drug users, masochists, schizophrenics, lovers—all BwO's play homage to Spinoza'.[17]

Along this line of argument, the pain in masochism acquires a completely new meaning: it is no longer conceived as a means for achieving pleasure but as a violent effort to divide desire from pleasure which is considered to be a transcendental measure. It is on this level that Deleuze and Guattari most vehemently contest not simply the psychoanalytic or Lacanian understanding of masochism but, most importantly, also Deleuze's early reading of masochism which is now dismissed as too psychoanalytical:

> Doubtless, psychoanalysis demonstrated that desire is not subordinated to procreation, or even to genitality. That was its modernism. But it retained the essentials; it even found new ways of inscribing in desire the negative law of lack, the external rule of pleasure, and the transcendent ideal of phantasy. Take the interpretation of masochism: when the ridiculous death instinct is not invoked, it is claimed that the masochist, like everybody else, is after pleasure but can only get it through pain and phantasied humiliations whose function is to allay or ward off deep anxiety. This is inaccurate; the masochist's suffering is the price he must pay, not to achieve pleasure, but to untie the pseudobond between desire and pleasure as an extrinsic measure. . . . In short, the masochist uses suffering as a way of constituting a body without organs and bringing forth a plane of consistency of desire.[18]

IV

We are now in a position to see how Deleuze and Guattari's revision of masochism challenges directly what they take to be the psychoanalytic (or even transcendental) reading of masochism, based on the phallus and castration, which they see as transcendental intruders into the otherwise consistent and self-sufficient immanence of desire. In fact, Deleuze and Guattari also oppose desire and pleasure because they understand pleasure as an equivalent of the phallus which is conceived as an *organ* in the literal sense: a principle of organisation according to which the body is organised around erogenous zones or regions of the body which, as such, function as a source of pleasure/enjoyment (partial drives in the Lacanian sense). This conception pretty much corresponds to the classical idea of the phallus in psychoanalysis which is not articulated simply as a material physical organ but rather as a structural place (a signifier of castration which symbolically marks erogenous zones of the body as regions of *jouissance*) according to which *jouissance* itself is territorialised. So when Deleuze and Guattari posit an equivalence between the masochist and the *BwO*, this hypothesis should be grasped precisely in the sense of the Body *without* Organ/Phallus, that is, as the body which is subtracted from the Organ/Phallus which symbolically marks erogenous zones as regions/territories of *jouissance* on the surface of the body. As Éric Alliez maintains, this has immediate political consequences. In fact, the liberation of desire from the tyranny of the Organ/Phallus will

> be a line of flight out of the *organisations* of the Father-State, starting with this organism of the phallus-man to which the masochist opposes a suffering that neutralises it (by *suspending* the organisation of the organs), undoing its hierarchical organicity (instead of re-organising the hierarchy of bodies on the basis of sex, of the Organ which bears witness to the 'extreme sensibility of organisation' [de Sade]).[19]

We can see here the true motive for Deleuze and Guattari's alleged 'anti-phallocentrism': the phallus should be rejected or excluded precisely insofar as it is an organisational principle for the territorial division of the body and marks the erogenous zones as privileged regions of pleasure. This organisation of the surface of the body, in turn, corresponds to the paternal or sovereign organisation of the state territory which not only implies a social and political hierarchy but is, as Stuart Elden has argued in a Foucauldian manner, something essentially calculable and measurable (and should thus be conceived as modern technology of power).[20] Such a principle of state organisation is, by definition, hostile and logically incompatible with nomadic and deterritorialised social (non)organisation[21] and with the nomadic character of desire as well.

Yet although Deleuze and Guattari's rejection of the psychoanalytic concept of the phallus might be clear at the terminological level, their position remains much more ambiguous in conceptual terms. In fact, there seems to be two different ways of rejecting the concept of the phallus or, more precisely, of devaluating its role as the principle of the territorial division of body. On the one hand, the phallus can be rejected directly as a transcendental intruder, that is, as something foreign which contaminates the preexisting surface of the body from the outside; however, on the other hand, it can be also be devaluated or suspended by overlapping the surface of the body and the erogenous regions of pleasure. By extending erogeneity to the totality of the bodily surface, in other words, one suspends the privileged and exclusive role of few peculiar, selected regions. This reading might contradict the terminology employed by Deleuze and Guattari, but it can achieve plausibility, especially if put in the context of Deleuze and Guattari's take on the figure of the Father and Oedipus in relation to Kafka's literature. If they think desire in terms of the 'escape',[22] this implies, on the one hand, that territory and territorialisation block the flow of desire by enclosing it within some peculiar closed spaces—and the figure of the father is problematic above all because, in the context of Kafka, he gave up on his desire and allowed for his own territorialisation within the family triangle and the dominant or major culture. However, on the other hand, the solution Deleuze and Guattari propose in relation to this father's impasse is precisely not to give up upon his desire but rather to expand it over and beyond the territory in which it was enclosed ('to find a path there where he didn't find any'[23]). In other words, the expansion of desire over the territory implies the very deterritorialisation of the latter. The photo of the father should be thus enlarged until 'absurdity' and expanded to the map of the world: 'The photo of the father, expanded beyond all bounds, will be projected onto the geographic, historical, and political *map* of the world in order to reach vast regions of it'.[24]

Doesn't the same go for the concept of the phallus too? Rather than directly rejecting the concept, Deleuze and Guattari seem to open up the possibility of conceiving the devaluation of the phallus in terms of its expansion until the point of absurdity, so that now the phallus does not mark only some particular and anatomically predisposed zones of the body but is expanded to cover the whole bodily surface. The *BwO* is here constituted in a paradoxical manner, that is, in such a way that it in itself becomes—immanently—the Organ/Phallus. The phallus as the signifier of castration, which functions as an organisational principle according to which pleasure is territorialised, was articulated in terms of the transcendental (external) principle, but its expansion beyond selected regions to all bodily surfaces implies its very immanentisation. Importantly, this immanence is now somehow overlapping with transcendence. Or, better yet, the immanence of the expanded phallus of the *BwO* (which implies a total overlapping between pleasure and desire as endless flow) now takes the position of the former transcendence which was eliminated from the immanence/transcendence opposition. This is by far best expressed in another concept Deleuze and Guattari introduce in relation to the *BwO*, that is, the concept of an 'absolute Outside' according to which the old metaphysical Self is transformed. In fact, a field of immanence or *BwO* doesn't mean simply the enclosure of the old metaphysical Self within the boundaries of the body, dismissing all of the external world and its influence upon it. Rather, the field of immanence signifies the absolute Outside, in which the very difference between inside and outside is somehow dissolved. As they put it, 'The field of immanence is not internal to the self, but neither does it come from an external self or a nonself. Rather, it is like the absolute Outside that knows no Selves because interior and exterior are equally part of the immanence in which they have fused'.[25] In short, the topology of the absolute Outside points to the a-subjective position beyond the phallus (and castration) which is close to what Jacques-Alain Miller coined as 'extimacy'; the absolute Outside is furthermore advanced along the very devaluation of the phallus and castration, yet this devaluation occurs only through the radicalisation and absolutisation of these two concepts. Instead of the limited libidinisation of the selected zones of the body alone, the topology of the absolute Outside thus implies the absolute libidinisation of the whole bodily surface.

V

Recapitulating what we have developed thus far in this chapter, we can say the following: Deleuze and Guattari rearticulate masochism via the figure of *BwO*, which is characterised by the plane of consistency that maintains the immanence of desire as neatly as possible separated from any transcendental 'measures' (fantasy, the phallus, pleasure, etc.). In an openly anti-psychoanalytic and anti-phallocentric way, they argue for a rejection of pleasure which is now seen as a 'rotten idea' or an 'intruder' into the consistency of desire rather than being considered the end-goal achieved through pain. The anti-Oedipal character of desire is thus preserved through its link to nomadism and deterritorialisation. The latter, in fact, points to the topological position of the absolute Outside with respect to the territorialised and Oedipalised spaces of the state and the family triangle.

To give a hint of what will be discussed in part IV, which will be dedicated to the exploration of ontology and perversion in Lacanian psychoanalysis, I will argue that Lacan is far closer to Deleuze's analysis than we might expect. Far from simply opposing Deleuze on this point, what Lacan is searching for under the headline of 'formulas of sexuation' and especially 'feminine *jouissance*' as 'beyond phallus' in his *Seminar XX* is similar to what Deleuze and Guattari were looking at in *Anti-Oedipus* and *A Thousand Plateaus*: the question of how to say 'No!' to the Other.

This is what Deleuze and Guattari's concept of the absolute Outside, on the one hand, and Lacan's concept of subjective destitution, on the other, point towards. However, already these two concepts imply the very difference between Deleuze and Guattari's and Lacanian psychoanalysis: while the former maintains the alternative between Oedipal and anti-Oedipal positions towards the human psyche, the latter actually introduces a third choice which is epitomised by Jacques-Alain Miller's distinction between pre-Oedipal and pre-linguistic drives in psychoanalysis. In summary, we will see that the articulation of pre-Oedipal drives, not simply as anti-Oedipal or free floating but as already shaped by the hole in the Other (the point of primal repression around which partial drives circulate), is precisely the point where Deleuze and Guattari's vitalist position diverges from Lacan's psychoanalysis.[26]

NOTES

1. Daniel W. Smith, 'The Concept of the Simulacrum: Deleuze and the Overturning of Platonism', *Continental Philosophy Review* 38, no. 1–2 (2005): 116.
2. Gilles Deleuze and Félix Guattari, *A Thousand Plateaus: Capitalism and Schizophrenia*, trans. Brian Massumi (Minneapolis and London: University of Minnesota Press, 1987), 6.
3. Éric Alliez, 'Deleuze with Masoch', trans. Alberto Toscano, in *Deleuze and Psychoanalysis: Philosophical Essays on Deleuze's Debate with Psychoanalysis*, ed. Leen de Bolle (Leuven: Leuven University Press, 2010), 124.
4. Gilles Deleuze and Félix Guattari, *Kafka: Toward a Minor Literature*, trans. Dana Polan (Minneapolis and London: University of Minnesota Press, 1986), 10.
5. Hereafter abbreviated as *BwO* in the text.
6. Deleuze and Guattati, *A Thousand Plateaus*, 152.
7. Gilles Deleuze, 'Coldness and Cruelty', in *Masochism: Coldness and Cruelty and Venus in Furs*, trans. Jean McNeil, ed. Gilles Deleuze and Leopold von Sacher-Masoch (New York: Zone Books, 1991), 71.
8. Ibid.
9. Ibid.
10. Sigmund Freud, 'Three Essays on the Theory of Sexuality', in *The Standard Edition of the Complete Psychological Works of Sigmund Freud, Vol. VII*, ed. James Strachey (London: Vintage, 2001), 210. As far as this distinction is concerned, Aaron Schuster recently goes so far as to speak about '*two contrasting ontologies of pleasure*. It is both Aristotelian and Platonic, aimless immanent activity [fore-pleasure] and teleologically driven punctual satisfaction [end-pleasure]' (Aaron Schuster, *The Trouble with Pleasure: Deleuze and Psychoanalysis* [Cambridge, MA: MIT Press, 2016], 115).
11. Deleuze, 'Coldness and Cruelty', 70.
12. Besides Schuster (Schuster, *The Trouble with Pleasure*, 97–126), this topic was discussed in detail by Peter Klepec, *Dobičkonosne strasti: Kapitalizem in perverzija 1* [Profitable Passions: Capitalism and Perversion 1] (Ljubljana: Society for Theoretical Psychoanalysis, 2008), 247–86.
13. Gilles Deleuze, *Essays Critical and Clinical*, trans. Daniel W. Smith and Michael A. Greco (Minneapolis and London: University of Minnesota Press, 1997), 53–54.
14. Ibid., 157.
15. This point of the transformation of such concepts as desire, pleasure, subjectivity, etc. on the basis of the central role of the body and corporeality in the later Deleuze period was the subject of the in-depth discussion of Elizabeth Grosz's book *Space, Time and Perversion* (London and New York: Routledge, 1995); see especially part III titled

'Perverse Desire', 140–228. This book might be considered as a pioneer work which opened up the space for what was later consolidated as vitalist or neomaterialist current in contemporary critical thought and philosophy.

16. Deleuze and Guattari, *A Thousand Plateaus*, 157.

17. Ibid., 154.

18. Ibid., 154–55.

19. Alliez, 'Deleuze with Masoch', 123.

20. See, for instance, Stuart Elden, 'Land, Terrain, Territory', *Progress in Human Geography* 34, no. 6 (2010): 799–817.

21. On the very peculiar relationship between state organisation which functions according to the principle of territorialisation and the deterritorialised nomadism, see Eugene Holland, *Nomad Citizenship: Free-Market Communism and the Slow-Motion General Strike* (Minneapolis and London: University of Minnesota Press, 2011).

22. Deleuze and Guattari, *Kafka*, 10.

23. Ibid.

24. Ibid.

25. Deleuze and Guattari, *A Thousand Plateaus*, 156.

26. Although this is justifiably taken as the point of radical divergence between Deleuze's and Lacan's positions, it is necessary to mention here Andreja Zevnik's book *Lacan, Deleuze and World Politics: Rethinking the Ontology of the Political Subject* (London and New York: Routledge, 2016), which is one of the rare systematic attempts to reconcile and read together Lacan and Deleuze as far as the political implications of the Oedipus complex are concerned.

Part III

Beyond Metaphysics? Perversion in Agamben's Philosophy of Language and Political Philosophy: *Theatrum Politicum*

FIVE

Perverse Sphinx Against Oedipal Metaphysics

(Anti-)Metaphysics of Perversion in Agamben's Critique of Derrida and Freud

I

In chapter 1, we already underlined the fact that perversion is certainly not a central theme in Agamben's philosophy. Even more, considering the fact that Agamben addresses this issue rarely and in a sporadic manner (which is also the main reason why this issue is completely absent from the vast scholarship on Agamben's philosophy), we could even say that perversion is anathema to Agamben's work. Yet if one could agree that perversion is not a central issue for Agamben, its marginality does not imply it is of less importance. Quite the opposite, the lack of secondary accounts on this topic becomes rather striking as soon as we notice the significant role and place Agamben assigns to the structure of perversion in general, and particularly to the Freudian concept of the fetishist's disavowal within his entire work. The most explicit and in-depth discussion Agamben gives on this concept is surely the last part of his early book *Stanzas* (originally published in 1977) titled 'The Perverse Image: Semiology from the Point of View of the Sphinx'.[1] Agamben here addresses a severe critique towards the metaphysical legacy of modern semiology, insofar as the latter, through the concept of the linguistic sign, violently represses the original difference between signifier and signified, and between thought and being, marked by the barrier that irreversibly divides the two levels (S/s). In other words, the violent core of metaphysics, and of semiology, as its modern variation, consists precisely in the repression of this barrier between signifier and signified:

> From the point of view of signification, metaphysics is nothing but the forgetting of originary difference between signifier and signified. Every semiology that fails to ask why the barrier that establishes the possibility of signifying should itself be resistant to signification, falsifies, with that omission, its own most authentic intention. In Saussure's formula, 'linguistic unity is double', the accent has been placed now on the pole of the signifier, now on that of the signified, without ever putting into question the paradox, insuperable for Saussure, that had testified on behalf of his own formulation.[2]

Before we engage more in detail with the question of why and how the fetishist's disavowal represents, for Agamben, a privileged way of facing and thinking the paradox of the linguistic barrier which internally divides the linguistic sign conceived as unity, it is worthwhile and necessary to highlight the somewhat 'esoteric' context in which Agamben writes this thesis. In fact, Agamben here formulates his criticism towards metaphysics and semiology through an implicit polemical dialogue with Derrida's deconstruction—a dialogue which will become manifest in later works. As Kevin Attell pointed out in his groundbreaking study,[3] this critical stance towards Derrida's deconstruction is essential for an understanding of Agamben's early reflections on language as well as of his entire political philosophy of the *Homo Sacer* period. Attell's merit is in pointing out how Agamben's and Derrida's respective interpretations of Kafka's famous parable 'Before the Law', in which they set up their respective and contradictory views regarding the status of the messianic event, is actually anticipated in their much more remote and apparently marginal polemical dialogue concerning the issue of the linguistic difference as a condition of possibility of signification. For us, it is also significant that it is within the same discussion that Agamben unfolds his thesis that the fetishist's disavowal is the best possible way for grasping the paradox of the linguistic bar which the metaphysics of signification and semiology try to repress. However, the main problem of Attell's otherwise brilliant reading of Agamben-Derrida's 'esoteric dossier',[4] as he puts it, is that he fails or intentionally avoids approaching it from the angle of perversion opened up by Agamben himself. This is quite surprising because Agamben deploys the concept of the fetishist's disavowal precisely as the most efficient means for overcoming the metaphysics of signification and the Western metaphysical tradition as such. Introducing perversion in the context of this disagreement between Agamben and Derrida will, in turn, enable us to see where exactly Agamben misreads Freud's concept of the fetishist's disavowal and the far-reaching (negative) consequences this misreading has for Agamben's thought. In fact, as Lorenzo Chiesa and Frank Ruda convincingly argue, Agamben himself, by identifying 'perversion with that which paves the way to the abyss of the signifier (its void), that is, the irreducible non-correspondence between the signifier and the signified', and, consequently, by opposing and privileging perversion (disavowal) over (metaphysical) neurosis (repression), fails to see that, from a Lacanian perspective, it is, on the contrary, rather 'the pervert [who] disavows this abyss in a way that is possibly more "metaphysical" than the neurotic's repression'.[5] In other words, while Agamben might be right in emphasising the necessity of thinking the paradox of the linguistic bar as a possible way out of the metaphysics of signification, he, however, wrongly suggests that this task can be accomplished through the fetishist's disavowal. As I will argue, this suggestion is based on Agamben's misreading of the difference between the mechanism of repression and the repressed content itself within the clinical picture of perversion. Instead of addressing the void of the signifier or the point of the primal repression (*Urverdrängung* or fundamental ontological negativity)[6] which constitutes the supposedly metaphysical mechanism of repression or the barrier, the pervert disavows this point by directly fetishising the repressed content itself, thus making the negativity of primal repression a new transcendental, that is, metaphysical principle. Differently put, instead of overcoming the metaphysics, the pervert suspends this process and delays its fulfilment endlessly. I will thus proceed by, firstly, highlighting the main points of disagreement between Agamben and Derrida regarding the interpretation of Kafka's parable 'Before the Law' in order to, secondly, trace this disagreement back into their respective views on the language and the paradox of the bar.

II

As is well known, Kafka's parable 'Before the Law' is (although also published as a separate short story) a part of the novel *The Trail*: the priest in the cathedral tells Joseph K. a story about the 'man from the country', who comes before the widely opened door of the Law and is about to enter. Yet there is an 'enigmatic doorkeeper'[7] standing before the Law who prohibits the man from the country access. The prohibition the doorkeeper embodies is, however, of a very peculiar nature. It is not a physical prohibition, nor it is a categorical or absolute prohibition; instead it is rather similar to an undetermined and, as the story reveals later on, an endless postponement of the moment of entry.[8] This endless postponement or delay of the moment of entrance is, furthermore, supported by the uncanny idea that this concrete doorkeeper and this concrete door are only the first in an endless series of doors and guardians who follow. Though it would seem there is a chance for the man from the country to actually enter the Law, the Law ultimately appears to be nothing but the endless process of entering without ever actually entering. The man from the country is thus forced to sit down before the door contemplating the doorkeeper for the rest of his life.[9] Just before his death, the man from the country asks the doorkeeper why, in all these years, nobody apart from himself has come asking for permission to enter the Law. In other words, the man from the country wonders why he is actually the only person who wants to get through the door. The doorkeeper gives him the famous and widely interpreted answer: '"No one else could be granted entry here, because this entrance was intended for you alone. I shall now go and shut it"'.[10]

Although this last scene of closing the door that was meant only for the man from the country has long been a point of critical contention (Cacciari, Agamben, Derrida), Attell stresses that, in Derrida's interpretation, the distinctive character of this scene can be grasped only if one reads it against the background of the rest of the parable—which seems to be of even greater importance. In fact, according to Attell, Derrida's main focus is on the structure of the prohibition enunciated by the doorkeeper. As we have already mentioned, this prohibition has a structure of permanent delay or postponement of the act of entering and this structure is what Derrida calls *différance*: 'The present prohibition of the law is not a prohibition in the sense of an imperative constraint; it is a *différance*'.[11] Derrida's concept of *différance* points here to the *a-topic* structure of the form of law in which there is no place (in the sense of *topos*) where one could enter. And this is why the subject who may want to enter is doomed to an endless and always delayed process of entering without ever being able to really enter the law. The paradox of a so-defined *a-topic* form of the law is thus that it does not represent merely the unsurpassable threshold of the law but its enigmatic foundation—its force which derives precisely from the fact that the law is *a-topical*: '*différance* that not only is impassable, but whose play of deferral and nullification is the fundamental (non-)source and (non-)origin of the law'.[12] Following Attell, what is really crucial in Derrida's 'differential topology' or 'atopology'[13] of the form of the law is that it relates to the man from the country in the form of abandonment. Consequently, 'the impassabilty of the paradoxical ban-structure indicates precisely the insuperability of *différance*'.[14] This leads Attell to the conclusion that *différance* is the unsurpassable condition of possibility of the law itself.

Therefore the final scene of the doorkeeper shutting the door should be read against the background of the concept of *différance* at work in the previous endless postponement of entering. So if *différance* as *a-topos* is the (non)foundation of the law embodied in the multiplication of entrances and doorkeepers, so that the otherwise punctual and singular act of entry turns into the never-ending process of entering, then, from Derrida's perspective, the whole parabola should be read as a linear regression which can only end up in death. Roughly put, death is simply the consequence of the shutting of the door insofar as this act actually implies the abolition of *différance*. This is why Agamben states that, from a Derridean perspective, the concluding moment of shutting the door is actually not an event but an anti-event (or an apology of the defeat) because, as Derrida writes, it is '"an event that happens not to happen"'.[15] However, before discussing this moment of difference between Agamben's and Derrida's respective interpretations of the end of the parable, let us briefly stay with correspondence between Derrida's articulation of *différance* in the context of the law and within his conception of language. As Derrida suggests, *différance* as an unsurpassable condition of the law (which is in force without significance) corresponds exactly to the linguistic concept of difference, which is the negative condition of possibility of language as system. Language should be conceived, according to Saussure, as a system of negative differences so that each linguistic unity is defined in negative differential relation to other unities (as different from other). Of course, this implies that no linguistic unity exists outside language as a system of negative differences, which led Saussure to conclude that this system is actually without positive terms and all the differences are only negative.[16] Moving from these premises, Derrida stated that each linguistic unity thus exists only in the 'play of *différance*' with other linguistic unities, that is, in play with other signifiers or signified concepts. *Différance* is thus only 'the non-full, non-simple, structured and differentiating origin of differences. Thus, the name "origin" no longer suits it'.[17] In short, *différance* is, for Derrida, an absent 'origin' of language.

Considering the fact that Derrida opposed himself to scientific linguistics because he 'casts Saussure as a vehement defender against the heresy of the written sign',[18] that is, as an advocate of phonetic against writing or of phonology against grammatology, it becomes clear why he must propose a different understanding of the law. The latter, for Derrida, is not something one should enter; instead it is a text which should be deciphered: 'He [the man from the country] wants to see or touch the law, he wants to approach and "enter" it, because perhaps he does not know that the law is not to be seen or touched but deciphered'.[19] Against this background, Derrida draws the conclusion that precisely because the man from the country 'cannot read', he wants to enter the law, which means that he wants to enter something which is impossible to enter because there's no place at all to enter the law. In other words, because he wants to enter the law which one cannot enter but only read, the man from the country falls into the endless play of *différance* which can only end up in death as an anti-event.

III

Unlike Derrida, Agamben reads the concluding scene of the parable (the moment the doorkeeper shuts the door) as an event which *does happen*. Namely, the moment of closing the door, for Agamben, is not simply an episode in line with the previous narrative in the sense of being its logical conclusion but rather represents its anti-dialectical reversal. The door of the law is something ontologically opened and by closing it one also closes up the fundamental ontological disposition of the law: its being 'in force without significance'. According to Agamben, the man from the country, by endlessly contemplating the doorkeeper, thus forcing him to shut the door, succeeds in overcoming the structure of the law which actually seeks or invites one to decipher the enigma of its ontological openness. The main objection Agamben raises to Derrida's deconstruction is thus precisely the following: while the latter, on the one hand, by tracing back the play of *différance* in the heart of the law, succeeds in revealing its ontological structure, it, on the other hand, fails to go beyond this metaphysical threshold insofar as it envisions the deciphering of the enigma as a way out. In fact, the law is not something to be deciphered but something that lacks any meaning. From Agamben's angle, this overcoming consists of thinking the paradox of the bar at the level of language, the bar which enables signification as such. In this respect, Agamben acknowledges Derrida's value in his identification of the concept of *différance* in the heart of language which brings the metaphysics of signification to its very threshold, yet, for Agamben, Derrida fails to make another step forwards or beyond this threshold because he wrongly proposes a deciphering of the enigmatic message of the law to be the solution for such a metaphysical trap. *Différance* is still the structural element which points to the interpretation as deciphering of the secret message behind the external enigmatic signifier which is conceived as a *trace* of the otherwise absent meaning.[20] In so doing, Derrida establishes *différance* as the relation between the enigmatic secret meaning (significance) and its manifest expression (speech). This is why Agamben considers Derrida's *différance* as still essentially Oedipal. In fact, Agamben refers at this point to the ancient pre-metaphysical difference between the speech of the Sphinx and that of Oedipus, which he conceives as two fundamentally different sorts of speech.[21] The Sphinx's speech is fundamentally anti- or nonmetaphysical because it is precisely the mode of speech which makes manifest the original difference between signifier and signified, while Oedipus's speech, determined mostly by his unravelling of the Sphinx's puzzle, is precisely a metaphysical speech because it deciphers or translates one level to the other and therefore establishes a relation of subordination between the two. And it is at this point that Agamben encounters Freudian psychoanalysis, putting it on the same side along Derridean deconstruction by associating psychoanalysis precisely to the metaphysical mode of speech because it is supposedly determined by repression, hence by the Oedipus complex:

> The origin of this dissimulation—effected by the expressive unity of signifier and signified—of the fracture of presence was prefigured by

> the Greeks in a mythologeme that has always held a peculiar fascination for our culture. In the psychoanalytical interpretation of the myth of Oedipus, the episode of the Sphinx, although necessarily of essential importance for the Greeks, remains obstinately in the shadows; but it is precisely this aspect of the life of the hero that must here be put in the foreground. The son of Laius resolves in the simplest way 'the enigma proposed by the ferocious jaws of the virgin', showing the hidden meaning behind the enigmatic signifier, and, with this act alone, plunges the half-human, half-feral monster into the abyss. The liberating teaching of Oedipus is that what is uncanny and frightening in the enigma disappears as soon as its utterance is reduced to the transparency of the relation between the signified and its form, which the signified only apparently succeeds in escaping.[22]

According to Agamben, what is crucial in the story of Oedipus is not, as is usually assumed, incest; instead the crucial point concerns the divergence or difference between the speech of the Sphinx and that of Oedipus. Insofar as the latter resolves the enigma of the Sphinx's puzzle, it is identified by Agamben with the psychoanalytic interpretation or deciphering of the secret meaning behind the enigmatic signifier. In so doing, the speech of Oedipus represents metaphysical speech par excellence: this speech consists in translating one level (the external expression or the signifier) into another (hidden meaning behind its form), thus establishing the *relation* and hence the *unity* (the linguistic sign) between the two. Through the interpretation of the signifier, Oedipus violently appropriates the hidden meaning as something improper, that is, as something that does not belong to the signifier.

The speech of the Sphinx, in turn, represents for Agamben a completely different type of speech from Oedipus's. By avoiding the deciphering of the secret meaning, hence of translating one level into another, the Sphinx's speech succeeds in approaching the level of meaning without unifying it with (and subordinating it to) the level of manifest signifier. In other words, the Sphinx appropriates the hidden meaning without making it 'proper' through translation or deciphering but keeping the meaning at an indefinite distance from the signifier. In so doing, the Sphinx avoids the unification of meaning and the signifier in the form of the sign which is precisely what, according to Agamben, Freudian psychoanalysis and the metaphysics of signification more widely are doing when they interpret the unconscious content. Moreover, and most importantly, the Sphinx's speech also succeeds in making manifest precisely the barrier which irreducibly separates the two levels (of signifier and of signified): 'What the Sphinx proposed was not simply something whose signified is hidden and veiled under an "enigmatic" signifier, but a mode of speech in which the original fracture of presence was alluded to in the paradox of a word that approaches its object while keeping it indefinitely at a distance'.[23] The speech of the Sphinx is thus a speech which succeeds in keeping a distance between the form of the signifier and the improper meaning, thus making manifest the barrier between the two levels. According to Agamben, this paradox indicates a different, more original non-Oedipal speech which corresponds to an 'event of language'. The latter's characteristic is precisely a pure potentiality of the language, its *potentia potentiae*[24] in which, as in Musil's 'man without references' or in Bartleby's formula 'I prefer not to', the word is strictly detached from any reference (the object) in the words and every reference is detached from the word.

Before discussing more in detail Agamben's engagement with the fetishist's disavowal as a modern equivalence of the speech of the Sphinx, it is worthwhile briefly mentioning some important parallels between Agamben and Deleuze at this point. Similarly to Agamben, Deleuze sees the speech of the Sphinx as a divergent speech or a speech of simulacrum which, recall, overturns the Platonic model. As we have discussed in the previous part, Deleuze conceives of simulacrum as a divergent difference, which is not a positive negation, but rather corresponds to the question mark (?) or fold of, or in, being itself. This fold of being is best expressed precisely by the speech of the Sphinx, who communicates the puzzle which the Platonic model is simply unable to swallow. In other words, the speech of the Sphinx is an indefinite speech that communicates only communication itself and thus succeeds in devaluing or making inoperative the hierarchical relation between the essence (meaning) and appearance (signifier). What is more, here we find that the term 'event of language' that Chiesa and Ruda proposed to capture Agamben's conception of the speech of the Sphinx perfectly corresponds to (and actually originates in) Deleuze's understanding of this term, as set up in his *The Logic of Sense*. Communicating communication itself, in fact, brings language to its very limit at the point where it touches its extreme point of exteriority—the eternity beyond the historical actualisations of language. According to Deleuze, the privileged way of expressing this limit point of the language is the indefinite mode of the verb or undetermined infinitive which also corresponds to the temporal form of Aion: 'As it expresses in language all events in one, the infinitive verb expresses the event of language—language being a unique event which merges now with that which renders it possible'.[25] For Deleuze, the event of language is the Aion, so as for Agamben the Aion implies the anti-metaphysical eternal form-of-life—a life that is not deprived of or separated from its form by the metaphysical/biopolitical machine. As he writes exactly three decades later in his *The Kingdom and the Glory* (originally published in 2007), which genealogically traces back the origins of modern governmentality to the early Christian idea of *oikonomia* conceived of as an immanent order deprived of transcendental God: 'The empty throne, the symbol of Glory, is what we need to profane in order to make room, beyond it, for something that, for now, we can only evoke with the name *zoē aiōnios*, eternal life'.[26] In this respect, Chiesa and Ruda are absolutely right in calling the 'event of language' a 'force of life': form-of-life or *zoē aiōnios* is, from Agamben's perspective, inextricably connected with and co-dependent on the event of language, of communicating language itself, where what is said is language itself—its pure *potentia potentiae*. The event of language is a vital force of the form-of-life.

IV

Following Agamben, the Sphinx's speech is an example of such an 'event of language' insofar as it maintains the divergence between the proper and the improper, between hidden meaning and enigmatic signifier, without establishing an interpretation and without transmitting one level into another. Against this background, Agamben draws a general conclusion:

> Every interpretation of signifying as the relation of manifestation or expression (or, inversely, of coding and eclipse) between a signifier and a signified (and both the psychoanalytic theory of the symbol and the semiotic theory of language belong to this type) places itself necessarily under the sign of Oedipus; under the sign of the Sphinx must be placed every theory of the symbol that, refusing the model of Oedipus, focuses its attention above all on the barrier between signifier and signified that constitutes the original problem of signification.[27]

Agamben here places Freudian psychoanalysis along semiology as an example of Oedipal metaphysics precisely because he sees its main technique, which is interpretation, as analogous to the Oedipal deciphering of the Sphinx's puzzle: a translation of the unconscious content or hidden meaning into the manifest word or signifier. Such a translation has, for Agamben, two negative consequences: on the one hand, it obfuscates the problem of the barrier which is the fundamental paradox of signification, and, on the other hand, it completely extinguishes the unconscious content by appropriating it by the manifest conscious word, that is, by bringing it completely onto the side of the signifier:

> The Oedipal interpretation of the speech of the Sphinx as a 'coded speech' secretly governs the Freudian conception of the symbol. Psychoanalysis in fact presupposes the splitting of discourse into an obscure speech by means of improper terms, based on repression (which is that of the unconscious), and into a clear speech of proper terms (which is that of the consciousness). The passage ('the translation') from one discourse to the other properly constitutes analysis. This necessarily presupposes a process of 'desymbolisation' and of progressive reduction of the symbolic: the 'drying of the Zuider Zee', which according to Freud substantiates the psychoanalytic process, is, once concluded, the equivalent of a complete translation of unconscious symbolic language into conscious sign. The myth of Oedipus

> therefore dominates the horizon of analysis in a manner much more profound than its critics heretofore thought. Not only does it furnish the content of interpretation, it guides and structures the fundamental attitude of analytic discourse itself in its self-positioning before the Sphinx of the unconscious and its symbols. As Oedipus discovers the hidden meaning of the enigma of the Sphinx, and, in so doing, frees the city from the monster, so analysis rediscovers the latent thought behind the manifest symbolic cipher and 'heals' the neurosis.[28]

According to Agamben, the main problem of a so-conceived analytic procedure is the fact that it erases the barrier between signifier and signified, or between consciousness and a repressed unconscious meaning. As such, this barrier is the marker for the phenomenon defined by Freud as *Ichspaltung*. This phenomenon is, according to Agamben, strictly correlative to the speech of the Sphinx, which, instead of translating the discourse of the unconscious into that of consciousness, rather avoids this deciphering, and in this way makes present and manifest the barrier which irreducibly divides the two levels.

It is at this point that Agamben opposes the phenomenon of the fetishist's disavowal, as defined by Freud himself, to Freudian analysis, conceived as a process of deciphering of unconscious meaning. For Agamben, fetishism is a privileged mode of keeping the difference between consciousness and the unconscious and therefore of the barrier which separates the two sides. In Freud's case of the child's encounter with the castration of the mother, this barrier means his or her 'compromise' between knowledge of castration of the mother and the illusion of universal possession of the penis (counterdesire):

> In the conflict between perception of reality that moves him to renounce his phantasm, and his counterdesire that moves him to renounce his perception, the boy in fact does neither one nor the other, or, rather, he does both at once, arriving at a unique compromise. On the one hand, with the help of a particular mechanism, he repudiates the evidence of his senses; on the other, he recognises and assumes the reality of that evidence by means of a perverse symptom. The space of the fetish is precisely this contradiction; the fetish is simultaneously the presence of that nothingness that is the maternal penis and the sign of its absence. As both a symbol of something and its negation, the fetish can maintain itself only with the provision of an essential laceration, in which the two contrary reactions constitute the nucleus of a true and proper splitting of the ego (*Ichspaltung*).[29]

In this way, the fetishist's disavowal (*Verleugnung*) allows an alternative type of appropriation, foreign to metaphysics. In this alternative model, appropriation is accomplished without transference or translation of the secret repressed meaning of the unconscious into the manifest level of expression:

> The *Verleugning* presents us with a process in which, by means of a symbol, man succeeds in appropriating an unconscious content without bringing it to consciousness. . . . In this gesture of the fetishist, who succeeds in appropriating his own hidden treasure without unearthing it, the ancient wisdom of the Sphinx, which repels by receiving and receives by repelling, once again comes to life. And just as the analyst can perhaps learn something from the pervert as far as pleasure is concerned, so too perhaps Oedipus can learn something from the Sphinx about symbols.[30]

V

Here, Agamben's criticism towards Freud seems to be convincing, even disarming. In fact, his reading of the fetishist's disavowal as opposed to the psychoanalytic technic of interpretation, whereby the latter is conceived as the translation of the unconscious content into a manifest word, which apparently relies upon the unity of two poles within the linguistic sign, corresponds to the most widespread understanding of Freud's concept of the unconscious. The latter is usually conceived precisely as a negation of the consciousness, assuming a latent repressed material to be unearthed and brought into the consciousness. This conception leads to the related idea that consciousness and the unconscious are actually lying on the same level as symmetrical oppositions. Against this background, there is only one step forwards: towards the articulation of psychoanalytic interpretation as a technique of translation of the unconscious content into a manifest conscious word.

And yet, as Alenka Zupančič has argued many times over the past decade, this interpretation (although grounded in some of Freud's texts) is still a weak reading of the Freudian concept of the unconscious, according to which the latter is simply the negation of the consciousness. This reading inevitably leads us to the simplistic idea that the unconscious concerns a lack of knowledge or awareness of something which can be recuperated in the analytic practice. In other words, this idea presupposes the positive object which is repressed in the unconscious and hence the task of analysis is to bring it back again into the realm of consciousness. Following this conception, the unconscious is mostly characterised by a lack of knowledge *about* something (which is thus considered as unconscious) and could be even translated as 'not conscious'.[31] In this respect, the goal of analysis would be precisely to put the subject in the position to appropriate or recuperate the unconscious object by means of analytic interpretation; to make him 'know' something he didn't know. In other words, the task of analysis would be to make the subject conscious of his unconscious or repressed content.

According to Zupančič, a strong interpretation, in turn, posits the unconscious not simply as the positive negation of the consciousness, but as essentially characterised by the ontological negativity inscribed in conscious knowledge itself—the negativity contained in the Lacanian notion of the barred or inexistent big Other (Ⱥ).When Freud himself pointed out that the unconscious is something inaccessible to the consciousness, this did not simply imply the same structure of two separate levels whereby the subject would now be constrained with ontological limitations in the analytic process of appropriating the unconscious content. On the contrary, the unconscious, insofar as it is characterised by the ontological negativity or the gap (implied by the lack of the first, primally repressed signifier), implies a hole in conscious knowledge itself. The unconscious is thus not something merely opposite to and separated from conscious knowledge; rather, it is something inscribed and at work in conscious knowledge itself, so to speak. What is truly unconscious is not the repressed content but the lack in knowledge. And as Zupančič does not fail to add, this leads to the very 'paradoxical redoublement' of knowledge itself:

> The unconscious (in its very form) is the 'positive' way in which the ontological negativity of a given reality registers in this reality itself, and it registers in a way which does not rely on the simple opposition between knowing and not knowing, between being or not being aware of something. . . . To be 'unconscious of something' does not mean simply that one does not know it; rather, it implies a paradoxical redoublement, and is itself twofold or split: it involves *not knowing that we know* (. . . that we don't know).[32]

Now we are in a position to better locate the most problematic point in Agamben's praise of perversion: what the pervert does, with the help of the mechanism of disavowal, is turn this disposition upside down. By directly fetishising unconscious knowledge ('not knowing'), he turns the lack of knowledge into knowledge itself. In other words, he first transforms the lack of knowledge into an object of identification in order to elevate it in this way up to the level of a transcendental principle: instead of 'not knowing that we know (. . . that we don't know)', the pervert posits himself as the one who 'knows that he does not know', that is, as one who has a knowledge about ontological negativity itself. To repeat Agamben's own words: the 'analyst can perhaps learn something from the pervert as far as pleasure is concerned'.

What Agamben misses in this context is the fact that the Freudian *Ichspaltung* (Lacanian barred subject) is precisely not the same as this ontological negativity which is the main characteristic of the unconscious; rather, the subject (which is, according to Lacan, by definition split between two signifiers or signifying dyad) emerges in the empty place left by the primally repressed signifier (what Freud calls primal repression) which constitutes ontological negativity. The subject is thus the effect of the latter or its representative in positive reality. As Zupančič argued,

> Simply put: the subjective split between the signifying dyad [presence-absence] constitutive of alienation is the result of the fall of some first signifier, which is to say of the signifier as *one*. The logic of the signifier (and the subject as that which one signifier represents for another signifier) only starts with two, with the signifying dyad. On the level of the first signifier there is not yet a subject, nor a signifying logic or chain. However, the latter does not occur by means of a second signifier being added to the first, it emerges by means of the 'repression' of the first signifier *at its place* (or 'instead' of it).[33]

To be precise, the distinction between the signifier and the place of its inscription is the key for the explanation of why signifiers, which themselves alone have no meaning at all, are able to generate a meaning as their effect. Because the signifying chain is established at the empty place of the first, primally repressed signifier, the subject emerges as the effect of the signifying chain. More precisely still, the subject emerges in the moment when the signifier crosses over the barrier and passes onto the side of the signified. Importantly, this moment which Lacan defines as the effect of metaphor (substitution of one signifier for another) is also the moment of the emergence of significatory effect or meaning. The subject thus functions as an extra-linguistic reference point in material reality or as a bearer of the meaning: 'metaphoric structure, indicating that it is in the substitution of signifier for signifier that a signification effect is produced that is poetic or creative, in other words, that brings the signification in question into existence. . . . This crossing [of the bar] expresses the condition for the passage of the signifier into the signified, whose moment I pointed out above by provisionally conflating it with the place of the subject'.[34] However, what should be added here is that this crossing of the signifier onto the side of the signified, which produces the significatory effect or meaning while also enabling the emergence of the subject, is constituted only through the further subjective fantasmatic relation with the object *a*, a reminder or leftover of the primal repression ($\$\lozenge a$), which is metonymically contained in the signifying chain. In other words, the subject functions as a bearer of the meaning only to the extent that it constitutes itself in the fantasmatic relation with the otherwise traumatic reminder of the primally repressed signifier.

Following this conception, we can now truly grasp the metaphysical (rather than anti-metaphysical) core of perversion: the pervert, by fetishising the unconscious content, disavows precisely the gap of the unconscious, constituted by this ontological negativity of the primally repressed signifier. In so doing, he reverses the fantasmatic relation between the subject and the object and directly identifies himself with the partial object or remainder of the primally repressed signifier ($a\lozenge\$$). That is to say, instead of addressing the negativity at stake, which is not separated but inscribed in the positive reality itself, the pervert actually disavows it by means of turning this negativity itself into a positive, imaginary object of imaginary identification. And in so doing, he ultimately elevates this negativity or the lack of knowledge to the level of new transcendental principle. As Lacan suggests already in the 'Subversion of the Subject', perversion 'barely accentuates the function of desire in man, insofar as desire institutes the dominance—in the privileged place of jouissance—of object *a* in fantasy, which desire substitutes for Ⱥ. . . . Only my formula for fantasy allows us to bring out the fact that the subject here makes himself the instrument of the Other's jouissance. . . . To return to the fantasy, let us say that the pervert imagines he is the Other in order to ensure his own jouissance'.[35] In short, the pervert introduces himself precisely as the one who turns the lack of knowledge into the object of knowledge (about *jouissance*) itself: the object he is sure he possesses thus succeeds establishing himself in the position of the transcendental instance of the Other.

In the next chapter, I will show how this misreading is mirrored in Agamben's conception of messianism as a post-religious phenomenon and in the perverse structure of messianic time. However, I will do this through a close reading of Freud's concept of the fetishist's disavowal by arguing that, contrary to Agamben's conviction, the perverse suspension of time at work in his concept of messianic time represents rather its very short circuit: the messianic impotence to completely overcome religion.

NOTES

1. Giorgio Agamben, *Stanzas: Word and Phantasm in Western Culture*, trans. Ronald L. Martinez (Minneapolis and London: University of Minnesota Press, 1993), 133–58.
2. Ibid., 137.
3. See Kevin Attell, 'An Esoteric Dossier: Agamben and Derrida Read Saussure', *ELH* 76, no. 4 (2009): 821–46.
4. Ironically enough, Attell borrows this term from Agamben himself. In fact, this is the term Agamben assigns to a tacit and anonymous polemical dialogue between Walter Benjamin and Carl Schmitt regarding political theology and the concept of violence. Without ever naming each other, Schmitt wrote his 1922 essay *Political Theology* as an answer to Benjamin's 'Critique of Violence', published just a year earlier in *Archiv für Sozialwissenschaften und Sozialpolitik* of which Schmitt was a regular reader. See on this Giorgio Agamben, *State of Exception*, trans. Kevin Attell (Chicago: University of Chicago Press, 2005), 52.
5. Lorenzo Chiesa and Frank Ruda, 'The Event of Language as Force of Life: Agamben's Linguistic Vitalism', *Angelaki* 16, no. 3 (2011): 179 (endnote).
6. This point was already briefly discussed in part I and will be analysed in more detail in part IV.
7. Attell, 'An Esoteric Dossier', 822.
8. 'Before the Law there stands a doorkeeper. A man from the country comes to this doorkeeper and asks to be allowed into the Law, but the doorkeeper says he cannot let the man into the Law just now. The man thinks this over and then asks whether that means he might be allowed to enter the Law later. "That is possible", the doorkeeper says, "but not now". Since the door to the Law is open and the doorkeeper steps to one side, the man bends down to see inside. When the doorkeeper notices that, he laughs and says, "If you are so tempted, why don't you try to go in, even

though I have forbidden it? But remember, I am powerful. And I am only the lowest doorkeeper. Before each room you will pass through there is a doorkeeper, each one more powerful than the last. The sight of just the third is too much even for me"' (Franz Kafka, *The Trail*, trans. Mike Mitchell [Oxford: Oxford University Press, 2009], 153–54; translation modified).

9. 'As a result of his years of studying the doorkeeper, he has come to recognise even the fleas in his fur collar' (ibid., 154).

10. Ibid., 155.

11. Jacques Derrida, 'Before the Law', trans. Avital Ronell, in *Acts of Literature*, ed. Derek Attridge (London and New York: Routledge, 1991), 202.

12. Attell, 'An Esoteric Dossier', 823.

13. Derrida, 'Before the Law', 208, 209. See also Attell, 'An Esoteric Dossier', 825.

14. Attell, 'An Esoteric Dossier', 824.

15. Derrida cited in Giorgio Agamben, *Homo Sacer: Sovereign Power and Bare Life*, trans. Daniel Heller-Roazen (Stanford, CA: Stanford University Press, 1998), 57.

16. Saussure writes: 'Everything that has been said up to this point boils down to this: in language there are only differences. Even more important: a difference generally implies positive terms between which the difference is set up; but in language there are only differences *without positive terms*' (Ferdinand de Saussure, *Course in General Linguistics*, trans. Wade Baskin [New York: McGraw-Hill, 1966] 117).

17. Derrida cited in Attell, 'An Essoteric Dossier', 831.

18. Attell, 'An Esoteric Dossier', 829.

19. Derrida, 'Before the Law', 197.

20. In order to remain within the scope of this book, I consciously avoid the discussion whether and to what extent Agamben's reading of Derrida (reading Saussure) is correct. I limit myself to only highlight the main points of this discussion with respect to their relevance for Agamben's later critique of Freud and his deployment of perversion as an allegedly anti-metaphysical strategy. For Derrida's engagement with Saussurean linguistics, especially with the relationship between the sign and the trace, see Arthur Bradley's brilliant book *Derrida's* Of Grammatology (Bloomington and Indianapolis: Indiana University Press, 2008), 56–78.

21. See Agamben, *Stanzas*, 138–39.

22. Ibid., 137–38.

23. Ibid., 138.

24. Giorgio Agamben, *The Coming Community*, trans. Michael Hardt (Minneapolis and London: University of Minnesota Press, 1993), 36.

25. Gilles Deleuze, *The Logic of Sense*, trans. Mark Lester with Charles Stivale (London: The Athlone Press, 1990), 185.

26. Giorgio Agamben, *The Kingdom and the Glory: For a Theological Genealogy of Economy and Government*, trans. Lorenzo Chiesa (with Matteo Mandarini) (Stanford, CA: Stanford University Press, 2011), xiii.

27. Agamben, *Stanzas*, 138–39.

28. Ibid., 145.

29. Ibid., 145–46.

30. Ibid., 146–47.

31. Alenka Zupančič, *What* Is *Sex?* (Cambridge, MA: MIT Press, 2017), 16.

32. Ibid.

33. Alenka Zupančič, 'On Repetition', *Sats — Nordic Journal of Philosophy* 8, no. 1 (2007): 41.

34. Jacques Lacan, 'The Instance of the Letter in the Unconscious, or Reason Since Freud', in *Écrits*, trans. Bruce Fink (London and New York: W. W. Norton and Co., 2006), 429.

35. Ibid., 697, 699.

SIX

Messianism between Religion and Post-Religion

On the Perverse Structure of the Messianic Time

I

In his monumental work *Homo Sacer: Sovereign Power and Bare Life,* Agamben puts forwards the thesis that messianism seems to represent the limit point at which all three biggest monotheisms, Christianity, Islam, and Judaism, seem to exceed themselves as religions: 'In monotheism, messianism thus constitutes not simply one category of religious experience among others but rather the limit concept of religious experience in general, the point in which religious experience passes beyond itself and calls itself into question insofar as it is law'.[1] We could say that, in Agamben's view, messianism here clearly implies the opening of a new, nonreligious dimension 'beyond religion', a dimension in which 'religious experience passes beyond itself', as he states. In this chapter, rather than simply opposing Agamben's claim by arguing that messianism has a religious character as well, I will try to show the very paradoxical and ambiguous nature of this passage from religion into the nonreligious dimension, as represented by messianism. To be more precise, I will henceforth call 'post-religious' this interval between a bare opposition between religion and nonreligion, where messianism is evidently located. Therefore I will argue neither for messianism being already an atheism, insofar as is understood by Agamben here as a nonreligious phenomenon, nor will I argue for messianism being just another kind, albeit post-religious, of religious experience. Instead I will propose the thesis that Agamben's messianism must be, in the last instance, understood as a peculiar radicalisation of religion rather than its overcoming: insofar as it is the 'limit concept', the point at which 'religious experience passes beyond itself', messianism certainly implies the passage from religion to another nonreligious dimension; yet this passage is itself infinite, and so messianism represents a peculiar point at which this transition is stuck. In other words, I will try to show that messianism is neither a simply religious nor a nonreligious experience but a post-religious experience, and as such deeply marks the point at which religion overcomes itself, and yet also that this overcoming or transition to another dimension is itself infinite from the temporal point of view. In this sense, the prefix 'post-' in the term 'post-religious', which characterises messianism, must not be understood in the sense of the simple transition of religion to another dimension of nonreligious experience but rather as the very inability of religion to fulfil this transition or bring it to the end. Neither simply religion nor nonreligious experience, messianism rather signifies a specific inter-stage, in which religion, due to a peculiar perverse structure of messianic time, as we shall see, cannot completely accomplish its passage to another dimension. However, in order to properly develop this thesis, I will first briefly sum up the key conceptual line that led Agamben to his conclusion about messianism. I will thus begin with Agamben's very unusual understanding of the relation between religion and secularism and of the political theology of sovereignty in the context of his biopolitical theory.

Contrary to the generally accepted belief that modern secular political concepts, such as the 'laique state', are essentially nontheological and nonreligious and have their historical origin in the separation of the public sphere of the state from the private sphere of religious beliefs, Agamben suggests that there is no essential structural difference between religious power and modern state power. Both types of power share exactly the same structure of transcendence as the framework of their operation. According to Agamben, the real opposition is not between political theology and secularism but between secularism and profanity. For, in opposition to the 'political secularisation of theological concepts (the transcendence of God as a paradigm of sovereign power)', if we take Agamben's paradigmatic comparison that 'does nothing but displace the heavenly monarchy onto an earthly monarchy, leaving its power intact',[2] profanation 'neutralises what it profanes. Once profaned, that which was unavailable and separate loses its aura and is returned to use'.[3] Differently put, while secularisation 'guarantees the exercise of power by carrying it back to a sacred model', profanation 'deactivates the apparatuses of power and returns to common use the spaces that power had seized'.[4] Profanation is the first political operation that, according to Agamben, finally disposes with the religious and, as we will see, the biopolitical core of modern sovereign politics.

II

According to Agamben, sovereignty as a political-theological concept has inherited from religion a sort of specific topological differentiation, that is, a separation that also refers to objects but only insofar as they are bound to a certain separate space that prohibits their use: 'Religion can be defined as that which removes things, places, animals, or people from common use and transfers them to a separate sphere. Not only is there no religion without separation, but every separation also contains or preserves within itself a genuinely religious core'.[5] The motive for this religious separation was, of course, the need to reproduce the model of scarification on which religion was based. At the core of this model, as René Girard[6] has shown in his exceptional study, was the idea of substitution, the substitution of people and Gods, and the purpose of this religious separation was precisely to provide the 'objects' of this ritual.

But as Agamben himself emphasises,[7] at a certain moment, an unusual doubling of this model emerged; this doubling referred to the emergence of a sphere that was separated also from the religious sphere of sacrifice itself. We could say that, in this case, the sphere under consideration was one of a double and therefore absolute exclusion in which people are excluded both from the sphere of civil law and the sphere of sacrifice. In *Homo Sacer* Agamben named this sphere the ban, and life in this sphere is precisely the life of the eponymous archaic figure of Roman law—*homo sacer*—'that may be killed and yet not sacrificed'.[8] It is precisely this sphere that is necessary for the biopolitical 'politicisation of bare life', which, according to Agamben, is nothing less than the 'decisive event of modernity',[9] and thereby also the foundational gesture of secularism as a modern event par excellence. Agamben defines this operation in the known terms of the inclusive exclusion of natural biological life, whose equivalent he finds in the Ancient Greek term *zoḗ*, into qualified forms of life denoted by the term *bíos*. It is precisely in this original gesture of the inclusive exclusion of bare life into political space that biopolitics assumes the place of the origin of metaphysics:

> Politics therefore appears as the truly fundamental structure of Western metaphysics insofar as it occupies the threshold on which the relation between the living being and the logos is realised. In the 'politicisation' of bare life—the metaphysical task par excellence—the humanity of living man is decided. In assuming this task, modernity does nothing other than declare its own faithfulness to the essential structure of the metaphysical tradition.[10]

What is crucial in Agamben's definition of the biopolitical foundation of metaphysics is, of course, the fact that the inclusive exclusion of bare life into political space concerns, first and foremost, a relationship, the relation between form and substance, between the forms of life and their biological content, which is common to all living beings. In other words, it concerns that which structural anthropology and psychoanalysis have defined as the inscription of the real into symbolic forms of identity, that which expresses a specific bond or contact between nature and the man-made order of culture or politics. In this sense, we can say that what lies at the core of modern political secularism, if we understand it in Agamben's sense of relation, is precisely a relational ontology as a specific form of capturing pure Being (bare life) in qualified forms of life, which, as Agamben unambiguously says, ultimately cannot exist in these forms otherwise than in the relation of exception or abandonment, and thus belongs to the very extimate edge of the interior exteriority of a political system.[11]

What Agamben is aiming at when he argues that this aporetic relation evokes a 'new politics', which, as he says, 'remains largely to be invented',[12] is nothing other than the deactivation and dissolution of this relation as the foundation of politics. This is what Lorenzo Chiesa has named Agamben's Franciscan or messianic nonrelational ontology.[13] More precisely, what the messianic event deactivates is precisely the religious limit or demarcation line that had delimited the specific space of the ban and, in general, the various and separate spheres of being as such. This was, as already mentioned, the main feature of modern political secularism as a still political-theological category. Messianism is thus nothing but the very internal limit or internal overcoming of religion, which Agamben himself unambiguously expresses by saying 'that the Messiah is the figure in which the great monotheistic religions sought to master the problem of law, and that in Judaism, as in Christianity or Shiite Islam, the Messiah's arrival signifies the fulfilment and the complete consummation of the Law. In monotheism, messianism thus constitutes not simply one category of religious experience among others but rather the limit concept of religious experience in general, the point in which religious experience passes beyond itself and calls itself into question insofar as it is law'.[14] As we mentioned at the beginning, Agamben here seems to define messianism as a merely nonreligious phenomenon or, more precisely, as a nonreligious element within religion itself.

Having summarised Agamben's argumentation, which leads him to assuming a paradoxical (post-religious) status of messianism in respect to religious experience, it is now necessary to provide a deeper inquiry into the structure and logic of this phenomenon. By inquiring into the ontological implications of messianism as well as into its representative figures, I will try to show the connection between this structure and that of perversion because Agamben himself throughout his work explicitly sustains this connection, claiming that both messianism and perversion are examples of a 'new politics' beyond metaphysics and religion. However, as we have seen in the previous chapter, and will further argue here, Agamben, in his reading of Freud's fetishism from his early work *Stanzas*, obscures the contradiction inherent in perversion and hence misses the contradiction inherent in messianism too. And it is only through this connection between messianism and perversion that the paradoxical status of messianism as a post-religious phenomenon can be seen, in the sense that it takes place in a temporal interval in which the process of religion's self-overcoming precisely doesn't come to an end but is rather stuck.

III

In order to proceed with the argument started here, I find it no coincidence that in his *The Time That Remains: A Commentary on the Letter to the Romans,* Agamben dedicates a sustained philosophical, hermeneutic, philological, and genealogical analysis to the first ten words of Paul's Letter to the Romans, which, he argues, encapsulate the entire idea of messianism.[15] He continues to insist on the conception of messianism as the form of life that is wholly transformed into writing, that is, as a phenomenon of complete indiscernibility between life and law. Put otherwise, the messianic dimension of the complete indiscernibility of life and law proceeds from an operation that abolishes both spheres with one move. According to Agamben, this happens precisely with Benjamin's 'real' state of exception, which is nothing but another name for the messianic event:

> We have seen the sense in which law begins to coincide with life once it has become the pure form of law, law's mere being in force without significance. But insofar as law is maintained as pure form in a state of virtual exception, it lets bare life . . . subsist before it. Law that becomes indistinguishable from life in a real state of exception is confronted by life that, in a symmetrical but inverse gesture, is entirely transformed into law. The absolute intelligibility of a life wholly resolved into writing corresponds to the impenetrability of a writing that, having become indecipherable, now appears as life. Only at this point do the two terms distinguished and kept united by the relation of ban (bare life and the form of law) abolish each other and enter into a new dimension.[16]

This point can be explained in another way, that is, in strictly political-ontological terms. By deactivating the internal limit that at the same time separates and connects bare life as 'pure Being'—the immediate and undetermined Being, which is precisely Being as nothing, nothing that is Being[17]—and the empty form of the law in the sphere of the ban, real state of exception actually causes the emergence of a zone of 'absolute indiscernibility between immanence and transcendence, between this world and the future world'.[18] This zone of indiscernibility between immanence and transcendence should be understood in Deleuze's terms of the *plane of immanence,* which elsewhere Agamben names 'absolute immanence'.[19] It is a place where the very difference between Being and nothing is abolished and where there is no longer any difference between this world and the other worlds, between higher and lower forms of existence, between their inclusion and exclusion. This formulation perhaps best encapsulates the basic thesis of Agamben's messianic political ontology: *everything exists*.[20] With this move to 'absolute immanence', every transcendence, every hierarchical difference or separation of various forms of life, which is the fundamental condition of religion, is abolished. In this sense, Agamben's differentiation between secularism and messianism has to be grasped as a difference between the religious and the nonreligious, or perhaps atheistic, models of politics.

Nevertheless, as we said at the beginning, this crucial dimension of Agamben's political ontology can also be explained via another figure who shares a place alongside Paul in a series of figures of 'new politics' but who also introduces a certain new perspective upon that politics. This is the literary figure of Bartleby the scrivener as an *exemplum* of the ontology of potentiality as Agamben develops it on the basis of his specific interpretation of Aristotle. The starting point of this interpretation is Aristotle's differentiation between potentiality (*dynamis*) and actuality (*energeia*).[21] According to Agamben, this differentiation implies a definition of potentiality as a privation of actuality or Being: 'Potentiality is therefore essentially defined by the possibility of its non-realisation which is what the term *hexis* means: the availability of privation'.[22] On the basis of this insight, Agamben generalises a distinction within the concept of potentiality itself: 'For Aristotle, all potential to be or to do something is always also potential not to be or not to do (*dynamis mē einai, mē energhein*), without which potentiality would always already have passed into actuality and would be indistinguishable from it. . . . The "potential not to" [*adynamia*] is the cardinal secret of the Aristotelian doctrine of potentiality, which transforms every potentiality in itself into an impotentiality'.[23]

If potentiality is essentially the potentiality 'not to' (do or be), this means that it belongs to the order of contingency, which is here opposed to the order of necessity. According to Agamben, it is precisely the ban of the first on account of the domination of the second that fundamentally determines the Western ethical tradition, and theology is mostly 'to blame' for such a state: 'Since Aristotle stated that all potentiality is also potentiality not (to be or do), the theologians were forced to strip God of all potential to be and to will at the same time that they affirmed his omnipotence. If God had the potential to be, he could also not be, which would contradict his eternity. On the other hand, if God were capable of not wanting what he wants, he would be capable of wanting non-Being and evil, which is equivalent to introducing a principle of nihilism into God'.[24]

On the basis of these suppositions, Agamben derives a formal comparison between Aristotle's definition of potentiality and Bartleby's formula 'I would prefer not to'. In Agamben's opinion, the scrivener's 'refusal' to perform the assigned tasks is not a classical refusal as a negation of something but precisely an active inactivity in the sense of disconnecting the possibility from the necessity of its realisation of potentiality from actuality. As Deleuze, who Agamben refers to at this crucial point, says, 'the formula "disconnects" words and things, words and actions, but also speech acts and words—it severs language from all reference, in accordance with Bartleby's absolute vocation, *to be a man without references*, someone who appears suddenly and then disappears, without reference to himself or anything else'.[25] In other words, Bartleby's formula 'opens a zone of indistinction between yes and no',[26] thereby deactivating the relation that connects real existence with its symbolic framework given by language, and this formula ultimately collapses both levels into one immanence of becoming. Thus, Bartleby is once more a figure that, in this regard, is strictly correlative to the figure of the Messiah. It is no coincidence that Deleuze concludes his essay about Bartleby with two general conclusions that refer to Melville as the bearer of becoming and Bartleby as the new Christ: 'Because there are so few authors in America, and because its people are so indifferent, the writer is not in a position to succeed as a recognised master. Even in his failure, the writer remains all the more the bearer of a *collective enunciation*, which no longer forms part of literary history and preserves the rights of a people to come, or of a human becoming. A schizophrenic vocation: even in his catatonic and anorexic state, Bartleby is not the patient, but the doctor of a sick America, the *Medicine-man*, the new Christ or the brother to us all'.[27]

Deleuze's adjective 'new' before the name of Christ should not be understood as a doubling of the figure of the Messiah but rather as a shift of emphasis compared to the traditional conception of the Messiah as a son of God. The new Christ, which is here a synonym for the 'brother to us all', thus denotes a sort of an anti-paternal figure,[28] just as it denotes a figure of the anti-law for Agamben. At this decisive point, we should recall an essential detail regarding Deleuze's idea of 'the exclusion of the father', namely, that for Deleuze, Bartleby is ultimately derivative of a more original and paradigmatic anti-paternal figure—the figure of the masochist as the embodiment of one of the two basic perversions.[29] It is precisely this connection that brings us to a certain, until now overlooked, connection between Deleuze and Agamben, that is, the figure of *perversion* or, more specifically, of masochism as the meta-figure that stitches together everything that Deleuze develops as a continuation of Nietzsche's project of overturning Platonism, on the one hand, and that Agamben develops in terms of messianic and post-metaphysical new politics, on the other.

In this respect, and as already mentioned in a previous chapter, it is not surprising that Agamben in *Stanzas* recognises in the fetishist disavowal exactly the same stance as he later finds in messianism: an anti-metaphysical stance which completely overcomes the neurotic or Oedipal structure of metaphysics. I will now continue the critical examination of Agamben's misreading of Freud's theory of fetishism begun in the previous chapter by focusing in more detail on Lacan's reading of this concept. This move to Lacan's further unfolding of the Freudian concept of fetishism will enable us to show, firstly, the correlation between perversion and messianism indicated earlier, and secondly, how Agamben, by misreading Freud at least in part, overlooks the very reason why the perverse structure of messianism represents the problem rather than the solution, with regard to overcoming the religious and metaphysical structure of Western biopolitics.

IV

In Freud's theory, a fetish is notoriously known as a substitute. However, Freud insists that this is not a general substitute for everything that is lacking in reality, but rather a specific substitute, a 'substitute for the woman's (the mother's) penis that the little boy once believed and—for reasons familiar to us—does not want to give up'.[30] Precisely because the fetish is not a general but rather a specific substitute for a specific organ (the mother's penis, which is lacking at the imaginary level), it is essentially tied to the experience of woman's castration, hence of sexual difference as such. As Lacan stresses regarding this point, the essential function of the fetish is that it constitutes a phallic object of the phallus properly speaking. Namely, if the fetish is the mask or cover, it is the cover not for something hidden behind it but rather for the lack itself. In this sense, the phallus constitutes itself essentially as absent, so that Lacan could claim that 'it is the absence of the penis that makes her the phallus, the object of desire'.[31] This emergence of the phallus as absent is inextricably connected with the fetish so that the latter constitutes a material support for the former. The fetish constitutes a curtain or veil, which covers the imaginary lack, constitutive for the symbolic value of the phallus, which determines sexual difference.[32] In this sense, the fetish is constitutive for a certain 'beyond', a certain 'behind the veil', which constitutes the field of the phallus. In other words, the fetish is the projection of the absence on the curtain, which fixes its image only by indicating that which is behind it—nothing, which appears as the absent object only in this context. As Lacan put it, 'Absence is depicted on the veil. This is nothing but the function of the curtain as such. It acquires its value, its being, and its consistency exactly insofar as it constitutes that on which the absence is projected and imagined'.[33]

However, this characteristic of the fetish as veil led Freud to the discovery of another characteristic, which is even more important in the constitution of the fetish, namely, the process of its constitution. As he put it,

> It seems rather that when the fetish is instituted some process occurs which reminds one of the stopping of memory in traumatic amnesia. As in this latter case, the subject's interest comes to a half-way, as it were; it is as though the last impression before the uncanny [*unheimlich*] and traumatic one is retained as a fetish. Thus the foot or shoe owes its preference as a fetish—or a part of it—to the circumstance that the inquisitive boy peered at the woman's genitals from below, from her legs up; fur and velvet—as has long been suspected—are a fixation of the sight of the pubic hair, which should have been followed by the longed-for sight of the female member; pieces of underclothing, which are so often chosen as a fetish, crystallise the moment of undressing, the last moment in which the woman could still be regarded as phallic.[34]

The comparison between the fixation of the gaze in fetishism and 'the stopping of memory' in traumatic amnesia is certainly not coincidental. This clearly indicates the primacy of trauma in the constitution of the fetish, which is only a secondary reaction to the traumatic experience. However, there is a condition on which traumatic experience depends too. As Alenka Zupančič claims, the trauma is not the reason why something is experienced as traumatic and then repressed. Rather, the repression or, more precisely, primal repression, the repression of the signifier as the first phase of repression, is that which opens up the possibility for a traumatic experience: 'It is not that we repress a signifier because of a traumatic experience related to it, it is rather because this signifier is repressed that we can experience something as traumatic (and not simply as painful, frustrating etc.)'.[35] This is why Freud insisted so much on assuming the fetishist's disavowal within the process of repression and not on their separation:[36] there is a reason why the sight of castration is experienced as traumatic, and why the subject reacts to it by the constitution of the fetish. This reason is established with primal repression. In order to relate itself to a specific traumatic situation, experienced by the sight of the woman's castration, which is then disavowed, the fetish must be conditioned by the (primal) repression, insofar as it is the very condition of possibility for the traumatic experience as such. Otherwise, the fetish would not be a substitute for a specific organ (the mother's penis) as Freud insisted but rather a substitute for any kind of object.

It is precisely this aspect that explains the whole constellation of fetishism. As already mentioned, Freud's comparison between the fixation of sight or the constitution of the curtain and the stopping of memory implies the whole line of sight, which is at a determined moment suspended. Lacan calls this line 'history' or the course of history and defines it as a signifying chain or a succession of signifiers. This is why the stopping of sight shouldn't be understood as an occasional stopping or snapshot without any previous preparation. On the contrary, Lacan insists that we are dealing here with the 'remembrance of covering', which implies something behind, which is covered. In other words, it implies the course behind the veil: 'Remembrance of covering, *Deckerinnerung*, is not simply an occasional snapshot, it is the interruption of history, the moment in which the history is stopped and fixed, and in which at the same time indicated the course of its own movement beyond the veil'.[37]

It's important to add here that for Lacan, the stopping of the course of the signifying chain and the fixation of the image not only compares with the stopping of a film tape, that is, with the so-called screen-shot, but also assigns to the image a complete conceptual value by associating it with the linguistic concept of metonymy.[38] The metonymic character of fetishist disavowal lies precisely in a fixed image, a curtain, which preserves the illusion of a certain 'beyond', regardless of the concrete experience of its inexistence. This point of metonymic projection of the image and the displacement of desire 'beyond' the curtain is conveyed best in Freud's basic example of fetishism, in the so-called shine at the nose [in German *Glanz auf der Nase*] of one of his patients. According to Freud, this phrase must be read in English, which was the language of the patient's infancy: namely, the German word *Glanz* (shine) is phonetically inseparable from English word 'glance', so that 'shine at the nose' becomes set as 'glance at the nose' and nose becomes the object fetish. Lacan's commentary: 'You see here how the historical chain, which may contain the whole phrase, even more, a phrase in a forgotten language, enters in the game and projects itself at the point on the veil'.[39]

In drawing this part to a close, we can turn back to Agamben's reading of Freud's disavowal. What Agamben misreads in Freud is exactly the co-dependence of disavowal and repression. Both depend on the first moment of repression, on the so-called primal repression, which is a condition of possibility for traumatic experience. Therefore disavowal in no way deactivates the mechanism of repression (and the return of the repressed, which is the moment of constitution of the symptom). Moreover, if primal repression constitutes the very point at which interpretation (for Agamben, the metaphysical operation par excellence) constitutively fails, insofar as this repression is the condition for interpretation and for the unconscious as such and not vice versa, disavowal rather withholds the interpretation exactly before it touches its own breaking point, which is not the point of total interpretability but rather the point of the incompleteness of interpretation. By doing so, disavowal holds up the illusion of a positive reality behind the interpretation, behind the fetish as a mask for nothing. In other words, disavowal, by projecting and fixing the image at the veil, essentially constitutes the infinite realm behind the veil, which is the realm of the phallus. Rather than escaping metaphysics, perversion in this way keeps the subject in its vice. In the last part of the chapter, I will thus turn back to the initial paradox of messianism and its relation to religion, focusing on a specific structure of messianic time and its correlation to this stopping of the image, or disavowal, which constitutes perversion.

V

In concluding this chapter, I want to propose that Lacan's definition of the fixation of sight as the stopping of the course of history, which determines the constitution of fetishism, in fact enables us to see properly what is at stake in Agamben's theory of the messianic event and messianic time. Messianic time is here actually perverse time in the sense that, at the point of its stopping, it simultaneously indicates a certain course of time beyond its own end. In this sense, messianic time establishes itself precisely as that time which, in the last instance, disavows its own end by indefinitely displacing its actualisation into a realm of the traumatic 'beyond'.[40]

It seems necessary to focus again here, albeit briefly, on Agamben's rather violent criticism of Derrida's interpretation of the messianic event. Although Agamben explicitly rejects Derrida's interpretation of the messianic event as an anti-event or an 'event that succeeds in not happening',[41] and claims, to the contrary, that messianism is an event that actually happens, a closer reading shows that, in his own definition of messianism, Agamben nevertheless also presupposes a temporal postponement or suspension. Despite his general rhetoric and attempts at defining the temporal structure of the messianic event as the opposite of waiting, as the opposite of the suspension or the postponement of an event, there is a rather decisive point in *The Time That Remains* where Agamben's definition of messianic time as '*the time that time takes to come to an end*, or, more precisely, the time we take to bring time to an end, to achieve our representation of time',[42] brings him unusually close to Deleuze's early conception of suspense in Masoch as well as to Derrida's conception of messianic postsecularism. Indeed, Agamben writes, 'Paul decomposes the messianic event in two times: resurrection and *parousía*, the second coming of Jesus at the end of time. Out of those issues the paradoxical tension between an *already* and a *not yet* that defines the Pauline conception of salvation. The messianic event has already happened, salvation is already accomplished, and yet, in order to be really achieved it needs a supplementary time'.[43]

In view of the above, messianism is thus ultimately traversed by a postponement, a temporal suspension between an *already* and a *not yet*; it is a paradoxical synthesis of *yes* and *no*, which thus become emphatically undistinguishable. But on the other hand, it seems as if this emphatic indistinguishability produces precisely what it seeks to abolish, that is, an absolute 'not yet', an absolute suspension of the time needed to bring time to an end. This is precisely the point of the messianic temporal dynamics: a *katechon* in an intensified form. If the classical image of the *katechon*—as we know it from Paul's *Second Letter to the Thessalonians* (2 *Tes* 2, 6–7)—is the image of the pure form of the law that 'blocks the *anomos*',[44] then the eschatological image of *katechon* is the image of an anomie that has already happened—the end of time has already occurred—and yet its full realisation has been delayed, which is why the time of anomie is precisely the messianic *time that remains*. It is a postponement of the completion of the very end of time, which necessarily lasts forever precisely because the end of time had already happened. Therefore we could say that what Agamben fails to see is that the endless postponement of the actualisation of the end of time is strictly co-dependent with the constitution of the Messiah as a fetish, which only serves to construct an infinite temporal realm within the time of the messianic event. In this context, we should also recall that the structure of messianic time as a postponement of the completion of historical time corresponds precisely to the time Deleuze detected in analysing the functioning of postdisciplinary societies of control: 'in control societies you never finish anything', on the basis of which Deleuze immediately deduces the fundamental principle of '*endless postponement*'.[45] This feature clearly shows how the very fact of the impossibility of completion has turned into the dominant principle of the functioning of Western societies. At the general level, this simply means that between historical time and messianic eternity there is an intermediate time or, to put it better, the indistinction and simultaneous distinction between historical and messianic time within the messianic event bring us precisely to the eternity of historical time, not in the sense of the eternity of chronology, but eternity as the suspension or the postponement of the transition of historical time into eternity. In other words, what is really eternal is postponement itself or the eternity of the time of the end.

If we now return to the initial question of the relation between messianism and secularism as a political-theological concept, then we could say something along these lines: Agamben's messianism founds itself not so much in the suspension of the historical, that is, secular time, but in a perverse suspension of its completion or accomplishment. If secularism necessarily, according to its etymology, implies a 'relationship with the secolo',[46] if it is therefore immanently bound to historical time, then messianism literally means 'post-secularism': post-secularism, or post-temporality, that which emerges at the end of secularism, after historical time has been finished. As we have said, the very idea of the messianic event as understood by Agamben means that at the end of historical time there appears not simply eternity as the opposite of history but precisely messianic time as the time needed to bring historical time, which has already ended, to an end. The end of history and secularism means precisely the impossibility of their ending. This is why Agamben can say that the messianic event is immanent to and simultaneously different from historical time:

> The messianic event is considered through a bi-unitary figure. This figure probably constitutes the true sense of the division of the single Messiah (like the single Law) into two distinct figures, one of which is consumed in the consummation of history and the other of which happens, so to speak, only the day after his arrival. Only in this way can the event of the Messiah coincide with historical time yet at the same time not be identified with it, effecting in the *eskhaton* that 'small adjustment' in which, according to the rabbi's saying told by Benjamin, the messianic kingdom consists.[47]

In this double figure of the Messiah, messianism ultimately always involves two kinds in one and the same concept: secularised historical Christianity and the Christianity of the messianic event as the time of the end of historical secular Christianity that cannot be brought to an end. To be precise, messianism is the permanent postponement (that converges on the impossible) of this completion of the time of the end of historical Christianity and historical time. This feature is again similar to masochism, where it is not the whipping itself that is suspended but the raised whip that does not finish its movement with a direct dynamic strike upon the body. If we formulate this point in a more general way, then we could say that *messianism is the end of secularism in the precise sense of the impotency of its completion, accomplishment, conclusion*. In this sense, 'the end' should be understood precisely in the paradoxical meaning that Heidegger refers to when talking about 'the end of philosophy' (as metaphysics): 'The old meaning of the word "end" means the same as place: "from one end to the other" means from one place to the other. The end of philosophy is the place, that place in which the whole of philosophy's history is gathered in its most extreme possibility. End as completion means this gathering'.[48] This means that messianism is not secularism's simple opposite but merely a radicalised, concentrated version of secularism (as a religious phenomenon) that cannot end. Thus, the messianic time is precisely a 'not yet' that sets up the immanent temporal suspension of this time that has already ended as a transcendental principle. It is in this sense that we could say that messianism has to do precisely with a sort of an ideological illusion of an immanent temporal transcendence without immanence, the future in the present that has already ended. In more topological terms, messianism replaces the duality of symbolic order by disavowing the gap in immanence itself, producing with this a surface of an absolute immanence without any gap, which is simultaneously redoubled in the absolute transcendence of full meaning (Kafka's law as life that is only studied) that cannot ever be reached precisely because of its limitlessness. This is why messianism is in the last instance neither merely a religious nor a nonreligious experience but rather a paradoxical post-religious experience placed at the very extimate position of internal exteriority within religion, at the indefinite temporal interval in which religion overcomes itself—yet this overcoming cannot be accomplished.

NOTES

1. Giorgio Agamben, *Homo Sacer: Sovereign Power and Bare Life*, trans. Daniel Heller-Roazen (Stanford, CA: Stanford University Press, 1998), 56.
2. Giorgio Agamben, 'In Praise of Profanation', in *Profanations*, trans. Jeff Fort (New York: Zone Books, 2007), 77.
3. Ibid., 77.
4. Ibid.
5. Ibid., 74.
6. See René Girard, *Violence and the Sacred*, trans. Patrick Gregory (Baltimore, MD: Johns Hopkins University Press, 1979).
7. Agamben, 'In Praise of Profanation', 77.
8. Agamben, *Homo Sacer*, 8.
9. Ibid., 4.
10. Ibid., 8.
11. The extimate position of bare life proceeds precisely from its structural symmetry with the position of the sovereign exception: 'Here the structural analogy between the sovereign exception and *sacratio* shows its full sense. At the two extreme limits of the order, the sovereign and *homo sacer* present two symmetrical figures that have the same structure and are correlative: the sovereign is the one with respect to whom all men are potentially *homines sacri*, and *homo sacer* is the one with respect to whom all men act as sovereigns' (ibid., 84).
12. Ibid., 11.
13. See Lorenzo Chiesa, 'Giorgio Agamben's Franciscan Ontology', *Cosmos and History: The Journal of Natural and Social Philosophy* 5, no. 1 (2009): 111–15.
14. Agamben, *Homo Sacer*, 56.
15. Giorgio Agamben, *The Time That Remains: A Commentary on the Letter to the Romans*, trans. Patricia Dailey (Stanford, CA: Stanford University Press, 2005).
16. Agamben, *Homo Sacer*, 55.
17. This formulation is based on a simultaneous reading of two of Agamben's seemingly contradictory theses. Referring to Heidegger, Agamben says, 'Being is nothing other than the ban of the being' (ibid., 59). But it is precisely this ban that equalises Being and nothing; in the ban, life lives as nothing that is Being. For only with this presupposition can Agamben insist that Benjamin's nihilism precisely *is* the nullification of nothing: 'Confronted with the imperfect nihilism that would let the Nothing subsist indefinitely in the form of a being in force without significance, Benjamin proposes a messianic nihilism that nullifies even the Nothing and lets no form of law remain in force beyond its own content' (ibid., 53). The question that we leave open here and only suggest a possible answer for is whether the basis of Agamben's deduction is not precisely Hegel's main thesis from the second volume of *The Science of Logic* that says precisely this: Being is nothing.
18. Agamben, *The Time That Remains*, 25.
19. See Giorgio Agamben, 'Absolute Immanence', in *Potentialities: Collected Essays in Philosophy*, trans. Daniel Heller-Roazen (Stanford, CA: Stanford University Press, 2000), 220–39.
20. It seems that this interpretation finds its explicit confirmation on the last page of Agamben's 'Absolute Immanence', dedicated to Deleuze's last essay 'Immanence: A Life': 'In this dimension, there will be little sense in distinguishing between organic life and animal life or even between biological life and contemplative life and between bare life and the life of the mind. Life as contemplation without knowledge will have a precise correlate in thought that has freed itself of all cognition and intentionality. Theōria and the contemplative life, which the philosophical tradition has identified as its highest goal for centuries, will have to be dislocated onto a new plane of immanence. It is not certain that, in the process, political philosophy and epistemology will be able to maintain their present physiognomy and difference with respect to ontolo-

gy. Today, blessed life lies on the same terrain as the biopolitical body of the West' (ibid., 239; translation modified).

21. For a more precise and in-depth analysis of the entire distinction and its consequences, see Giorgio Agamben, 'La potenza del pensiero', in *La potenza del pensiero — saggi e conferenze* (Vicenza: Neri Pozza, 2010), 281–96.

22. Ibid., 285; my translation.

23. Giorgio Agamben, 'Bartleby, or On Contingency', in *Potentialities*, 245.

24. Ibid., 253.

25. Quoted in ibid., 255.

26. Ibid., 255.

27. Gilles Deleuze, *Essays Critical and Clinical*, trans. Daniel W. Smith and Michael A. Greco (Minneapolis: University of Minnesota Press, 1997), 90.

28. 'Melville will never cease to elaborate on the radical opposition between fraternity and Christian "charity" or paternal "philanthropy". To liberate man from the father function, to give birth to the new man or the man without particularities, to reunite the original and humanity by constituting a society of brothers as a new universality. In the society of brothers, alliance replaces filiation and the blood pact replaces consanguinity. Man is indeed the blood brother of his fellow man, and woman, his blood sister: according to Melville, this is the community of celibates, drawing its members into an unlimited becoming' (ibid., 84).

29. As we have already mentioned, in his 'Coldness and Cruelty' (in *Masochism: Coldness and Cruelty and Venus in Furs*, trans. Jean McNeil and Aude Willm [New York: Zone Books, 1991]), Deleuze writes, 'The masochist thus liberates himself in preparation for a rebirth in which the father will have no part' (66), and, 'In the case of masochism the totality of the law is invested upon the mother, who expels the father from the symbolic realm' (90). Recall that, for Agamben, sovereign 'right over life and death' originates in the Roman 'formula *vitae necisque potestas*, which designates not sovereign power but rather the unconditional authority [*potestà*] of the *pater* over his sons' (Agamben, *Homo Sacer*, 87).

30. Sigmund Freud, 'Fetishism', in *The Standard Edition of the Complete Psychological Works of Sigmund Freud, Vol. XXI*, ed. James Strachey (London: Vintage, 2001), 152–53.

31. Jacques Lacan, 'The Subversion of the Subject and the Dialectic of Desire in the Freudian Unconscious', in *Écrits*, trans. Bruce Fink (London and New York: W. W. Norton & Company), 699.

32. 'Exactly insofar as it [the phallus] is there or is not there, and only insofar as it is there or is not there, is the symbolic differentiation between the sexes established' (Jacques Lacan, *Le Seminair, livre IV: La relation d'objet* [Paris: Seuil, 1994], 153; my translation).

33. Ibid., 155.

34. Freud, 'Fetishism', 155.

35. Alenka Zupančič, 'On Repetition', *Sats — Nordic Journal of Philosophy* 8, no. 1 (2007): 39.

36. 'A new technical term is justified when it describes a new fact or emphasises it. This is not the case here. The oldest word in our psycho-analytic terminology, "repression", already relates to this pathological process. If we wanted to differentiate more sharply between the vicissitude of the *idea* as distinct from that of the *affect*, and reserve the word "*Verdrängung*" ["repression"] for the affect, then the correct German word for the vicissitude of the idea would be "*Verleugnung*" ["disavowal"]' (Freud, 'Fetishism', 153).

37. Lacan, *La relation d'objet*, 157; my translation.

38. Ibid.

39. Ibid., 158; my translation.

40. Note how this suspension of time also echoes in Deleuze's interpretation of Masoch: 'What becomes essential is waiting or suspense as a plenitude, as a physical and spiritual intensity. The rituals of suspension become the novelistic figures par excellence, with regard to both the woman-torturer who suspends her gesture, and the

hero-victim whose suspended body awaits the whip. Masoch is the writer who makes suspense, in its pure and almost unbearable state, the motivating force of the novel' (Deleuze, *Essays Critical and Clinical*, 54).

41. Quoted in Giorgio Agamben, 'The Messiah and the Sovereign: The Problem of Law in Walter Benjamin', in *Potentialities*, 174.

42. Agamben, *The Time That Remains*, 67.

43. Ibid., 69.

44. Roberto Esposito, *Immunitas. Protection and Negation of Life*, trans. Zakiya Hanafi (Cambridge, MA, and Malden: Polity Press, 2011), 63.

45. Gilles Deleuze, 'Postscript on Control Societies', in *Negotiations 1972–1990*, trans. Martin Joughin (New York: Columbia University Press, 1997), 179.

46. I again draw on Esposito (*Immunitas*, 60): 'Secularisation, in the literal sense of relationship with the secolo or "century", is entirely intrinsic to the Christian reality, unless we drastically bend Christianity toward some kind of Gnostic view'. Agamben's messianism as a postsecular new politics is precisely Christianity in the Gnostic sense mentioned by Esposito.

47. Agamben, 'The Messiah and the Sovereign', 174.

48. Martin Heidegger, 'The End of Philosophy and the Task of Thinking', in *Basic Writings*, (San Francisco, CA: Harper, 1977), 375. I rely here on Tadej Troha, who developed this point about (the impossibility of) the end of metaphysics in Heidegger in reference to Kafka in his 'Kafka and the Irreversible', *Critical Engagements: A Journal of Criticism and Theory* 8, no. 1–2 (2014): 157–79.

SEVEN

State of Exception and Sade's Biopolitical Manifesto

I

Having discussed Agamben's take on perversion in his early philosophical accounts of language, it is now the moment to move forwards and to analyse those few seemingly marginal, yet highly important, points within his political philosophy of the *Homo Sacer* project, where he brings perversion into play. In this chapter, I will try to show how Deleuze's idea of the "irreducibly dissymmetry"[1] between sadism and masochism is actually mirrored in Agamben's opposition between a virtual or sovereign state of exception on the one hand and the messianic or real state of exception which abolishes the former on the other. This argument will go beyond Agamben's own conception of sadism and masochism as a relation of 'complicity' which, as we will see, he sets out on many occasions. Roughly put, in *Homo Sacer: Sovereign Power and Bare Life*, Agamben rightly posits Sade's castle as a paradigmatic model of the contemporary state of exception in which the biopolitical politicisation of bare life is exercised over the physiological body of bare life; yet he then performs a standard conceptual slip by arguing for the complicity between the sadistic torturer and masochistic bare life within a desubjectivised world of the state of exception. As we have discussed at length in part II, Deleuze maintains that the world of perversion is a desubjectivised instrumental world without or beyond the symbolic structure of the Other, but he also claims that there is no complicity between sadist and masochist as far as Sade and Masoch are concerned. However, Agamben's unjustified argument about the complicity between sadist and masochist, which mirrors the relationship between sovereign power and bare life in the state of exception, does not thwart us to identify the logic of masochism elsewhere in Agamben's story. In fact, Deleuze's conception of masochism, which supposedly suspends the dynamic of sadistic institution by way of establishing a contractual (legal) subordination of the victim to the torturer, actually corresponds to Agamben's own appropriation of Benjaminian 'real state of exception' which Agamben considers as a messianic event. Specifically, by setting up the argument of how the latter succeeds in abolishing the virtual or sovereign state of exception in which a Sadean-Foucauldian biopolitical governmentality becomes operative, Agamben relies on the historical example of the seventeenth-century messianic movement lead by Sabbatai Zevi, the same movement which Deleuze argues to be the ideational inspiration for Masoch's writings and the political role of masochism.

To begin with, let us recall very briefly Deleuze's argument about the necessity of differentiating between sadism and masochism. When he argues that that 'there is between sadism and masochism an irreducible dissymmetry'[2] so that 'the names of Sade and Masoch have been used to denote two basic perversions',[3] instead of one general perversion, he does not speak from a meta-position that would represent an intersection of both but rather from the position of one of them—the position of masochism. For despite his constant comparative reading, from which he deduces a series of irreducible differences between sadism and masochism, it was the appearance of Masoch's novels that first made this comparison possible. Until then, there had been a tendency, which can still be found in many places today, to understand masochism and the masochist attitude as complementary to the sadistic position, with which it supposedly forms a harmonic whole, an ideal pair. According to Deleuze, Masoch, and retroactively also Sade, deserve credit precisely for being 'outstanding examples of the efficiency of literature',[4] insofar as each in his own way and with his own devices presents the 'unparalleled configurations of symptoms and signs'.[5] With their respective literary presentations of symptoms, both Sade and Masoch introduced a differentiation, even an irreducible dissymmetry, into the general concept of perversion, where masochism usually stood in the shadow of a much more exposed and discussed sadism as its complementary antipode. Such a conception led to the establishment of the compound signifier 'sadomasochism', which is still very present today and denotes a supposed synthesis of both attitudes into a harmonic whole. In this perspective, the lesson of Masoch's literary invention is quite the opposite. The attitude of his hero Severin could not be further from the attitude of a passive victim of sadistic will. Severin is a victim of his own will, which operates against the will of his woman torturer. As Deleuze constantly repeats, the masochistic contract 'implies not only the necessity of the victim's consent, but his ability to persuade, and his pedagogical and judicial efforts to train his torturer'.[6]

Following Deleuze, this general feature already traces out the obvious difference between the position of the masochist and that of the victim in sadism, who is objectified, impersonal element, raw material, so to speak, deprived of his or her will. As we will see, sadistic victims are more similar to what Agamben tries to formulate with the term 'bare life', while something quite the opposite holds for masochists—they are voluntary victims and as such establish the law as an apparatus of sacrifice in which they are inscribed. Deleuze's comparative reading of Sade and Masoch thus results in an exposition and conceptualisation of a series of irreducible differences[7] that more or less justify the former's entire argument which concerns the difference between the two basic perversions. Let us now focus on one specific difference listed by Deleuze which is particularly important for Agamben's conception of the state of exception and for the relation between sovereign power and bare life. This difference is the dissymmetry between the sadist's commitment to institutions and their simultaneous hostility to the law on the one hand and the masochistic celebration or creation of the law on the other. As Deleuze puts it,

> Sade's secret societies, his societies of libertines, are institutional societies; in a word, Sade thinks in terms of 'institutions', Masoch in terms of the 'contract'. The juridical distinction between contract and institution is well known: the contract presupposes in principle the free consent of the contracting parties and determines between them a system of reciprocal rights and duties; it cannot affect a third party and is valid for a limited period. Institutions, by contrast, determine a long-term state of affairs which is both involuntary and inalienable; it establishes a power or an authority which takes effect against a third party. But even more significant is the difference between the contract and institution with respect to what is known as a *law*: the contract actually generates a law, even if this law oversteps and contravenes the conditions which made it possible; institution is of a very different order in that it tends to render laws unnecessary, to replace the system of rights and duties by a dynamic model of action, authority and power.[8]

On this point, Deleuze does not allow for any ambiguity: on the one hand, the masochistic contract implies a formal symbolic regulation of relations between elements constituting the masochistic relation between the torturer and the victim. It is at the same time the condition of possibility of masochistic cruelty and the victim's pleasure. But in relation to sadism, whose condition of possibility is an institutional framework which takes place in anomy (a-*nomos*) precisely because of its specific dynamics whose aim is nothing but the creation of another, higher nature, a dynamics that constantly splits and traverses, patches up and completes this nature (in this process, as we shall see later, there are no victims in the strict sense of the word), masochism inverts the logic insofar as it establishes a paradoxical model of sacrifice. In masochism, we can speak precisely of the victim's inscription into a juridical relation as a victim or even a slave, which category masochists belong to, of course, out of their free will. That is why the juridical dimension is the key dimension in masochism, especially in its anti-dialectical relation to sadistic institutions.

The question that arises at this point is the following: Is not precisely this difference between the sadistic commitment to the institution and the creation of a law in masochism actually at the core of the difference that Agamben draws within the form of law, which manifests itself in two diametrically opposed forms of the state of exception? For despite all the rhetoric about the state of exception as the zone of indistinction between life and law, between fact and law, which is Agamben's constant concern, he in the end always preserves a double image of law, a view of the law from two diametrically opposed sides—Schmitt's imperfect nihilism of the sovereign exception and Benjaminian messianic nihilism which abolishes the duplicity of sovereign form of law that in its constitutive nothingness or void as a space in which the 'politicisation of bare life' takes place: 'Confronted with the imperfect nihilism that would let the Nothing subsist indefinitely in the form of a being in force without significance, Benjamin proposes a messianic nihilism that nullifies even the Nothing and lets no form of law remain in force beyond its own content'.[9] The anti-dialectical character of Benjamin's real state of exception or messianic event is then further associated, as we have argued in the previous chapter, with what Agamben calls that 'new politics', whose fundamental task consists in overcoming the metaphysical structure of law and the state of exception as its biopolitical essence. What, then, is this double image of law, one applying to the imperfect nihilism and the politicisation of bare life, and another to the messianic abolishment of the form of law by way of fully adopting this very form, thus bringing it to its qualitative transformation into the form-of-life itself?

II

As we know, the starting point of Agamben's treatment of the topic of *homo sacer* is a categorical lack in the field of jurisprudence concerning the connection between the state of exception as the suspension of juridical order *in toto* and this order itself. For according to Agamben, the understanding of this phenomenon as something outside the domain of law and thus without any connection to it was a constant within jurisprudence until Carl Schmitt.[10] It was with Schmitt that the state of exception became the object of jurisprudential thought, but, according to Agamben, this breakthrough does not suffice as a complete and accurate understanding of the problem. Agamben's objection to Schmitt is that he integrated the state of exception into law too quickly by declaring it to be a nonjuridical condition of possibility of law (the rule is determined by the exception) and thus an internal heterogeneity of law itself without which the latter could not exist. The Schmittian decision about the exception that first makes room for law thus relates to the decision on the relation between law and nonlaw, law and fact. In the positive sense, the juridical order is established only secondarily, after the establishment of this relation, for the original and primary relation of law is negative. As Jean-Luc Nancy has already noted, due to the law being devoid of significance, its original relation to life is one of ban or abandonment, the relation of a lapsus, a slipping of life outside the law. Such, in the last instance, is Nancy's reading of Kant's 'pure form of law' and it is no coincidence that Agamben followed him on this point.[11] According to Agamben, banning life into the special sphere of the internal extraneousness of law is nothing but the result of the fact that, since Kant, the law has been an empty form without significance and as such completely indeterminate. As Agamben puts it, 'In Kant the pure form of law as "being in force without significance" appears for the first time in modernity. What Kant calls "the simple form of law" (*die bloße Form des Gesetzes*) in the *Critique of Practical Reason* is in fact a law reduced to the zero point of its significance, which is, nevertheless, in force as such'.[12] He connects this reading of Kant to another key reference, that is, the abovementioned phrase 'being in force without significance', which Gershom Scholem and Walter Benjamin both used to define law in Kafka's parable 'Before the Law'. For it is precisely

> Kafka's legend [that] presents the pure form in which law affirms itself with the greatest force precisely at the point in which it no longer prescribes anything—which is to say, as pure ban. The man from the country is delivered over to the potentiality of law because law demands nothing of him and commands nothing other than its own openness. According to the schema of the sovereign exception, law applies to him in no longer applying, and holds him in its ban in abandoning him outside itself. The open door destined only for him includes him in excluding him and excludes him in including him. And this is precisely the summit and the root of every law.[13]

So the pure form of law generates a life that dwells in abandonment, which is not simply external to law, but is included precisely through this exclusion. Bare life is thus a result of the fact that the very form of law is empty, that bare life has no positive significance within this law apart from the relation of the abandonment. It is no coincidence that it is precisely in this paradoxical structure of the law that Agamben recognises a position of life which is symmetrical, but opposite to, the one taken on the sovereign exception by Schmitt.[14] In the form of law without significance, nothing else exists but the pure form of the relation between two figures: bare life and sovereign power. This is why we can say that it is Agamben himself who thus gives the best counter-arguments against his general thesis that in the logic of sovereignty there is a complete indistinction between life and law, where both spheres blend and coincide to the extent that no distinction between them is possible. The relation of ban here testifies to the fact that this indistinction is incomplete at best, that there still persists a minimal distinction between the two spheres, which makes the form of relation possible. This is why, in his *State of Exception,* Agamben can talk about the zone of anomie, the zone of the emptiness of law in the strict sense of the word.[15] For biopolitics to be possible as a 'politicisation of bare life', whereby the latter plays the role of a threshold in which the constant decision over life and death is taken, the existence of this sphere is—from the viewpoint of sovereignty—ontologically necessary.

The realm of biopolitics described earlier, which is represented by Schmitt's space of the exception, is *prima facie* quite similar to what Deleuze recognises as the institutional anarchic nature of sadism and its structurally motivated hostility to law. But we need not speculate on this because in a seemingly marginal but actually key passage in *Homo Sacer,* Agamben himself addresses Sade's *Philosophy in the Boudoir* and, more precisely, the famous pamphlet 'Make More of an Effort, Frenchmen, If You Want to Be Republicans', which he characterises as no less than 'the first and perhaps most radical biopolitical manifesto of modernity', insofar as in it Sade 'stages . . . the *theatrum politicum* as a theatre of bare life, in which the very physiological life of bodies appears, through sexuality, as the pure political element'.[16]

Before we come to discuss the anarchic institutional character of sadistic biopolitics in more detail, as well as its etymological connection with the Christian concept of trinity as proposed by Agamben, let us very briefly consider this connection between sadism and bare life via a Lacanian perspective. In fact, as will be further discussed shortly, Agamben does not fail to mention the explicit link pointed out by Sade between enjoyment and a so-conceived sadistic (bio)political power ('"there is no man", he [Sade] writes, "who does not want to be a despot when he has an erection"'[17]). This connection is important to mention because it puts into question the conventional view on sadism, where it is seen as essentially related to the suffering and pain of the other. For if Agamben insists that the biopolitical machine consists mostly in the production of the bare life of the other, this in fact implies the reduction of the latter to a zero point of subjectivity without symbolic mediation—because, to recall, Agamben sees the essential point of the state of exception in the mere unmediated relation between sovereign power and bare life. But what exactly does the term 'bare life' refer to here if we know that it does not concern the simple experience of physical pain—as evidenced by Agamben's analyses of concentration camp situations, which are not so much descriptions of torture as descriptions of specific anxious experiences of the uncanny position beyond life and death to which the figure of the

Muselmann refers.[18] In order to explicate this point, it seems apt to relate Agamben's concept to Lacan's thesis in his *Seminar X* on *Anxiety* according to which 'it is not so much the other party's suffering that is being sought in the sadistic intention as his anxiety'. And as Lacan immediately adds, 'I noted this with the little sign, $0'.[19] For Lacan, in other words, anxiety indicates the emergence of subjectivity reduced to the zero level of existence, which is to say, to the level of the pure subject which does not succeed in vanishing into the realm of the signifier (symbolic Other). More precisely, the subject is essentially the subject of the signifier, yet it functions as a 'vanishing mediator' (Žižek) which emerges only in the interval between two signifiers. This implies that the subject amounts to the very gap in the symbolic which revolves around the lack of the first (repressed) signifier. As we see, Lacan's formulation points to the state where the sadist's victim is reduced to the point where the subject, although still the effect of the signifier, is immanently detached from the latter and therefore from symbolic mediation as such. The moment of anxiety thus refers to the moment in which the victim is reduced to the status of bare life, as that which is directly confronted with the executioner without any mediation.

This correlation between bare life and the affect of anxiety seems even more justified if we remember that, in his *Seminar X* on *Anxiety*, Lacan additionally explains the affect of anxious paralysis with a matrix that defines the relation between the degree of the drive's thrust and the level of its tension, on the one hand, and the difficulty of symbolising this experience, on the other.[20] Anxiety as a zero degree of subjectivity is defined precisely as an extreme point characterised by the great tension caused by the movement of the drive, on the one hand, and the great difficulty of symbolising this experience by the subject, on the other. So anxiety thus entails a situation in which the subject is as close as possible to the real of the drive and as distant as possible from the signifier which would enable the subject to symbolise the intensity of the drive's pressure. What comes across as the effect of sadism in this concept—bare life in Agamben's terms—is precisely the subject's impotency of symbolising his position of the bare object in sadism. In Lacan's own words, 'In the sadist, anxiety is less concealed. It is even so barely concealed as to come right to the fore in the fantasy, which makes the victim's anxiety a required condition'.[21] From this premise, Lacan further argues that, although the main intention of the sadist is the anxiety of the other being, the sadist nevertheless misses this point precisely because, under the superego's pressure, his ultimate aim is elsewhere: 'to realise God's jouissance'.[22] Here—and with this we are bringing to a close this excursus to Lacan's concept of anxiety—God's *jouissance*, being the ultimate aim of the sadist, reveals the synthesis, enacted by the instance of the superego, of the ontological negativity (the lack of the signifier in the Other) signalised by the affect of anxiety and the imperative of *jouissance*. The anxiety of the other is thus instrumentalised for the higher purposes of achieving the moment of God's *jouissance* which constitutes the ultimate aim of the sadist—God's *jouissance* which also means Father's *jouissance* as a fantasmatic unlimited *jouissance* of the father, as seen by his sons. This is why Lacan states that God is 'there and everywhere in Sade's text'.[23] In short, the modern biopolitical production of bare life within the framework of sadistic anarchic institutions can thus be grasped as a *modern political-economic theology of jouissance*.[24]

III

Let me now focus on the way in which Agamben extends this realm of what we might call the sadistic exceptional space of the production of bare life, a realm which is, in Lacan's perspective, reduced to the experience of anxiety. I will now concentrate on Agamben's genealogical research into the origins of what he considers to be not only 'a decisive technical term in the strategy of Foucault's thought', at least from the mid-1970s on, which is precisely the period when Foucault intensively worked on the notions of biopolitics and, more broadly, of 'governmentality', and also one of the rare terms or notions that 'occupy the place of one of those terms that he [Foucault] defines, critically, as "the universals" (*les universaux*)'.[25] This term is, of course, the term 'apparatus', which David Kishik, the English translator of Agamben's short essay 'What Is an Apparatus?', uses to translate the French term *dispositif* used by Foucault. More specifically, I will focus on Agamben's genealogical discovery of the origins of the 'apparatus', which goes 'well beyond the chronological limits that Foucault assigned to his genealogy, to the early centuries of Christian theology, which witness the first, tentative elaboration of the Trinitarian doctrine in the form of an *oikonomia*'.[26] If Agamben argues that Foucault's basic insights into the notion of biopolitics as it appeared in the nineteenth century can and should be extended to the twentieth-century concentration camps as the 'exemplary place of modern biopolitics',[27] then he also says something similar, and yet completely opposite, about the origins of the notion of 'apparatus' in the Ancient Greek *oikonomia*. Instead of continuing Foucault's analysis of biopolitics and governmentality in the passage from the nineteenth to the twentieth century, Agamben thus traces the origins of biopolitics not to the nineteenth century but much further back into the past, to, as he puts it, 'the early centuries of Christian theology'.

In comparison with the previous volumes of *Homo Sacer* (*Homo Sacer, The Remnants of Auschwitz, State of Exception*), which focus primarily on the crucial intersection between modern biopolitics and the political theology of sovereignty, Agamben's book *The Kingdom and the Glory* and the short text 'What Is an Apparatus?' put forward a slightly different perspective, introducing the paradigmatic transhistorical duplicity of

Western politics.[28] To be precise, biopolitics is here displaced from the dimension of political theology onto the context of the second paradigm, Christian *oikonomia,* which constitutes the second axis of the inextricable nexus between political theology and economic theology of the West. As Agamben announces his main line of investigation at the very beginning of *The Kingdom and the Glory,*

> One of the theses that we shall try to demonstrate is that two broadly speaking political paradigms, antinomical but functionally related to one another, derive from Christian theology: political theology, which founds the transcendence of sovereign power on the single God, and economic theology, which replaces this transcendence with the idea of an *oikonomia,* conceived as an immanent ordering—domestic and not political in strict sense—of both divine and human life. Political philosophy and the modern theory of sovereignty derive from the first paradigm; modern biopolitics up to the current triumph of economy and government over every other aspect of social life derive from the second paradigm.[29]

The antinomical but functional relation between political and economic theology emerges out of the problem of divine ontology in the early centuries of Christianity. If, on the one hand, political theology, especially in the work of Carl Schmitt, insists on the notion of God as an inseparable unity from which derives the idea of unity of sovereign power—as opposed to liberal idea of the division of power—then economic theology, on the other hand, faces precisely the necessity of the split of God, and it is exactly this problem that was at the core of the debate among the Church Fathers between the second and fifth centuries. More precisely, this disunity or split of God, which emerged in the second century as the problem of the Trinity, raised the spectre of reintroducing polytheism into Christian monotheism, insofar as the seeming plurality contained in the notion of the Trinity did not fit the idea of a single and undivided God. The Church Fathers solved this problem with a unique interpretation of God as One, yet also divided into two inherently related spheres of being and practice. In other words, the Fathers provided an idea of God, who is ontologically One in the celestial world but who appears practically in the terrestrial world as the Trinity, which is precisely the way the God of beyond governs the world and life on earth as *oikos.*

The philosophical source for this elaboration of Agamben's is Aristotle's *Metaphysics,* where Agamben stresses the problem of the twofold determination of the object of metaphysics: 'Those who have some familiarity with Aristotle's philosophy know that one of the fundamental exegetical problems that still divides interpreters is that of the double determination of the object of metaphysics: separate being and being as being'.[30] According to Agamben, what really fits this aporia within the object of metaphysics, with its simultaneous attempt to maintain two aspects of being, is precisely a mutual articulation between transcendence and immanence. The concept, which allows Aristotle this articulation and, consequently, the salvation of the aporia, is the concept of 'order' (*taxis*):

> Transcendence, immanence, and their reciprocal coordination correspond here to the splitting of the object of metaphysics, and to the attempt to keep together the two figures of being. Yet the aporia lies in the fact that order (that is, a figure of relation) becomes the way in which the separate substance is present and acts in the world. The eminent place of ontology is in this way displaced from the category of substance to that of relation, of an eminently practical relation. The problem of the relation between transcendence and immanence of the good thus becomes that of the relation between ontology and praxis, between the being of God and his action. . . . In any case, *taxis*, order, is the apparatus [*dispositivo*] that makes possible the articulation between separate substance and being, of God with the world. *Taxis* names their aporetic relation. . . . In other words, without this being one of his aims, Aristotle transmitted to Western politics the paradigm of the divine regime of the world as a double system, formed, on the one hand, by transcendent *archē*, and, on the other, by an immanent concurrence of secondary actions and causes.[31]

It is clear that, in Agamben's view, the crucial role is here occupied by the apparatus of order or, better, the order as apparatus, which, though aporetically, keeps the split or fracture of God *within* God himself. If Agamben equates this split with divine *oikonomia*, it is precisely because the relation between transcendence and immanence, between God as being and his actions, functions so that the immanent order of actions, metaphorically associated with the management of the *oikos*, situates itself at the place of the absent God. Or to put it the other way around, God constitutes himself as an undivided being (being as being) only by way of leaving his place free for his an-archic (literally: 'without *archē*') immanent actions. In this sense, we might say that immanence and *oikonomia* are nothing but the anarchic mode of appearance of God, which means that they occupy the very place of transcendence of *archē*. This is why Agamben directly refers to Benjamin's and Pier Paolo Pasolini's insights about the very anarchical character of power as such:

> *The fracture between being and praxis, and the anarchic character of the divine* oikonomia *constitute the logical place in which the fundamental nexus that, in our culture, unites government and anarchy becomes comprehensible. Not only is something like a providential government of the world possible just because praxis does not have any foundation in being, but also this government—which, as we shall see, has its paradigm in the Son and his* oikonomia*—is itself intimately anarchic. Anarchy is what government must presuppose and assume as the origin from which it derives and, at the same time, as the destination toward which it is traveling. (Benjamin was in this sense right*

> *when he wrote that there is nothing as anarchic as the bourgeois order. Similarly, the remark of one of the Fascist dignitaries in Pasolini's film* Salò *according to which 'the only real anarchy is that of power' is perfectly serious.)*[32]

According to Agamben, Foucault's notion of the apparatus (*dispositif*) originates precisely in Aristotle's so-conceived divine and anarchic *oikonomia* because the Latin translation of *oikonomia*, provided by the Church Fathers, is exactly *dispositio*, from which derives the French term *dispositif*. As Agamben clearly put it, 'The Latin term *dispositio*, from which the French term *dispositif*, or apparatus, derives, comes therefore to take on the complex semantic sphere of the theological *oikonomia*. The "dispositifs" about which Foucault speaks are somehow linked to this theological legacy'.[33] The function that the term 'apparatus' played in early Christian theology was, together with the previously described semantic connotations, to solve the problem or danger of reintroducing polytheism into Christian monotheism. If the Holy Trinity is the apparatus par excellence, it is because it represents the very pluralistic appearance in the terrestrial world of a one and only God from the celestial world, and it is in this way that the absent God governs and manages the world and living beings that He created. Yet there is also something not *lost* in this translation but rather *added* to it. Namely, it is only in Christian theology, and particularly in the term 'apparatus', that something which might still be concealed in the Greek *oikonomia* becomes fully apparent. As already mentioned, the Church Fathers used this Aristotelian category in order to save the Christian God from the polytheistic threat, insisting on the interpretation according to which 'God, insofar as his being and substance is concerned, is certainly one; but as to his *oikonomia*—that is to say the way in which he administers his home, his life, and the world that he created—he is, rather, triple'.[34] Yet on the other hand, they added a kind of violent and substantial connotation to this very formal meaning of *oikonomia*. In the passage from Greek *oikonomia* to Christian *dispositio* or apparatus, what is added is a violent aspect of capturing, controlling, orienting, etc. The term 'apparatus' in this context does not only refer to the multiple agency of a terrestrial divine government but even more so to its practices of capturing living beings in its own governmental net. Not surprisingly, unlike Foucault, who usually used the term 'apparatus' adjectively, speaking of this or that concrete apparatus, Agamben goes on to insist that a general definition of apparatus can be deduced from all of Foucault's concrete uses of the term: 'Further expanding the already large class of Foucauldian apparatuses, I shall call an apparatus literally anything that has in some way the capacity to capture, orient, determine, intercept, model, control, or secure the gestures, behaviors, opinions, or discourses of living beings'.[35] By saying this, Agamben's intention is certainly to emphasise the very strategic nature of the apparatus as such, insofar as it is a privileged mechanism to confront some urgent or critical situation. The apparatus is therefore the general mechanism or the means for solving precisely those kinds of situations. In Agamben's account, the apparatus, precisely to the extent that it is a strategic concept, can thus function as the main mechanism of modern biopolitical governmentality.

IV

At this point, we can, perhaps, turn back to Agamben's argument from *Homo Sacer*, where he argues for the sadistic nature of the state of exception and modern biopolitics. For if Agamben is right to draw this parallel between biopolitics and sadism, he then immediately makes a standard slip by falsely recognising the masochistic attitude in the position of bare life, which leads him to the inappropriate concept of sadomasochism. As he puts it,

> The growing importance of sadomasochism in modernity has its root in this exchange. Sadomasochism is precisely the technique of sexuality by which the bare life of a sexual partner is brought to light. Not only does Sade invoke the analogy with sovereign power ('there is no man', he writes, 'who does not want to be a despot when he has an erection'), but we also find here the symmetry between *homo sacer* and sovereign, in the complicity that ties the masochist to the sadist, the victim to the executioner.[36]

Thus, we could say that Agamben correctly diagnoses the correlation between sadism and law as the empty form which banishes bare life before this very form in the exceptional space—the space that Agamben further associates with the economic-theological origins of Foucauldian governmentality and the concept of apparatus. However, as we see in the last passage, Agamben then incorrectly extends Sade's anarchic institution of the state of exception to the supposedly general problem of sadomasochism as a symmetrical and compatible intersubjective structure which links the bare life to the torturer or the 'victim' to the 'executioner'. If we take into account Deleuze's arguments regarding the difference and asymmetry between sadism and masochism, that is, two attitudes between which there precisely is no 'complicity', then we are forced to assess Agamben's thesis as entirely inappropriate. There is a peculiar irony also in the fact that Agamben's conclusion, that is, the very idea of sadomasochism as 'complicity that ties the masochist to the sadist, the victim to the executioner' stands in direct contradiction to Agamben's concept of *homo sacer*, whose characteristic is precisely the impossibility of being sacrificed, so it is impossible to be a victim in the strict (sacrificial) sense of the term. In fact, Agamben precisely opposes bare life to the status of the sacrificial victim in his controversial thesis that the term 'Holocaust' should be rejected as a proper name for the extermination of the Jewish people:

> The wish to lend a sacrificial aura to the extermination of the Jews by means of the term 'Holocaust' was, from this perspective, an irresponsible historiographical blindness. The Jew living under Nazism is the privileged negative referent of the new biopolitical sovereignty and is, as such, a flagrant case of a *homo sacer* in the sense of a life that may be killed but not sacrificed. His killing therefore constitutes, as we will see, neither capital punishment nor a sacrifice, but simply the actualisation of a mere 'capacity to be killed' inherent in the condition of the Jew as such. The truth—which is difficult for the victims to face, but which we must have the courage not to cover with sacrificial veils—is that the Jews were exterminated not in a mad and giant holocaust but exactly as Hitler had announced, 'as lice', which is to say, as bare life. The dimension in which the extermination took place is neither religion nor law, but biopolitics.[37]

The concept of *homo sacer* does not imply any mutual or compatible relation between the sadist and the masochist, between the executioner and the victim, precisely because sadism does not presuppose any victim and masochism, on the other hand, does not presuppose bare life as such. As we said earlier in reference to Lacan, the sadistic logic underlying the Nazi's extermination of the Jewish people produces bare life, understood precisely as the subject's impossibility of being inscribed in the symbolic order as a victim. If Agamben's identification of bare life and masochism is wrong, though, then we are still left with the question: Which conceptual figure within Agamben's philosophy does the masochist's attitude actually correspond to?

V

In the rest of this chapter, I would like to propose that the Deleuzian figure of the masochist is metonymically included in Agamben's concept of the messianic or messianic event. To do so, we should take into account another image of law which is, at least in Agamben's perspective, opposed to the sovereign form of law described earlier, which is characterised by the incomplete indistinction between law and life. How does Agamben formulate this other image of law? This second view on the form of law originates in a detail Agamben noticed in Benjamin's Thesis VIII on the concept of history, where the latter distinguishes between two kinds of state of exception:

> The tradition of the oppressed teaches us that the 'state of emergency' in which we live is not the exception but the rule. We must attain to a conception of history that is in keeping with this insight. Then we shall clearly realise that it is our task to bring about a real state of emergency.[38]

According to Agamben, the state of exception that became the rule is actually a virtual state of exception, which allows bare life to exist as indeterminate in the sphere of the ban. The real state of exception, however, is the one in which he sees the possibility of a postmetaphysical 'new politics', insofar as it represents a life which is entirely transformed into law and which thus annihilates or deactivates law. Life that is entirely transformed into law produces a situation where there is no life left outside the law that could be politicised, and which makes the metaphysical and biopolitical 'politicisation of bare life' impossible. As Agamben puts it,

> We have seen the sense in which law begins to coincide with life once it has become the pure form of law, law's mere being in force without significance. But insofar as law is maintained as pure form in a state of virtual exception, it lets bare life (K.'s life, or the life lived in the village at the foot of the castle) subsist before it. Law that becomes indistinguishable from life in a real state of exception is confronted by life that, in a symmetrical but inverse gesture, is entirely transformed into law. The absolute intelligibility of a life wholly resolved into writing corresponds to the impenetrability of a writing that, having become indecipherable, now appears as life. Only at this point do the two terms, distinguished and kept united by the relation of ban (bare life and the form of law), abolish each other and enter into a new dimension.[39]

Do not these two images of law, which here appear as two kinds of the state of exception (sovereign and messianic), correspond precisely to Deleuze's conceptualisation of the difference between sadism and masochism? More specifically, doesn't the second image of law as a life that is entirely transformed into law correspond precisely to the masochist's relation towards law, which apparently achieves the abolition of the incomplete indistinction between life and law in the first sadistic image? It seems that Agamben's strategy of overcoming and abolishing the virtual state of exception in the situation of the ban is precisely the strategy of the masochist as one whose life as such is entirely transformed into law and codified, the one whose life becomes intelligible. Let us remember that the extreme form of a masochistic contract is precisely enslavement as the moment when there is no life left outside the law. In Agamben's terms, we could thus say that the masochist is precisely a bare life that, through its complete transformation into law, actually changes its position into that of a victim and does not allow any life to exist outside the apparatus of sacrifice. Life that could not be sacrificed establishes its own symbolic horizon as a victim and is thus inscribed in the symbolic order of exchange.

Here, again, we come across a parallel with Lacan's *Seminar X*, where he argues that the intention of every true masochist is precisely to provoke 'God's anxiety' by way of establishing himself as a pound of flesh. As he puts it, 'whether he becomes a dog under the table or a piece of merchandise, an *item* dealt with by contract, sold amongst other objects put on the market. In sum, what he [the masochist] seeks is his identification with the common object, the object of exchange. It remains impossible for him to grasp himself for what he is, inasmuch as, like all of us, he is an [object] *a*'.[40] As Lacan continues later in *Seminar X*, 'This anxiety, which is the masochist's blind aim because his fantasy masks it for him, is scarcely less, in real terms, what we might call God's anxiety'.[41] Surprisingly or not, this concept of a masochist whose ultimate aim is to make God's anxiety emerge by means of his legal adoption of the status of the slave, resembles many figures in Agamben's work. For instance, not only does Paul's messianism, which is Agamben's paradigmatic figure of the real state of exception, involve Paul's declaration of his own slavery—let us remember the first four words in Paul's Letter to the Romans, which according to Agamben encapsulate the entire idea of messainism: 'Paulos Doulus Christi Iesu', 'Paul, a slave of Christ Jesus'—but also in *Homo Sacer* Agamben characterises Joseph K.'s life itself as the trial, so life that is completely undistinguishable from law. In his words, 'The existence and the very body of Joseph K. ultimately coincide with the *Trial*; they become the *Trial*'.[42]

The masochistic nature of the real state of exception or messianic event becomes even clearer if we take into account Agamben's own interpretation of the meaning of the letter K. in Joseph K.'s name. As opposed to many interpreters of Kafka, including his close friend Max Brod, who have for a long time insisted that the letter K. in the name of the figure of Josef K. actually stands for Kafka himself, Agamben posits the opposite thesis, namely, that K. does not mean Kafka, but *kalumnia,* and even more so *kalumniator*.[43] *Kalumniator* or *kalumnia*—both concepts of Roman law—refer to a false accuser or the process of false accusation or self-accusation respectively. Agamben reports that, in the time of Roman law, such a process represented a dangerous threat to the legal system.[44] The danger of self-accusation was based precisely on the key meaning that the concept of accusation had for law as such. Accusation is, as Agamben claims, a legal 'category' par excellence; it is the central element of the law, law as such is based on accusation. In his characteristic manner, Agamben bases his argument on the etymology of accusation, saying that accusation is 'perhaps, the juridical "category" *par excellence* (kategoria, in Greek, means accusation), without which the entire edifice of the law would crumble: the implication of being in the law. The law is, that is to say, in its essence, accusation, "category"'.[45] In the process of self-calumniation, of self-accusation, the subject implicates itself in law, which is thus created by the subject's self-accusation. Self-accusation generates law, it is itself law, but in an extremely paradoxical way. The danger of the process of self-calumniation is therefore related precisely to the fact that, in this process, the foundations of law as such were 'on trial'. It is therefore not surprising that, in ancient Rome, they marked the *kalumniator* by branding the letter K on his forehead. Self-accusation or self-calumniation is thus at the same time the implication of a subject into the law and an attempt at the latter's deactivation or transgression. For Agamben, this submission to the law, and implication within the legal system, is in a strict sense possible only through the process of self-accusation. And it is precisely in the process of self-accusation by which Josef K. triggers the trial against himself[46] that Agamben also sees a strategy by which the subject tries to deactivate the law as a metaphysical category.

Doesn't this strategy again resemble the strategy of Deleuze's Masoch and the logic of masochism more generally? For in Masoch, Deleuze saw an attitude that, in its absurd submission to the law, is capable of subverting the metaphysical law itself. According to Deleuze, this gesture explains the meaning of masochistic humour and the fact that a masochist is a logician of consequences. In masochism, Deleuze says there is

> a demonstration of the law's absurdity. The masochist regards the law as a punitive process and therefore begins by having the punishment inflicted upon himself; once he has undergone the punishment, he feels that he is allowed or indeed commanded to experience the pleasure that the law was supposed to forbid. The essence of masochistic humour lies in this, that the very law that forbids the satisfaction of a desire under threat of subsequent punishment is converted into one which demands the punishment first and then orders that the satisfaction of the desire should necessarily follow upon the punishment.[47]

That is why for Deleuze, and Agamben as well, a masochist is 'rebellious in his submission'.[48] Such a submission is precisely the essential strategy by which the masochist overturns the symbolic structure of the family triangle revolving around the figure of the father.

In *The Use of Bodies*, the last volume of the *Homo Sacer* project, Agamben revealingly brings into play the Aristotelian figure of the slave in order to completely reverse the standard moralistic view on this figure.[49] As Arthur Bradley has pointed out recently in his outstanding reading, beyond the strict legality which establishes the slave as a property of the master, Agamben completely inverts the meaning of Aristotle's famous 'naturalistic' definition, according to which the slave is a subhuman 'living tool' used by the master and capable of being disposed by him. 'Yet', as Bradley argues, 'Agamben seeks to turn this ideological argument on its head by claiming that what is at stake in natural slavery is the exact opposite of the reduction of a human being to a sub-human animal, object or tool'.[50] Insofar as the slave is the master's tool or object, he becomes part of his master's (human) body as his 'organ', therefore he constitutes the threshold in which takes place the 'becoming fully human of the living being'[51] and in which inside and outside, immanence and transcendence are completely blurred. Precisely to the extent that the slave is subordinated to the master and his body is disposable for the use, he cannot be regarded simply as an inhuman object extraneous to the master but rather constitutes an integral part of master's human body.

This is why, as Bradley continues, 'in this expanded sense, the slave becomes the last privileged figure for what Agamben famously calls a "form of life" in which, rather than being biopolitically opposed, isolated and captured, *zoē* and *bíos*, life and form, essence and existence irreducibly coincide with one another'.[52] There is absolutely no coincidence that, in order to further develop his argument, Agamben immediately draws upon Artemidorus's *Interpretation of Dreams* (note the Freudian title) and the latter's analogy between masturbation and the sex with the slave, which reveals that the slave and the hand are mutually exchangeable. In the seemingly autonomous activity of the partial object, whether it is hand or slave, subjectivity is 'becoming-outside'[53] and thus transforming the relation of subordination into the nonrelational form-of-life. As Bradley further stresses, precisely this act 'of the self on the self' corresponds, for Agamben, 'to the ontology of immanence, to the movement of autoconstitution and of autopresentation'[54] which Agamben further explains by recourse to Spinoza's point regarding the Ladino verb *pasearse*. The latter in fact doesn't simply mean 'to take a walk'; 'it literally means "to walk-oneself": we constitute ourselves *as* selves in the act of walking, talking, kissing and so on'.[55] Such a definition, however, seems to correspond precisely to Freudian (pre-Oedipal) polymorphous perversion and to the autoerotic satisfaction of partial drives which Lacan considered precisely in terms of the self-reflective mode of the verb (for instance, '*making oneself seen*'[56]), which points to the *indifferent libidinal energy* which traverses the grammatical oppositions between passive and active, the very oppositions which, according to Freud, shape the circulation of the drives (seen/being seen; beat/being beaten; etc.). As we will see in the next part, the main difference between Agamben and Deleuze on the one hand and Lacan on the other lies in the fact that, for Lacan, the Other is already present in such self-reflective activity of the drives. In other words, if Deleuze and Agamben, on the one hand, think perversion in terms of a neat separation of the pleasure from sexuality, Lacan, on the other hand, shows that this separation is impossible to achieve. In any case, this perverse autoerotic approach to sexuality is once more brought to the core of what Agamben seeks to articulate as a 'new politics', which can be regarded also as a new 'ontology of immanence'. There is absolutely no coincidence that Agamben once again refers to the self-reflective mode of the verb and to a problematic notion of sadomasochism in his discussion of the concept of 'use', arguing that '*sadomasochism exhibits the truth of use, which does not know subject and object, agent and patient*'.[57] This is even more surprising if we consider that only two paragraphs later Agamben makes explicit reference precisely to Deleuze and his concept of masochism as that which 'implies the neutralisation of the law through its parodic exaggeration'.[58] However, from Deleuze's point of view, masochism is politically plausible only insofar as it does not imply the synthesis of sadism and masochism in the concept of sadomasochism.

In many ways, all these structural and logical similarities between Deleuze's take on masochism and Agamben's take on the messianic event seem to ultimately converge in yet another crucial figure: Sabbatai Zevi, who was the leader of a seventeenth-century messianic movement. According to Deleuze, as we have discussed earlier, the figure of Zevi very much inspired Masoch in his writings on masochism and on the political role of minorities within the Austrian empire one century later. Not surprisingly, when Agamben suggests that messianism is actually 'a theory of the state of exception—except for the fact that in messianism there is no authority in force to proclaim the state of exception; instead, there is the Messiah to subvert its power',[59] he also suggests that, in such a messianic state of exception, the 'fulfillment of the Torah now coincides with its transgression. This is clearly affirmed by the most radical messianic movements, like that of Sabbatai Zevi (whose motto was "the fulfilment of the Torah is its transgression")'.[60] However, the fulfilment of the law occurs by means of the complete inscription of life into the law and this inscription as such reveals the repressed content of biopolitics, which is to say, its need to relate to life solely in the form of nonrelation or abandonment. By radicalising the virtual state of exception of sovereignty, Agamben argues that messianism thus reveals the biopolitical 'truth' of modern politics and succeeds in subverting the power of the form of law. What comes to take the place of sovereign power is thus the form-of-life, which is as such ungovernable from the point of view of the law. Summing up the argument of this chapter, we could say that, from Agamben's perspective, what succeeds in abolishing the imperfect transgression operating in the sadistic and anarchic institution of the state of exception that constitutes the core of modern biopolitical governmentality is precisely the masochistic attempt to inscribe into the law its very internal exteriority. Although Agamben wrongly posits the masochistic position as being in a relation of 'complicity' with the sadist in the virtual state of exception, we have seen how a masochistic strategy (as articulated by Deleuze) metonymically reappears in the figure of messianism, but also in the figure of the slave. The question we discussed in the previous chapter is, however, to what extent such a strategy—which involves the fetishistic approach towards the messianic ending of the historical time—actually succeeds in fulfilling its self-appointed task.

NOTES

1. Gilles Deleuze, 'Coldness and Cruelty', in *Masochism: Coldness and Cruelty and Venus in Furs*, trans. Jean McNeil, ed. Gilles Deleuze and Leopold von Sacher-Masoch (New York: Zone Books, 1991), 68.
2. Ibid.
3. Ibid., 15.
4. Ibid.

5. Ibid., 16.
6. Ibid., 75.
7. On the very last page of the essay 'Coldness and Cruelty', Deleuze summarises the difference at stake in eleven points: '(1) Sadism is speculative-demonstrative, masochism is dialectical-imaginative; (2) sadism operates with the negative and pure negation, masochism with disavowal and suspension; (3) sadism operates by means of quantitative reiteration, masochism by means of qualitative suspense; (4) there is a masochism specific to the sadist and equally a sadism specific to the masochist, the one never combining with the other; (5) sadism negates the mother and inflates the father, masochism disavows the mother and abolishes the father; (6) the role and significance of the fetish, and the function of the fantasy are totally different in each case; (7) there is an aestheticism in masochism, while sadism is hostile to the aesthetic attitude; (8) sadism is institutional, masochism is contractual; (9) in sadism the superego and the process of identification play the primary role, masochism gives primacy to the ego and to the process of idealisation; (10) sadism and masochism exhibit totally different forms of desexualisation and resexualisation; (11) finally, summing up all these differences, there is the most radical difference between sadistic *apathy* and masochistic *coldness*' (ibid., 134).
8. Ibid., 76–77.
9. Giorgio Agamben, *Homo Sacer: Sovereign Power and Bare Life*, trans. Daniel Heller-Roazen (Stanford, CA: Stanford University Press, 1998), 53.
10. Agamben discusses this extensively in part I ('The Logic of Sovereignty') of his *Homo Sacer*, 15–71, and—with more emphasis on Benjamin's 'esoteric' critique of Schmitt—in chapter 4 ('Gigantomachy Concerning a Void') of his *State of Exception*, trans. Kevin Attell (Chicago: University of Chicago Press, 2005), 52–64.
11. Jean-Luc Nancy, *L'imperativo categorico* (Torino: Besa Editrice, 2007), chapter 2 ('Lapsus judicii'), 43–71.
12. Agamben, *Homo Sacer*, 51.
13. Ibid., 49.
14. 'Here, the structural analogy between the sovereign exception and *sacratio* shows its full sense. At the two extreme limits of the order, the sovereign and *homo sacer* present two symmetrical figures that have the same structure and are correlative: the sovereign is the one with respect to whom all men are potentially *homines sacri*, and *homo sacer* is the one with respect to whom all men act as sovereigns' (Agamben, *Homo Sacer*, 84).
15. Agamben, *State of Exception*, 52–64.
16. Agamben, *Homo Sacer*, 134.
17. Ibid.
18. See Giorgio Agamben, *Remnants of Auschwitz: The Witness and the Archive*, trans. Daniel Heller-Roazen (New York: Zone Books, 1999), 41–86.
19. Jacques Lacan, *The Seminar of Jacques Lacan, Book X: Anxiety*, trans. A. R. Price (Cambridge, MA, and Malden: Polity Press, 2014), 104.
20. Sigi Jöttkandt, *First Love: A Phenomenology of the One* (Melbourne: re.press, 2010), 18–19.
21. Lacan, *Seminar X*, 164.
22. Ibid., 165.
23. Ibid.
24. This formulation might also encompass the past decade or so of Eric L. Santner's work, including his forthcoming contribution 'The Rebranding of Sovereignty in the Age of Trump: Toward a Critique of Manatheism' (in Eric L. Santner, Aaron Schuster, and William Mazzarella, *Sovereignty, Inc.* [Chicago: University of Chicago Press, forthcoming]). Also inspired by Agamben's idea of economic theology as the theological origin of modern biopolitics and governmentality, Santner provides an original reading in which he brings together Weber's Protestant ethic and the idea of modern disenchantment of the world, Marx's view on capitalism as a process of the 'self-valorisation of value', Freud's concept of the compulsion to repeat, and Foucault's

analysis of the primacy of the body and the biological in early modern capitalism, to argue that the essential characteristic of modernity is precisely the symbolic investment of the body with enigmatic signifiers which are then employed in the compulsory behaviours driving modern capitalist society and in what Santner calls the 'liturgical labour' in the context of the economic process of the 'branding of sovereignty'. On this, see also Eric L. Santner, *The Weight of All Flesh: On the Subject-Matter of Political Economy* (The Berkeley Tanner Lectures) (Oxford and New York: Oxford University Press, 2016), 23–129.

25. Giorgio Agamben, 'What Is an Apparatus?' in *'What Is an Apparatus?' and Other Essays*, trans. David Kishik and Stefan Pedatella (Stanford, CA: Stanford University Press, 2009), 1, 6–7.

26. Giorgio Agamben, *The Kingdom and the Glory: For a Theological Genealogy of Economy and Government*, trans. Lorenzo Chiesa (with Matteo Mandarini) (Stanford, CA: Stanford University Press, 2011), xi.

27. Agamben, *Homo Sacer*, 119.

28. See Sergei Prozorov, 'Why Giorgio Agamben Is an Optimist', *Philosophy and Social Criticism* 36, no. 9 (2010): 1055.

29. Agamben, *The Kingdom and the Glory*, 1.

30. Ibid., 83.

31. Ibid., 83–84.

32. Ibid., 64.

33. Agamben, 'What Is an Apparatus?', 11.

34. Ibid., 9–10; emphasis in original.

35. Ibid., 14.

36. Agamben, *Homo Sacer*, 134–35. Agamben repeats this argument on several other occasions (see, for instance, *The Remnants of Auschwitz*, 107–8, and, more recently, *The Use of Bodies*, trans. Adam Kotsko [Stanford, CA: Stanford University Press, 2016], 35).

37. Agamben, *Homo Sacer*, 114. However, sacrificial meaning is not the exclusive meaning of the term 'Holocaust'. Recently, I tried to develop a nonsacrificial meaning of this term based on my reading of László Nemes's film *Son of Saul* (see Boštjan Nedoh, 'When the Tiger Leaps into the Past: Holocaust, History and Messianic Materialism in Giorgio Agamben, Walter Benjamin and László Nemes' *Son of Saul*', *Angelaki* 24, no. 5 (forthcoming).

38. Walter Benjamin, 'Theses on the Philosophy of History', in *Illuminations*, trans. Harry Zohn, ed. Hannah Arendt (New York: Schocken Books, 1968), 257.

39. Agamben, *Homo Sacer*, 55.

40. Lacan, *Seminar X*, 105.

41. Ibid., 163. What seems to come to the fore here is an unexpected parallel: doesn't Lacan's distinction between 'God's jouissance' that we discussed earlier in relation to sadism and 'God's anxiety' as the aim of the masochist actually mirror Deleuze's 'irreducible dissymmetry' between sadism and masochism, the first relying upon the identification with the father and the negation of the mother, thus seeking precisely the absolute *jouissance* which is fantasmatically assigned to the position of the Father/God, whilst the masochist, by inversely identifying with the father as that who is beaten in the masochist, seeks precisely the father's anxiety which would be the sign of his symbolic collapse?

42. Agamben, *Homo Sacer*, 53.

43. At the very beginning, Agamben points out a not unimportant fact that while Kafka prepared for the legal profession, he studied the history of Roman law. See Giorgio Agamben, 'K.', in *The Work of Giorgio Agamben: Law, Literature, Life*, ed. Justin Clemens, Nicholas Heron, and Alex Murray (Edinburgh: Edinburgh University Press, 2008), 13. However, this point remains profoundly ambiguous insofar as Agamben, later on in the same essay, questions this strategy and proposes the figure of another K., that is, the land surveyor K. from Kafka's *The Castle* as more successful in achieving the abolishment of the internal boundary of the law. I developed this point in more

detail in my essay 'Kafka's Land-Surveyor K.: Agamben's Anti-Muselmann', *Angelaki* 16, no. 3 (2011): 149–61.

44. Agamben, 'K.', 13.

45. Ibid., 15.

46. The first sentence in *The Trial* is: 'Someone must have calumniated Josef K., he knew he had done nothing wrong, but, one morning, he was arrested'. Based on an analogy with the figure of the *kalumniator* from the Roman law, Agamben suggests that this 'someone' who calumniated Josef K. is Josef K. himself (Agamben, 'K.', 13).

47. Deleuze, 'Coldness and Cruelty', 88–89.

48. Ibid., 89.

49. For a critical overview, see Sergei Prozorov, 'Living *à la Mode*: Form-of-life and Democratic Biopolitics in Giorgio Agamben's *The Use of Bodies*', *Philosophy and Social Criticism* 43, no. 2 (2017): 144–63.

50. Arthur Bradley, 'In the Sovereign Machine: Sovereignty, Governmentality, Automaticity', *Journal for Cultural Research* (2018): online first, 5.

51. Agamben, *The Use of Bodies*, 16, quoted in Bradley, 'In the Sovereign Machine', 5.

52. Bradley, 'In the Sovereign Machine', 5.

53. Ibid., 6.

54. Agamben, *The Use of Bodies*, 29.

55. Bradley, 'In the Sovereign Machine', 6.

56. As Lacan puts it in *Seminar XI*: 'As to the relation between the drive and the activity/passivity, I think I will be well enough understood if I say that at the level of the drive it is purely grammatical. It is support, artifice, which Freud uses in order to enable us to understand the outward-return movement of the drive. But I have repeated four or five times that we cannot reduce it purely and simply to a reciprocity. Today I have shown in the most articulated way possible that each of the three stages, *a*, *b*, *c*, with which Freud articulates each drive, must be replaced by the formula of *making oneself seen*, *heard* and the rest of the list I have given' (Jacques Lacan, *The Seminar of Jacques Lacan, Book XI: The Four Fundamental Concepts of Psychoanalysis*, trans. Alan Sheridan [London and New York: W. W. Norton and Co., 1998], 200).

57. Agamben, *The Use of Bodies*, 35.

58. Ibid., 36; translation modified.

59. Agamben, *Homo Sacer*, 57–58.

60. Ibid., 57.

Part IV

Not Without the Other: Ontology and Perversion in Lacanian Psychoanalysis: *Theatrum Analiticum*

EIGHT

Why Perversion Is Not the Norm of the Drive

Polymorphous Perversion from Freud to Lacan

I

We can sum up what we have elaborated so far as follows: in Deleuze's and Agamben's respective philosophical projects, perversion has a privileged, although not exclusive, role in fulfilling the task of overturning/renewing (Deleuze) or overcoming (Agamben) the structure of classical metaphysics. Generally, there are two basic features of perversion that both Deleuze and Agamben employ in their respective philosophical enterprises. On the one hand, a deactivation and suspension of the law, which by definition pertains to the function of the father around which revolves the whole neurotic social structure. On the other, the operations of suspension and deactivation of the law are accompanied by the counter-operations of the affirmation and elevation of the mother by means of the fetishist's disavowal and the art of fantasy, that is, more generally, by means of an idealisation of the divergent difference and an elevation of the simulacrum on the surface. In Agamben, this gesture corresponds to the messianic suspension of sovereignty and the form of law which holds bare life in the position of abandonment by means of the inclusive exclusion. However, as I have argued, messianic time in Agamben has itself the structure of perverse suspension which means his idea of a 'new politics' is completely in line with his early praise of perversion and the fetishist's disavowal.

Both Deleuze's and Agamben's positions thus epitomise not only a vitalist critique of psychoanalysis, which is thus considered to be a metaphysical (and biopolitical) practice par excellence but, even more importantly, a kind of anti-Lacanian appropriation of Freud. This appropriation occurs at the point of apparent identity between perversion and the drive, that is, at the point, also noticed by Lacan, of apparent equivalence between the structure of perversion and the structure of the drive. Roughly put, there are two existing interpretations, which are mutually exclusive, of Freud's theory of the drive as set up in his 'Three Essays on the Theory of Sexuality' (1905): a vitalist and a psychoanalytic interpretation. The vitalist interpretation argues that the drive should be considered as a kind of preexisting natural given which is only afterwards subjected to a repression prescribed by external cultural norms. To be sure, such norms are considered to be shaped by the Oedipus complex and by the phallus as the signifier of castration. According to this view, the difference between sexes is established only after the agents of the symbolic (the Oedipus complex and the phallus) intervene. The equivalence between perversion and the partial drives set up by Freud himself is here located on the pre-subjective and pre-individual level of impersonal singularity which apparently avoids being subjected to the pressure of those cultural norms which trigger the process of repression. Freud's crucial thesis, according to which '*neurosis is, so to speak, the negative of perversion*',[1] is interpreted as the basis of temporal difference, as if there were some preexisting primordial and pre-Oedipal state of libidinal economy which would be subjected to repression and cultural regulation imposed by the Other (paternal metaphor/prohibition) only afterwards. As Lacan phrases this position, 'As if that which is hidden in the unconscious in the case of neurosis would stand under the blue sky and in some sense in a free state in the case of perversion'.[2] This sort of vitalist reading of perversion clearly founds itself upon the illusion, if not fantasy, that the pervert successfully avoids castration (even by fully identifying with it, as in the case with masochism) which is precisely defined as that peculiar psychic mechanism that puts the subject of the signifier in a disjunctive position with respect to *jouissance*. In other words, the vitalist reading of perversion implies, as Alenka Zupančič observes, a neat separation between sexuality and the drive or *jouissance*. As Lacan does not fail to add in this regard, 'perversion would be the drive which was not elaborated by the Oedipal and neurotic mechanism; it would be pure and simple survival or the insistence of the irreducible, partial drive'.[3]

Contrary to this argumentative line, Lacan categorically and insistently contends the following: 'Freud, contrarily, sufficiently shows that no perverse structuration, however primitive . . . , can be articulated otherwise than as the means, support, the element of something, which in the last instance cannot be imagined, understood, and articulated as in, from and through the process, organisation and articulation of the Oedipal complex'.[4] In order to simplify this apparently complex and dense passage, we can say that Lacan, here, emphasises the fact that the drive alone is nothing primordial or natural and as such does not concern any kind of 'physics of the body'. On the contrary and in accordance with the theorem of primal repression, the drive is fixed with the hole of primal repression, that is, with the primally repressed signifier which shapes the drives as partial. This, of course, implies that, first, even if the drive might be articulated outside the Oedipus complex, it cannot be grasped outside the concept of primal repression and of the phallus as the signifier of castration, and, second, that there is fundamental structural difference between perversion, which is by definition Oedipal, and the drive, which is non-Oedipal, yet not pre-symbolic. According to Jacques-Alain Miller, Lacanian psychoanalysis introduces here a new dimension which is foreign to philosophical readings of perversion (the latter oscillating between Oedipal and anti-Oedipal conceptions of the drive only). This dimension concerns the distinction between the symbolic (which founds itself upon the repression of the primal signifier) and the stage of Oedipus, which comes into play only afterwards, so that the pre-Oedipal stage of libidinal economy should not be grasped as pre-linguistic. As he puts it, 'In Lacan's view, however, the pre-Oedipal drive is not pre-linguistic or raw; the drive is a highly elaborate concept compared to "natural needs". The drive is not primitive and "pre-Oedipal drives" are not pre-linguistic. What Lacan called the Other is already there in the drive'.[5] As we will soon see, Lacan locates the famous name-of-the-father precisely at this point of the barred Other, conceived as a *locus* set up by the primally repressed signifier or primal repression. In this respect, it will also become comprehensible why Lacan in the last phase of his teaching argued that perversion should be understood as *père-version* (literally: father-version), that is, as a version or '*a call to the father*',[6] so as Woman as one of the versions or names of the father is possible only as *père-version*. In order to deconstruct some of the most important passages in Lacan's construction of the previously mentioned theses, it thus seems plausible to begin with the way the drive and perversion interrelate in Freud's 'Three Essays' and then proceed further with Lacan's articulation of this relation.

II

In Freud's early 'Three Essays' (1905), we find the first systematic analysis of perversion. However, in these essays, perversion achieves a central status only indirectly, that is, through the issue of what Freud calls 'sexual aberrations'. This term also figures in the title of the first of the three essays and epitomises Freud's intention to rethink the libido on the basis of its 'aberrations' from biological sexual norms or copulation in heterosexual relationships. Freud thus presupposes the libido as a norm which consists of two basic features: on the one hand, it assumes a genital/coital sexual interaction (the sexual aim) with a person of an opposite gender (the sexual object), with the ultimate purpose of human reproduction.

'Sexual aberrations' indicate above all two kinds of 'deviation' from this so-conceived sexual norm: an aberration with respect to the sexual object and an aberration with respect to the sexual aim. The main topics that Freud lists under the first kind of aberrations, that is, with respect to the sexual object, are what he calls 'inversions':[7] bi- and homosexuality, paedophilia, zoophilia, etc. In short, what these phenomena have in common is that the presupposed sexual drive is not directed towards a person of the opposite gender. What is more, the genital aspect of sexuality is nevertheless usually if not always emphasised. This is why these kinds of aberrations do not give ground for unfolding a more robust theory of perversion; in fact, they are even not considered as specifically perverse by Freud. The scope of Freud's engagement with this systemisation of different aberrations lies elsewhere: it gives him a general insight, with far-reaching consequences, into the relationship between the sexual drive and sexual object which the 'biological norm' sees as inextricably bound together. Freud, on the contrary, argues that this bond between drive and object should be separated—and this is one of the main features of perversion:

> It has been brought to our notice that we have been in the habit of regarding the connection between the sexual drive and the sexual object as more intimate than it in fact is. Experience of the cases that are considered abnormal has shown us that in them the sexual drive and the sexual object are merely soldered together—a fact which we have been in danger of overlooking in consequence of the uniformity of the normal picture, where the object appears to form part and parcel of the drive. We are thus warned to loosen the bond that exists in our thoughts between drive and object. It seems probable that the sexual drive is in the first instance independent of its object; nor is its origin likely to be due to its object's attractions.[8]

As mentioned, this unbinding of drive and the object has far-reaching consequences insofar as it puts into question the biological norm, that is, the idea of the innate sexual interest of one sex for another sex. From the standpoint of psychoanalysis, the problem which should thus be addressed instead of being taken for granted is that of sexuality as such, including the most conformist heterosexual relationships: 'Thus from the point of view of psycho-analysis the exclusive sexual interest felt by men for women is also a problem that needs elucidating and is not a self-evident fact based upon an attraction that is ultimately of a chemical nature'.[9]

The fact that sexuality is in itself contradictory can be best observed, perhaps, in another kind of aberration, that is, in aberrations which relate to the sexual aim. For if the genital function is still present and not fully suspended in aberrations which relate to the sexual object, in the other set of aberrations the situation is different. On this point precisely, Freud introduces more sharply the question of perversion, which he defines according to two of its basic features: he considers perversions those 'sexual activities which either (*a*) extend, in anatomical sense, beyond the regions of the body that are designed for sexual union, or (*b*) linger over the intermediate relations to the sexual object which should normally be traversed rapidly on the path towards the final sexual aim'.[10]

Following these considerations, it is clear that Freud, here, grants to perversion a large part of what is usually considered to be the territory of sexuality, so that he has to conclude not only that every single engagement of partial objects such as the anus or mouth should be considered as perverse but 'that foreplay is perverse',[11] as Miller has put it. On this preliminary point, perversion ends up being defined negatively: it encompasses all excitations and the activities of partial drives which are not strictly genital or copulative. What seemingly comes to the fore here is the neat separation between and independence of the drives and sexuality: libido as the sexual drive is able to achieve satisfaction even without copulation or genital satisfaction. The conclusion that Lacan takes from this consideration is that the sexual drive—the drive towards the opposite sex—actually does not exist; the only thing that exists are partial, a-sexual drives which only partially represent sexuality in the human psyche by circulating around the symbolically contaminated erogenous zones of the body (anus, mouth, ears, eyes). As Miller has it, 'Lacan's thesis here is that there is no drive toward the opposite sex'.[12]

In any case, the fact that Freud provides a pretty large preliminary definition of perversion leads him to admit the insufficiency of such a broad definition with respect to the clinical scope of psychoanalysis.[13] He is thus forced to propose a narrower definition of perversion by way of distinguishing between perversion as a symptom and what Miller calls 'generalised perversion' which could also be regarded as a 'perversion of everyday life'. As we have already argued in chapter 4, 'ordinary perversion' actually corresponds to foreplay (which indeed involves partial objects and fetish) as the moment of fore-pleasure which leads towards copulation (end-pleasure), but perversion as a symptom is characterised by the reversal between fore-pleasure and the moment of end-pleasure (copulation), so that the foreplay becomes itself the end-pleasure. As Freud argues, 'If a perversion, instead of appearing merely *alongside* the normal sexual aim and object, and only when circumstances are unfavourable to *them* and favourable to *it*—if, instead of this, it ousts them completely and takes their place in *all* circumstances—if, in short, a perversion has the characteristics of exclusiveness and fixation—then we shall usually be justified in regarding it as a pathological symptom'.[14] As already mentioned, Freud clearly stresses that we are dealing with perversion as pathological in the clinical sense only when a nongenital activity of partial drives permanently takes the place of genital sexuality without ever becoming or ending up in the latter.

It was perversion, conceived as this neat separation between genital sexuality and partial drives in adults, that directed Freud to investigate in more detail infantile sexuality, which is for him a decisive moment in what we might call his phylogenetic reconstruction of the drive. It is here that Freud acknowledges the connection between partial drives and partial objects which belong to the erogenous zones of the body. The latter are those anatomical holes on the surface of the human body that, in a peculiar way, connect the human organism with the outside world and which have a biological function in helping the child as an organism to survive. Roughly put, Freud is convinced that the repetition of the drive emerges out of the repeated satisfaction of biological needs (eating, for instance) which produces a surplus of excitation/pleasure. In his preliminary definition, the drive is thus a demand which insists beyond the satisfaction of biological needs but emerges out of the latter. And importantly, the 'erogeneity' of erogenous zones derives precisely from this surplus of excitation/pleasure which is linked to the activities of anatomical holes:

> It was the child's first and most vital activity, his sucking at his mother's breast, or at substitutes for it, that must have familiarised him with this pleasure. The child's lips, in our view, behave like an erogenous zone, and no doubt stimulation by the warm flow of milk is the cause of the pleasurable sensation. The satisfaction of the erogenous zone is associated, in the first instance, with the satisfaction of the need for nourishment. To begin with, sexual activity attaches itself to functions serving the purpose of self-preservation and does not become independent of them until later.[15]

For Freud, this surplus of pleasure in the process of satisfying biological needs leads to the later independence of the repetition of the partial drives, which insist beyond biological satisfaction and self-preservation. The satisfaction of the drive beyond biological need thus implies the transgression of the pleasure principle, which was itself established as a principle on the basis of the pleasurable repetition of satisfying biological needs. This detachment of the drive from the biological functions of the organs has, however, another important implication: the drive does not follow the rhythm of the demand for satisfaction of biological needs. On the contrary, the drive is a constant force (*konstante Kraft*) and as such is essentially different from what Freud calls 'instincts'.[16] While the latter come from the external world and allow the subject to deal with that world by way of 'escape' (Freud's example: if the light of the sun falls onto our eye, we can simply shut it down), the drive is a constant force coming from within the human organism and seeks satisfaction (Freud's examples: the dryness of the mucous membrane of the pharynx or an irritation of the mucous membrane of the stomach). In his commentary on the distinction between biological needs and the constant force of the drive, Lacan thus argues that the 'constancy of the thrust forbids any assimilation of the drive to a biological function, which always has a rhythm. The first thing Freud says about the drive is, if I may put it this way, that it has no day or night, no spring or autumn, no rise and fall. It is a constant force'.[17]

Furthermore, Freud identifies another important characteristic of the so-conceived partial drives and of the whole field of pre-genital sexual activity as such: its autoerotism. In the period of latency, the satisfaction of the partial drives is achieved through the child's own body. It is only after the emergence of sexual difference and the Oedipus complex that the child experiences the fear of castration and is forced to take its place within the field of sexual difference by identifying with one sexual identity. Consequently, Freud argues that it is here that the synthesis of the pre-genital partial drives under the primacy of the genitals occurs. From now on, the fear of castration forces the child to employ the partial drives for reproductive purposes, hence apparently directing him or her towards the opposite sex. This, in turn, enables Freud to consider the autonomy of the pre-genital partial drives which have not yet been synthesised under the primacy of the genitals, precisely in terms of the 'polymorphously perverse disposition'[18] which should be repressed and synthesised afterwards:

> The characteristics of infantile sexual life which we have hitherto emphasised are the facts that it is essentially autoerotic (i.e. that is finds its object in the infant's own body) and that its individual component drives are upon the whole disconnected and independent of one another in their search for pleasure. The final outcome of sexual development lies in what is known as the normal sexual life of the adult, in which the pursuit of pleasure comes under the sway of the reproductive function and in which the component drives, under the primacy of a single erogenous zone [the genital], form a firm organisation directed towards a sexual aim attached to some extraneous sexual object.[19]

According to Miller, Freud's articulation of perversion posits polymorphous perversion as a kind of natural disposition, and the task of the Oedipus complex would be in this case the synthesis of mutually independent partial drives under the primacy of the genitals. It is here that Lacan's articulation of the drive and, consequently, of perversion substantially differs from Freud's—although one should admit that this different articulation is only made possible due to Freud's later invention of the concept of primal repression which we will soon discuss. Miller thus sums up the difference at stake as follows:

> The sexual *Tribe* thus does not go toward the opposite sex. There are multiple impulses, multiple drives, and psychoanalysis points to the

> problem of the integration of multiple drives. We have to recognise that the concept of perversion, the original concept of perversion, has been perverted. According to Freud, children are naturally polymorphously perverse. Thus for Freud, perversion is natural, that is, primary. Perversion is more primal than the norm, that norm being secondary or even cultural for Freud—though not for Lacan. In psychoanalysis, there is a problematic of normalisation, of normative integration of multiple drives.[20]

From a Freudian perspective, the persistence of polymorphous perversion in the life of the adult points in the first place to the failed normalisation/synthesis of the pre-genital partial drives under the primacy of the genital. Relatedly, for Freud, the aim of his analysis is to accomplish this normalisation by way of the subject's acceptance of castration and his full identification with one of the sexes—which, importantly, includes the possibility, for instance, of a homosexual identification with the (biologically) opposite sex (which is why Freud cannot be considered as a biological essentialist). However, for Lacan, perversion is articulated precisely as a solution for this failed normalisation, which is epitomised in his famous claim that 'there is no such thing as sexual relationship'. As Miller further argues,

> It is clear in Lacan's work that, as there is no sexual *rapport*—no fixed sexual formula, as he puts it—perversion takes the place of what doesn't exist as a fixed sexual formula. Perversion means innovation, invention of ways of relating to the opposite sex; perversion is a way of relating to the opposite sex. Woman remains present at the very core of male homosexuality. . . . What Freud calls the synthesis of the partial drives under the primacy of the genital organs finds a very simple, logical translation in Lacan's work in the tension or opposition between object *a* and the phallus. Lacan shows that the primacy of the genitals is a negative primacy, that is, that object *a* is connected with minus phi ($-\phi$), which translates the Freudian primacy of the genitals, but takes into account castration.[21]

The crucial distinction between Freud's and Lacan's respective conceptions of perversion thus concerns the question of whether there are non-normalised residues (pre-genital partial drives which have not been synthesised under the primacy of the genitals), which imply that the drive is something unframed or raw, or whether all drives have already undergone normalisation so that they are not raw but 'cooked', as Miller has it. However, what enables Lacan to modify Freud's initial position is precisely his further elaboration of another highly important Freudian concept, which is that of primal repression. In fact, the concept of primal repression, which we already tackled in previous chapters, enables Lacan to introduce a third dimension which is located in between the false opposition between the Oedipal and non-Oedipal drives. Before we come to discuss this fundamental point more in detail, let us first complete our overview of Miller's reading. Following his initial line of argument, Miller further advances two interrelated theses which are truly innovative yet also highly problematic or ambiguous at the least. On the one hand, he proposes a renewed definition of Lacan's main concept, that is, of the object *a* as the object of the partial drive (libido object). The latter is no longer conceived as a real reminder of symbolisation, around which the drive circulates (gaze, voice, etc.), but as a satisfaction gained from this repeating circulation itself—the object *a* is now satisfaction as object:

> What is the libido object? It isn't material. The Freudian drive, which is a satisfaction-seeking *Treib*, doesn't seek any object in particular. It seeks satisfaction. The object that corresponds to the drive is *satisfaction as object*. That is what I would like to propose today, as a definition of Lacan's object *a*: object *a* is satisfaction as an object. Just as we distinguish between instinct and drive, we have to distinguish between the chosen object and the libido object, the latter being *satisfaction* qua *object*.[22]

Following this renewed articulation of the object *a* as satisfaction as object, Miller, on the other hand, does not fail to further argue for a peculiar identity between perversion and the drive as satisfaction seeking: 'But this makes no sense if we do not admit that the drive is by its very nature perverse, and that perversion is the norm of the drive'.[23] Although this thesis seems innovative, and even resonates with other more recent interpretations of perversion in psychoanalysis,[24] it should be carefully examined in detail before we accept it. One of the reasons to be suspicious towards such a thesis is Lacan's own worry about the unjustified equation between the structure of perversion, which by definition contains the subject and the structure of the drive, which Lacan famously defines as the 'headless subject': 'I stress that the drive is not perversion. What constitutes the enigmatic character of Freud's presentation derives precisely from the fact that he wishes to give us a radical structure—in which the subject is not yet placed. On the contrary, what defines perversion is precisely the way in which the subject is placed in it'.[25]

III

In order to explain the difference between perversion and the drive, which will enable us also to comprehend why seemingly pre-Oedipal drives are not also pre-linguistic or raw drives, that is, that they are necessarily shaped by the structure of the Other, it is now necessary to focus on Freud's brief essay on 'Repression'. Already at the beginning of this essay, Freud makes one crucial claim by insisting on repression's dependence on the differentiation between consciousness and unconsciousness. As he puts it, 'repression is not a defensive mechanism which is present from the very beginning, and . . . it cannot arise until a sharp cleavage has occurred between conscious and unconscious'.[26] However, this doesn't imply any preexistence of the unconscious to repression. In search of the mechanism which generates this difference between consciousness and unconsciousness, Freud introduces another, perhaps even more crucial, distinction between repression and primal repression (*Urverdrängung*). In fact, repression in the proper sense, 'repression proper', is only the 'second stage of repression', which consists in the 'after-pression [*Nachdrängen*]' of the 'derivatives of the repressed representative', symbolically associated with the primarily repressed. The process of repression is thus generated by a more original, yet not empirical, but rather real, primal repression:

> We have reason to assume that there is a primal repression, a first phase of repression, which consists in the psychical (ideational) representative of the drive [*die psychische (Vorstellungs-) Repräsentanz des Tribes*] being denied entrance into the conscious. With this a *fixation* is established; the representative in question persists unaltered from then onwards and the drive remains attached to it.[27]

Here the greatest attention needs to be paid to this crucial formulation: contrary to the standard understanding, Freud here clearly says that what is repressed is not the drive itself, but rather its '(ideational) representative [*(Vorstellungs-) Repräsentanz*]'. In this sense, primal repression by no means concerns the drive itself, nor does it concern its idea or representation but rather its representative or signifier as the 'subject's marker of this representation'.[28] Furthermore, the real character of primal repression consists in the fact that this primarily repressed representative is not at all something that would first be conscious and would be repressed only afterwards. Rather, as Alenka Zupančič has already stressed, this representative appears as already repressed for the first time. As she puts it,

> The 'primary repressed' marker or representative of the drive is something that has never been conscious, and has never been part of any subjective experience, but constitutes its ground. The logic of repression by association is the logic of what Freud calls the 'repression proper', whereas the primal repression is precisely not a repression in this sense. In it the causality usually associated with the unconscious is turned upside down: it is not that we repress a signifier because of a traumatic experience related to it, it is rather because this signifier is repressed that we can experience something as traumatic (and not simply as painful, frustrating etc.) and repress it.[29]

Only now does it become possible to fully grasp the relation between trauma and repression. If something traumatic is repressed, it is because it is by association connected with what is primarily repressed. Trauma is therefore dependent on, and determined by, primal repression and not vice versa. This becomes even clearer with regard to the traumatic status of the subject's alienation (between two signifiers), in the Lacanian reversal of Freud's conception of the so-called *fort-da* game from his 'Beyond the Pleasure Principle',[30] and explains why the subject ultimately only constitutes itself within the symbolic Other. In fact, Freud's usual interpretation of the game of *fort-da* is that this game already represents a subjective reaction to the trauma of birth, experienced as a first moment of unpleasure and determined by the physical separation between mother and child.[31] In other words, the *fort-da* game repeats the trauma of birth, the unpleasant moment of the departure of the mother, but in a reversed form: now the child is not a passive recipient of the mother's departure but rather reproduces that departure in an active way, which locates the child in the position of master over the presence and (traumatic) absence of the mother.

However, as Zupančič emphasises, this interpretation misses the crucial point made by Lacan: 'If the mother's departure is traumatic for the child, it is not simply because of her absence, but because of the split (*Spaltung*) it causes in the subject himself, and it is this split that the child's game repeats—he replays and repeats the fundamental alienation'.[32] It is in this repetition of the fundamental alienation that the reversed causality between (traumatic) alienation, which is subjected to repression proper, and primal repression begins to emerge:

> Alienation is not the cause of primal repression; rather, it is its effect or result. Simply put: the subjective split between the signifying dyad [presence-absence] constitutive of alienation is the result of the fall of some first signifier, which is to say of the signifier as *one*. The logic of the signifier (and the subject as that which one signifier represents for another signifier) only starts with two, with the signifying dyad. On the level of the first signifier there is not yet a subject, nor a signifying logic or chain. However, the latter does not occur by means of a second signifier being added to the first, it emerges by means of the 'repression' of the first signifier *at its place* (or 'instead' of it).[33]

Most importantly, there is a remainder, a leftover in the process of primal repression insofar as the drive, by circulating around the hole, produces its own object which Lacan terms 'object *a*'. This object is a fragment, a pound of flesh which the subject had to lose in order to subjectivise himself by vanishing into the signifier. Nonetheless, the subject remains attached to this constitutively lacking object through the constitution of the fundamental fantasy ($\$\Diamond a$). The fantasy, on the one hand, protects the subject against the real of the object (which may cause anxiety) while, on the other hand, it supports the metonymic sliding of desire from one empirical object to another. The object which constitutively lacks at its place thus establishes itself as the *cause* of desire—its lack causes the metonymic sliding of desire. However, the subject misperceives the object as if the latter would come from the realm of the Other. There are thus two interrelated 'effects' of this primal repression: on the one hand, the emergence of the phallus as a signifier of castration which contaminates the erogenous zones of the body and, on the other hand, a phallic object or object *a* in fantasy which constitutes simultaneously the subject's 'defense' against the constant force of the drive which circulates around the hole of primal repression and its support for the metonymic sliding of desire.

Turning back to the topology of primal repression, another aspect of the relation between primal repression and repression proper should be discussed. This aspect concerns their temporality or, rather, punctuality. In fact, both moments of primal repression, the repression of the first signifier, which appears as already repressed for the first time, and secondary repression proper (after-pression) do not appear in two different temporal moments but rather at the same time. From the temporal point of view, it is not that primal repression precedes repression proper *in time*; the primacy of primal repression doesn't mean that it precedes repression proper in the continuum of time but rather it concerns its structural role in the sense that it causes repression proper (repression by association) and determines it as secondary. This means that both stages of repression emerge punctually at the same time. In this sense, primal repression constitutes the structural place (*topos*) where the symbolic order or big Other as the place of the subject is established. The structural place is, however, only the reversal, the other side of the symbolic order; it is immanent to it and doesn't transcend it. In other words, primal repression constitutes a nonempirical and yet real immanent condition of possibility of the symbolic order of language.

Importantly, it is this constellation in which the partial drive is fixed by the hole of primal repression that causes the emergence of the symbolic order of language as essentially the order of binary oppositions. If Freud proposes to grasp the structure of the drive through grammatical oppositions (passive/active), it is thus due to the fact that the binary oppositions in the system of language emerge at the place of the minus One (lack of the first signifier) which also fixes the drive circulating around it and thereby triggers the libidinal investment of language. The repression of the first signifier thus introduces the difference between the signifier and the place of its inscription (signifying chain), and the former is invested precisely with the libido circulating around the same hole of primal repression. In *Seminar X* on *Anxiety*, Lacan captures this point by claiming that the '*a* is the cause of this ambivalence, of this yeah-and-nay'.[34] Precisely because language is libidinally invested by this *indifferent libidinal energy* and thus functions as a kind of 'vehicle' of the drive, speech is ambivalent and materialises the logic of linguistic differences.

This is already suggested by the—this time empirical—anecdote from which Freud developed his interpretation of the *fort-da* game. By mumbling '*fort-da*', Freud's grandson expresses his very first words, his first signifiers, which means that, from the temporal point of view, before those words there was no signifier which could be repressed afterwards at the place where the signifying dyad (*fort-da*) would then emerge. In this sense, primal repression is, again, the condition of possibility of language (as a system of differences), its structurally heterogeneous moment, which, however, emerges (as repressed) simultaneously with language and not in a previous positive reality. In short, the moment of primal repression is the moment of the emergence of the topological *place* of structure, which Lacan marked with the matheme of the barred Other (S[Ⱥ]) and explained as follows: 'There is a hole there and that hole is called Other. At least that is what I felt I could name it, the Other qua locus in which speech, being deposited . . . founds truth and with it, the pact that makes up for the non-existence of the sexual relationship, insofar as it would be conceptualised'.[35] For Lacan, the Other as symbolic order of signifiers is centred on the hole of primal repression, which, on the one hand, fixes the drive now circulating around this hole while, on the other hand, enabling the symbolic order of language to emerge. In other words, the fact that the speaking being is able to speak comes at the cost of the fact that there is a sexual relationship which cannot be said (the nonexistence of the sexual relationship corresponding to the primally repressed signifier). And it is François Balmès who further develops this link of the moment of primal repression with Lacan's axiom of the inexistence of the sexual relationship and the name-of-the-father: 'The unconscious as knowledge is itself dominated by a central fault or hole. S(Ⱥ) also writes down the hole of the primary repressed, which centres and limits all knowledge, and which finally coincides with the absence of the sexual relationship—Lacan will place here The-Name-of-the-Father, that is to say, God'.[36]

Yet as Alenka Zupančič points out many times, this point of negativity (primal repression) is also included in reality and in all existing sexual relationships as their integral part. It is not that the gap of primal repression is set on one level and the symbolic order of signifiers on the other; instead the gap or hole of primal repression is an integral part of the symbolic as such. Incidentally, following this theme, Lacan in his *Seminar XVIII* argues that these two points (the repression of the primal signifier and the phallus as a signifier of castration which emerges in the empty place left by the primally repressed signifier and contaminates the erogenous zones with enjoyment) should be taken in their simultaneity. Importantly, the sexual relationship does not exist (in the sense that ontological negativity shapes all actually existing relationships as precarious) for two interrelated reasons: on the one hand, because there is no signifier of such relationship while, on the other, because there is the phallus as excessive signifier-without-signified which emerges in the empty place left by the primally repressed signifier. In other words, the phallic signifier functions as an excessive obstacle, which emerges in the relation between sexes and prevents that such a relation would ever achieve the status of fantasmatic cosmic balance. As Lacan puts it in a comment on such an idea of cosmic balance or *yin/yang* (which is central in the later Deleuze as well), 'We are not dealing with the lack of the signifier, but with the obstacle which opposes itself to the relationship. The phallus, by stressing a certain organ, does not indicate simply the organ which is called penis including its physiognomy, nor indicates the function of copulation which can be ultimately attributed to such an organ. If we refer to the analytical texts, then the phallus undoubtedly points to the relation with jouissance'.[37] Phallus thus points not to the relation between the two subjects but rather to the relation between the subject and the lack of his own being at the place emerges partial *jouissance* emerges. Lacan explains this with the reference to the myth of the chimeric body of total *jouissance* which was, according to the myth, cut into two parts: man and woman. In this way, the libido was 'evacuated' from the body, remaining located only at the extime bodily orifices where the surface of the body goes from inside to outside thus—the position of the so-called lamella which Lacan defines as the real organ of *jouissance*.

This point becomes even more explicit in Lacan's *Seminar XX Encore* where he develops the theory of the 'other satisfaction' as a redefinition of the concept of *jouissance* articulated in the previous phase of his teaching.[38] If *jouissance* was previously defined as that which is mythically lost in the act of the subject's alienation so that the subject, insofar as it is constituted as the effect of the symbolic order of language, loses *jouissance*, what Lacan calls the 'other satisfaction' here, contrarily, signifies precisely the additional satisfaction of language, the satisfaction of 'blah-blah', of the stupid repetition of signifiers, which appears in the absence of immediate, direct satisfaction. This theory of the 'other satisfaction' is also an attempt to further develop the concept of surplus enjoyment set up by Lacan in his *Seminar XVII*.[39] However, it by no means implies a positive existence of any kind of original or primal satisfaction, which would precede the 'other satisfaction'. Rather, the *'other satisfaction' emerges at the place of the lack of primal satisfaction*, which already appears as lacking the first time, and which coincides with the inexistence of the sexual relationship. That is why Lacan insists that the 'other satisfaction', although it is privileged, is, from a structural point of view, second and not first. What is first is the inexistence of the sexual relationship—the moment of primal repression. As mentioned before, however, this still does not imply a logic of 'two levels'; instead it is a logic of one level only—with the constitutive hole as its integral part around which the symbolic is structured. Finally, this is also the reason why *jouissance* is subject to the process of repression: because as substitute, as the 'other satisfaction', it is incompatible with, or inappropriate for, the inexistence of the sexual relationship or primal repression, to which it is nevertheless symbolically connected by association. I cite at length:

> In the end, if this jouissance comes to someone (*celui*) who speaks, and not by accident, it is because it is a bit premature. It has something to do with the renowned (*fameux*) sexual relationship, concerning which he will have only too many occasions to realise that it doesn't exist. It is thus second rather than first. There are traces of it in Freud's work. If Freud spoke of *Urverdrängung*, primal repression, it was precisely because the true, good, everyday repression is not first—it is second. People repress the said jouissance because it is not fitting for it to be spoken. . . . Repression is produced only to attest, in all statements (*dire*) and in the slightest statement, to what is implied by the statement that I just enunciated, that jouissance is inappropriate—*non docet*—to the sexual relationship. It is precisely because the said jouissance speaks that the sexual relationship is not.[40]

Lacan's point here is simply that the *jouissance* or satisfaction of 'blah-blah' emerges only at the place of the primary repressed, at the place of the inexistence of the sexual relationship. As such, *jouissance* does not fit into this inexistence precisely because there is nothing into which it could fit. That is to say, the inexistence of the sexual relationship is not a positive but rather a negative measure in relation to which *jouissance* appears as always already inadequate or inappropriate. And this is why Lacan at the beginning of *Seminar XX* categorically claims that 'jouissance is what serves no purpose (*ne sert à rien*)'.[41] Insofar as it is an effect of the drive, *jouissance* serves no purpose precisely because the drive is fixed to its primarily repressed representative or to the inexistence of the sexual relationship. That is why sexuality, which steps into this place, is possible only through these partial drives, which are 'partial' precisely in relation to this inexistence—they cannot totalise sexuality, although they 'partially' represent it.[42] The 'total' sexual drive would mean precisely the reduction of sexuality to the level of biological reproduction, which would negate the postulate of the inexistence of the sexual relationship. In other words, no satisfaction of the drive is total because the totality of satisfaction doesn't exist for speaking beings. That's why *jouissance* is something traumatic and has to be repressed—because by association it is connected with the primarily repressed representative of the drive, which constitutes the inexistence of the sexual relationship.

IV

In this context, Alenka Zupančič has recently proposed a renewed definition of the death drive which encompasses the whole aforementioned mechanism where the hole of primary repression is the hole by which the partial drives are fixed. That is to say, the Freudian-Lacanian death drive contains the negative synthesis of the partial drives which are synthesised by the point of 'ontological negativity'[43] where Lacan locates the inexistence of the sexual relationship. This further implies that all partial drives are already shaped or framed by this mechanism from the very beginning and, importantly, prior to the emergence of any Oedipus complex, which can thus be regarded as only a secondary reaction. Drives are thus not 'raw' but 'cooked', as Miller has rightly argued: they circulate around the anatomical holes of the body due to the fact that these holes are symbolically 'contaminated' by the phallus as a signifier of the castration which is, along with the phallic object, the effect of primal repression.

We are now in a position to better comprehend what can be regarded as the problematic aspect of Miller's renewed definition of the object *a* in terms of satisfaction as object. As Zupančič further comments on this point, the drive does not seek any satisfaction: it is basically indifferent towards any satisfaction. The only instance that seeks and imposes satisfaction is not the drive but the superego.[44] Thus, satisfaction can be regarded only as by-product of the drive's circulation around the hole of primal repression, where it repeats the ontological negativity set up by primal repression. Drawing on Lacan's distinction between the aim and the goal of the drive from his *Seminar XI*, Zupančič argues,

> Satisfaction becomes *object* (starts to function as object of the drive) only because it gives body to this negativity, and not simply as satisfaction for the sake of satisfaction. In other words, if the drive wants (us) to repeat the surplus satisfaction, this is not because all it wants is to enjoy. The drive does not want (us) to enjoy. The superego wants (us) to enjoy. The superego (and its culture) reduces the drive to the issue of satisfaction (enjoyment), making us hostages to its vicissitudes, and actively blocking access to the negativity that drives it. In other words—and this is crucial—satisfaction (for the sake of satisfaction) is not the goal of the drive, but its *means*. This is what is profoundly disturbing about the 'death drive': not that it wants only to enjoy, even if it kills us, but that it wants only to repeat this negativity, the gap in the order of being, *even if this means to enjoy*. Enjoyment is the means, whereas the 'aim' is the repetition of the lack of being in the very midst of being.[45]

In short, the Freudian-Lacanian drive is, in the first place, indifferent towards enjoyment, which appears to be only the by-product of its circulation around the object *a*. The aim or the target of the drive is circulation itself, that is, the circulation around the lost object or the fragment of libido on the surfaces of the anatomical holes of the body. Put another way, the aim of the drive is the repetition of ontological negativity itself. Enjoyment as by-product is produced only due to the fact that the drive constantly fails to catch this negativity (which, however, is not prior to but rather simultaneous with the repetition itself). In other words, the subject enjoys because the vector of the drive, by repeating the ontological negativity and thus giving a body to it, in the end comes back again and again to the surface of the anatomical hole and therefore achieves its goal. So Miller's thesis, according to which the object of the drive is satisfaction as object, actually implies the reversal of the relationship between the aim and the goal of the drive and thus risks ending up in teleology (and theology). In this respect, Adrian Johnston is correct to recently define the Lacanian drive precisely as 'repetition-without-teleology'—as opposed to desire as 'teleology-without-repetition'.[46]

Furthermore, this clarification puts into question another one of Miller's theses, which posits perversion as the 'norm' of the drive. This thesis, which follows from his prior renewed definition of object *a* as satisfaction, actually implies the introduction of the superego's injunction to enjoy into the circulation of the drive. Although Miller is obviously far from being sympathetic towards such a vitalist reading of the drive, indeed he openly rejects it, this thesis is still strangely close to a form of vitalism. To argue that perversion is the norm of the drive, which implies the unjustifiable association of the circulation of the drive and the injunction of the superego, is to risk disavowing the crucial distinction in Lacan's psychoanalysis between the topological point of primal repression and the object *a*, thus opening up the space for a transcendentalisation of ontological negativity by way of the subject's direct identification with the object *a*. In contrast, Lacan argues, not for the substitution or overlapping, but rather for the separation and split between the barred Other and the object *a*,

> The aim of my teaching . . . is to dissociate *a* and A by reducing the first to what is related to the imaginary and the other to what is related to the symbolic. It is indubitable that the symbolic is the basis of what was made into God. It is certain that the imaginary is based on the reflection of one semblable in another. And yet, *a* has lent itself to be confused with S(Ⱥ). . . . It is here that the scission or detachment remains to be effectuated.[47]

However, this split between the (barred) Other and the object *a* does not imply that the drive is now somehow freed from the point of primal repression or ontological negativity. On the contrary, this split precisely unveils the structure in which the drive is shaped by the point of primal repression yet without the Oedipus complex and the superego. In fact, the superego agency consists of the fantasmatic nexus between the Other and the object. Following this line of argument in the next two chapters, we will first discuss the previously mentioned 'transcendentalisation' of ontological negativity in relation to Žižek's concept of 'Christian atheism' and Lacan's analysis of baroque perversion in order to, secondly, reelaborate the superego in order to explain its distinguishing sadistic character. We will thus reconstruct the as yet underthematised conceptualisation of the superego in psychoanalysis, which moves from the instance of prohibition (Freud) to the injunction to enjoy (Lacan).

NOTES

1. Sigmund Freud, 'Three Essays on the Theory of Sexuality', in *The Standard Edition of the Complete Psychological Works of Sigmund Freud, Vol. VII*, ed. James Strachey (London: Vintage, 2001), 165.
2. Jacques Lacan, *Le Séminaire, livre IV: La relation d'objet* (Paris: Seuil, 1994), 114.
3. Ibid., 120.
4. Ibid., 120–21.
5. Jacques-Alain Miller, 'On Perversion', in *Reading Seminars I and II: Lacan's Return to Freud*, ed. Richard Feldstein, Bruce Fink, and Maire Jaanus (New York: State University of New York Press, 1996), 315.
6. Ibid., 308.
7. 'The popular view of the sexual drive is beautifully reflected in the poetic fable which tells how the original human beings were cut up into two halves—man and woman—and how these are always striving to unite again in love. [Editor's Note: This is no doubt an allusion to the theory expounded by Aristophanes in Plato's *Symposium*. Freud recurred to this much later, at the end of chapter VI of *Beyond the Pleasure Principle* (1920).] It comes as a great surprise therefore to learn that there are men whose sexual object is a man and not woman, and women whose sexual object is a woman and not a man. People of this kind are described as having "contrary sexual feelings", or better, as being "inverts", and the fact is described as "inversion". The number of such people is very considerable, though there are difficulties in establishing it precisely' (Freud, 'Three Essays', 136; translation modified).
8. Ibid., 147–48.
9. Ibid., 146, note. This thesis, according to which even the most conventional heterosexual relation between man and woman should be taken as a problem seeking explanation, actually already anticipates Lacan's formula, that 'there's no such thing as sexual relationship'. It is worthwhile referring again to Alenka Zupančič's book *What* Is *Sex?* (Cambridge, MA: MIT Press, 2017), in which she unfolds the far-reaching consequences this thesis has for ontology, consequences which we will also explore in this book.
10. Ibid., 150.
11. Miller, 'On Perversion', 311.
12. Ibid., 313.
13. As he argues, 'No healthy person, it appears, can fail to make some addition that might be called perverse to the normal sexual aim; and the universality of this finding is in itself enough to show how inappropriate it is to use the word perversion as a term of reproach' (Freud, 'Three Essays', 160).
14. Ibid., 161.
15. Ibid., 181–82; translation modified.
16. Sigmund Freud, 'Instincts and Their Vicissitudes', in *The Standard Edition of the Complete Psychological Works of Sigmund Freud, Vol. XIV*, ed. James Strachey (London: Vintage, 2001), 118. Following contemporary terminological standards, I prefer to use the word 'drive' to name what was originally translated as 'instinct' and the word 'instinct' for what was translated as 'stimulus'. It is precisely the drive originating within the human organism that enables the subject to differentiate between inside and outside.
17. Jacques Lacan, *The Seminar of Jacques Lacan, Book XI: The Four Fundamental Concepts of Psychoanalysis* (hereafter abbreviated as *Seminar XI*), trans. Alan Sheridan (London and New York: W. W. Norton and Company, 1998), 165.
18. Freud, 'Three Essays', 191. In his discussion of the difference between infantile polymorphous perversion and the later synthesis of the drives in mature life, Freud confronts the riddle of the Sphinx, on which Agamben centres his whole discussion on perversion. For Freud, we can find an equivalent of the riddle of the Sphinx in the psychic life of children, and particularly in the enigmatic question 'where do babies come from?' (ibid., 195). The Oedipal 'deciphering' of this question would thus

amount to the synthesis of the partial drives under the primacy of the genitals and the acceptance of sexual difference and castration by the subject. However, Lacan argues—following his rearticulation of the Freudian drive on the basis of the concept of primal repression—that there is no difference between children and adults as far as the link between the drives and sexuality is concerned: 'With regard to the agency of sexuality, all subjects are equal, from the child to the adult—that they deal only with that part of sexuality that passes into the networks of the constitution of the subject, into the networks of the signifier—that sexuality is realised only through the operation of the drives in so far as they are partial drives, partial with regard to the biological finality of sexuality' (Lacan, *Seminar XI*, 176–77). As I will soon show, children and adults share the same position with regard to sexuality because 'the drive is precisely that *montage* by which sexuality participates in the psychic life, in a way that must conform to the gap-like structure that is the structure of the unconscious' (Lacan, *Seminar XI*, 176). This means that that sexuality must conform to the structure in which the drive is fixed with the point of primal repression (repression of the first, primal signifier).

19. Freud, 'Three Essays', 197; translation modified.

20. Miller, 'On Perversion', 313.

21. Ibid., 313–14.

22. Ibid.

23. Ibid.

24. See Dominiek Hoens, 'Toward a New Perversion: Psychoanalysis', in *Jacques Lacan and the Other Side of Psychoanalysis: Reflections on Seminar XVII*, ed. Justin Clemens and Russell Grigg (Durham and London: Duke University Press, 2006), 88–102.

25. Lacan, *Seminar XI*, 181–82.

26. Sigmund Freud, 'Repression', in *The Standard Edition of the Complete Psychological Works of Sigmund Freud, Vol. XIV*, ed. James Strachey (London: Vintage, 2001), 147.

27. Ibid., 148; translation modified.

28. Alenka Zupančič, 'On Repetition', *Sats—Nordic Journal of Philosophy* 8, no. 1 (2007): 39.

29. Ibid.

30. To recall the story, Freud once observed the child (his grandson) playing with a small gadget, a cotton reel which he controlled via the thread, throwing it away and then pulling it back while mumbling something like *fort-da* ('fort' [gone]-'da' [here]). See Sigmund Freud, 'Beyond the Pleasure Principle', in *The Standard Edition of the Complete Psychological Works of Sigmund Freud, Vol. XVIII*, ed. James Strachey (London: Vintage, 2001), 14–17.

31. See, for example, Sigmund Freud, 'Inhibitions, Symptoms and Anxiety', in *The Standard Edition of the Complete Psychological Works of Sigmund Freud, Vol. XX*, ed. James Strachey (London: Vintage, 2001), 161–62.

32. Zupančič, 'On Repetition', 41.

33. Ibid.

34. Jacques Lacan, *The Seminar of Jacques Lacan, Book X: Anxiety*, trans. A. R. Price (Cambridge, MA, and Malden: Polity Press, 2014), 302. To borrow Tadej Troha's nice formulation, the drive is a 'peculiar psychical quantity that traverses all dualisms' (Tadej Troha, 'On Ambivalence', *Problemi International* 1, no. 1 [2017]: 224).

35. Jacques Lacan, *The Seminar of Jacques Lacan, Book XX: Encore*, trans. Bruce Fink (London and New York: W. W. Norton and Co., 1999) (hereafter abbreviated as *Seminar XX*), 114. Insofar as the God is conceived here as the locus of the speech as such, this is the main reason why Lacan insists that 'as long as the things are said, the God hypothesis will persist' (ibid., 45).

36. François Balmès, *Dieu, le sexe et la vérité* (Paris: Erès, 2007), 29; my translation.

37. Jacques Lacan, *Le séminaire, livre XVIII: D'un discours qui ne serait pas du semblant* (Paris: Seuil, 2006), 67.

38. For a systematic overview of how the concept of *jouissance* evolves throughout Lacan's teaching, see a classic text by Jacques-Alain Miller, 'Paradigms of *Jouissance*', *Lacanian Ink* 17 (2000): 8–47.

39. Jacques Lacan, *The Seminar of Jacques Lacan, Book XVII: The Other Side of Psychoanalysis*, trans. Russell Grigg (London and New York: W. W. Norton and Co., 2007).

40. Lacan, *Seminar XX*, 61. On this topic as well as on the difference between the 'other satisfaction' and the 'Other *jouissance*', see Lorenzo Chiesa, '*Jouissance* in Lacan's Seminar XX: Prolegomena to a New Reading', in *The Care of Life: Transdisciplinary Perspectives in Bioethics and Biopolitics*, ed. Miguel de Beistegui, Giuseppe Bianco, and Marjorie Gracieuse (London and New York: Rowman & Littlefield International, 2014), 295–308. Chiesa also tackles this topic in his masterpiece *The Not-Two: Logic and God in Lacan* (Cambridge, MA: MIT Press, 2016), 1–21. In my reading of *jouissance*, I rely very much on this reading of Chiesa's, which I consider to be, along with Alenka Zupančič's, the best interpretation of *jouissance* in Lacan.

41. Lacan, *Seminar XX*, 3.

42. As Lacan does not fail to stress in Seminar XI, 'If all is confusion in the discussion of the sexual drives it is because one does not see that the drive represents no doubt, but *merely* represents, and partially at that, the curve of fulfilment of sexuality in the living being' (Lacan, *Seminar XI*, 177).

43. Zupančič, *What* Is *Sex?*, 16.

44. 'Nothing forces anyone to enjoy (*jouir*) except the superego. The superego is the imperative of jouissance—Enjoy!' (Lacan, *Seminar XX*, 3).

45. Zupančič, *What* Is *Sex?*, 104.

46. Adrian Johnston, 'Repetition and Difference: Žižek, Deleuze and Lacanian Drives', in *Lacan and Deleuze: A Disjunctive Synthesis*, ed. Boštjan Nedoh and Andreja Zevnik (Edinburgh: Edinburgh University Press, 2017), 186. As Johnston further proposes (187) in the view of the concepts of 'the axis of iteration' and 'the axis of alteration' developed in his early book *Time Driven* (see Adrian Johnston, *Time Driven: Metapsychology and the Splitting of the Drive* [Evanston, IL: Northwestern University Press, 2005], 256–332), the drive as 'repetition-without-teleology' corresponds to the 'axis of iteration', while the representational side of this topology, that is, desire as 'teleology-without-repetition' which includes the object *a* as object-cause of desire, corresponds to the 'axis of alteration'.

47. Lacan, *Seminar XX*, 83.

NINE

The Birth of Perversion from the Death on the Cross

Lacan, Žižek, and the Question of Christian Atheism

I

Having concluded the previous chapter by arguing once again for a distinction between the superego and the death drive, it is now time to focus in more detail on the (often misread) relation between psychoanalysis, Christianity, perversion, and atheism. This relation achieves the highest importance, especially in the context of the assumed overlap between analytic discourse and the structure of perversion. In fact, some interpretations take literally the fact that the upper level of the analytic discourse from Lacan's *Seminar XVII* is read as a perverse fantasy ($a\lozenge\$$).[1] So in this chapter I will argue that the way analytic discourse conceives of the inexistence of big Other (the fact that there is 'no Other of the Other' and thus no meta-language which would make of the symbolic order an enclosed totality or One) substantially differs from the perverse 'transcendentalisation' of the fact that the Other does not exist.

More specifically, I will argue that taking the theorem of the inexistence of the big Other (or the corresponding 'absence of sexual relationship' from Lacan's late period) as a *transcendental a priori* assumption, instead of an *immanent a posteriori* deduction, paves the way for a perverse shift which, far from being immune to the acknowledgement of the inexistence of the big Other, rather takes it as its own condition of possibility. Quite surprisingly, as I will soon show, the whole perverse arc stretches from the acknowledgement of the inexistence of the big Other to the moment this inexistence is 'transcendentalised' into the story or meaning that is already present in the Gospels and, more specifically, in the three versions of Christ's last words on the cross.

As Slavoj Žižek argues many times, what dies on the cross is not Christ as God's son or earthly representative but instead a God from beyond himself. Yet Žižek's argument is mostly based on the version of Christ's last words on the cross as written in Matthew 27:46 and Mark 15:34: 'My God, my God, why have you deserted me?' However, if we take into account the other two versions of the same event—in Luke 23:46, we read Christ's last words as 'Father, I put myself in your hands', while in John 19:30, we read 'Everything is done!'—we get nothing but the perverse inversion of the ontological catastrophe of the divine being, which is thus 'transcendentalised' into a positive story. That is to say, we get nothing but a perverse reversal of the originary atheist moment. As Lorenzo Chiesa nicely puts it, Christianity 'turns incompleteness into the definitive reason to believe in completeness'.[2]

Moreover, this reading is fully supported by Lacan's own reading of Christian 'polymorphous perversion', as it is depicted in Baroque art. This reading of the Baroque will enable us to distinguish between three apparently overlapping concepts: Christianity, perversion, and atheism. Finally, this reading will also enable us to clarify Žižek's defence of Christian atheism, which otherwise may remain ambiguous or even risk its own inversion into what Žižek elsewhere calls 'the perverse core of Christianity'.[3]

My twofold argument will thus involve the following. Firstly, in the following section, I will provide an overview of Žižek's arguments in favour of 'Christian atheism'. I will then explain the 'perverse reversal' that takes place in the event of Christ's death on the cross if we also take into account Luke 23:46 and John 19:30. In the third section, I will try to show how this interpretation agrees with Lacan's reading of Baroque Christian art and the exhibition of *jouissance* that is at work there. More precisely, Lacan's point regarding Baroque Christian art is that the perverse turn actually is the 'truth' of Christianity itself, as it appears in its historical concretisation. Finally, against this background, I will conclude by showing how Lacan's theorem of the inexistence of the big Other or sexual relationship cannot and must not be confused with the statement that there is no Other/God at all. Instead Lacanian criticism of ontology—which is also the way psychoanalysis differs from perversion—approaches ontology in, as Alenka Zupančič has put it, '*with-without*'[4] terms, which is to say, that fundamental negativity (the lack of the one/first signifier) as such is an integral part of the being/the symbolic Other. In other words, the lack of the first signifier is ontologically constitutive and formative for the constitution of being—the latter is thus *with-without* the first signifier which can thus also be articulated by the formulation 'with the inexistent Other'. This, however, by no means implies a (vitalist) ontology *without* the Other, which is the way vitalist thinkers such as Deleuze and Agamben think perversion.[5]

II

Throughout his career, Slavoj Žižek has notoriously defined himself as a 'Christian atheist' and defended a corresponding position of 'Christian atheism'.[6] When arguing in favour of this position, he includes a variety of examples which come from different domains, from theological tradition itself, to Hegelian philosophy and psychoanalysis. Nevertheless, the core of his argument still remains deeply rooted not only in a theological but also, or rather, more specifically, in a biblical context. In arguing for Christian atheism, Žižek refers mostly to two scenes from the Bible: the book of Job and Christ's death on the cross. As mentioned before, his reading of these two moments is principally inspired by Chesterton's reading of the story of Job and Hegel's interpretation of Christ's death on the cross. The main emphasis in Žižek's reading is thus put on the close interconnection between two stories because he reads the story of Christ's death on the cross as a repetition of the story of Job. Recalling Žižek's argument very briefly, the two stories reveal the fact that the transcendent God 'from beyond' is dead, or rather that it does not exist as a transcendental provider of meaning. The only form in which God exists is an immanent, earthly form, which is that of the Holy Spirit or the community of Christian believers. The death of God as a transcendent caretaker and his corresponding immanentisation in the form of the Holy Spirit represents, according to Žižek, the radically atheistic moment of Christianity. In order to properly explain this thesis, let us focus in detail on Žižek's reading of Job and the Crucifixion.

To consider Žižek's work as a whole, we cannot dismiss the story of Job as just one example among many. On the contrary, he considers this story as 'perhaps the first exemplary case of the critique of ideology in human history'.[7] Why so? He is not interested in providing a wider philological exegesis of the content; instead he focuses on some selected points in order to extract from them a lesson with universal validity. This is why he just barely surveys the content (all the particular incidents that happen to Job and which, taken together, make a gigantic catastrophe) of the story in order to focus on its conclusion in detail. According to Žižek, the moral of the story of Job is based on his radical rejection of the possibility that the catastrophe that struck him can have any meaning at all. In the face of all the incidents that affect him and his family, Job complains to God all the time, contesting the reasons why all this should happen to him. After some time, three of his friends (Žižek calls them 'theologians' or even 'ideologists') come to visit him with one task: to convince Job that there has to be some reason why all those tragic events have happened to him. In other words, they try to inscribe Job's catastrophe and a consequent suffering in a chain of *meaningful* causality: if B, therefore there must be A, because B can be caused only by A and not by some X (X stands for the meaningless or absent cause). As Žižek puts it,

> When the three theologians-friends visit him, their line of argumentation is the standard ideological sophistry (if you are suffering, you *must* by definition have done something wrong, since God is just). Their argumentation, however, is not confined to the claim that Job must be somehow guilty: what is at stake on a more radical level is the meaning(lessness) of Job's suffering. Like Oedipus at Colonus, Job insists on the utter *meaninglessness* of his suffering.[8]

According to Žižek, it is precisely the assumed meaning of an otherwise senseless catastrophic event that points to an exchange with the domain of the divine and therefore affirms God as a supreme, transcendent being. To assign a meaning to the catastrophe is to imply God as a supreme substance who is the 'cause' of all reality in the classic Aristotelian sense of the term. For Žižek, Job's rejection of the possibility that the catastrophe that occurred to him has any meaning means that he also contests the very ontological existence of God from above. However, there is another shift in the story, which is crucial: the fact that God somehow gives credence to Job's complaints, that he ultimately considers them as justified, is, for Žižek, the most powerful evidence that God is actually blaspheming himself alone. In other words, Žižek's point is not just that Job doesn't believe in God but also that even God doesn't believe in His own omnipotence—His acts are 'excessive' with respect to His will.

According to Žižek, the story of Christ's death on the cross repeats the same gesture of self-blaspheming by God as occurs in the story of Job. Here too, roughly speaking, there is no deeper meaning to this event, no transcendent exchange, according to the 'sacrificial' interpretations of the moment of Christ's death (God from above who sacrifices his Son). Quite literally: 'Christ's suffering is *also* meaningless, *not an act of meaning exchange*'.[9] Following Žižek, this implies the very suspension of God's position as the transcendental caretaker:

> Christ's death on the cross thus means that one should drop the notion of God as a transcendent caretaker who guarantees the happy outcome of our acts, the guarantee of historical teleology—Christ's death on the cross is the death of *this* God, it repeats Job's stance, it refuses any 'deeper meaning' that obfuscates the brutal real of historical catastrophes.[10]

For Žižek, this point is the origin of the distinctive 'atheist' character of Christianity, not only with respect to other religions but especially with respect to the standard form of atheism itself: 'In the standard form of atheism, God dies for men who stop believing in Him; in Christianity, God dies *for Himself*'.[11] In order to provide 'evidence' for the argument supporting this 'double kenosis' or 'double alienation',[12] that is, the overlap between man's alienation from God and God's alienation from himself,[13] Žižek refers precisely to Christ's last words on the cross before he dies: 'Eli, Eli, lema sabachthani?'—'Father, Father, why have you forsaken me?' (or, as another translation of this passage from Matthew 27:46 and Mark 15:34 goes: 'My God, my God, why have you deserted me?'). As previously mentioned, according to Žižek, this abandonment should be conceived in a double sense: on the one hand, as the abandonment of men from God, and, on the other hand, as the abandonment of God from Himself. This is why he concludes that what actually dies on the cross is not Christ as God's son or his earthly representative but the God from beyond Himself. Thus, what constitutes the 'atheist' core of Christianity is precisely the destruction of transcendence and the immanentisation of the divine by way of God's falling into his own creation through his incarnation in the body of Christ: 'God's self-alienation overlaps with the alienation from God of the human individual who experienced himself as alone in a godless world, abandoned by God who dwells in some inaccessible transcendent Beyond'.[14]

Here Žižek's Hegelian argument already seems clear enough. Yet it becomes even more convincing when completed with a corresponding Lacanian perspective. In fact, the overlapping double alienation (of men from God and of God from Himself) also crosses paths with Lacan's articulation of the big Other, that is, the symbolic order of linguistic reality which is constituted around the fundamental default or hole in its being. As we have already discussed,[15] Alenka Zupančič efficiently develops this point of Lacan's, stating that the fall of the one/first signifier is necessary for the emergence of the symbolic order of signifiers. This lack of the first signifier, which corresponds to the Freudian concept of primal repression, is thus constitutive for the order of signifiers (the signifying chain) which emerges at this empty place. The subject's alienation in the Other (his split between the signifying dyad) can be thus conceived as the 'effect' of this fall of the first signifier.[16] This originary gap finally corresponds to the Freudian articulation of the unconscious as such, conceived not as a secret 'treasure' to be unearthed in the course of an analytic process (Agamben) but instead as the gap which constitutes the very mechanism of repression. The aforementioned 'with-without' formulation proposed by Zupančič, which sums up the constitutive role of the lack of the first signifier, is thus the best way to grasp the fact that, for Lacan, the unconscious goes beyond the being/nonbeing opposition, and thus opens up the space for a 'third dimension': 'Indeed, what became apparent at first to Freud, to the discoverers, to those who made the first steps, and what still becomes apparent to anyone in analysis who spends some time observing what truly belongs to the order to the unconscious, is that it is neither being, nor non-being, but the unrealised'.[17] The expression 'the unrealised' indicates precisely that the gap of the unconscious not only affects being but also, and more fundamentally so, it is constitutive for being itself. In other words, the gap of the unconscious leaves traces in the very way the being *is* (inherently 'contaminated' with jokes, slips of the tongue, dreams, etc.), hence it cannot be dismissed as an unthinkable nonbeing.

According to Lacan, then, what the subject is supposed to encounter in traversing the fundamental fantasy at the end of the analytic process is not simply the object but rather the lack in the Other or, better yet, the split between the object and the Other.[18] This split also marks the very moment of meaninglessness, that is to say, the point where the subject *qua* meaning, set up by the structure of the fantasy, experiences his subjective destitution or lack of meaning.

Turning back to Žižek's argument concerning the question of Christian atheism, we can now conclude that the atheism inherent to Christianity is essentially dependent on the inexistence of a transcendental Being as a provider of meaning of our earthly lives. The moment of atheism within Christianity thus comprises the immanentisation of the divine: the transcendent God is replaced by the immanent, earthly community of the believers (the Holy Spirit) which can rely only on itself without any transcendental guarantee for the success of its actions. In this respect, the moment of the death of God can be, at least at first glance, associated with the moment of traversing the fundamental fantasy in the analytic process.

Yet although I agree with Žižek's articulation of this singular moment of atheism in monotheism, his line of argument necessitates in my view an essential supplement without which it cannot resist the perverse reversal that the inexistence of the big Other already undergoes in the Gospels. As we know, in addition to the version of Christ's last words on the cross that appears in Matthew 27:46 and Mark 15:34 ('My God, my God, why have you deserted me?'), which Žižek mainly refers to in his argumentation, there are two other versions which should not be taken as mutually exclusive but rather as *complementary* to the first. In Luke 23:46, recall, we read Christ's last words as 'Father, I put myself in your hands', while in John 19:30 we read 'Everything is done!'

As previously mentioned, my suggestion is that if we take these three versions together, that is, as complementary rather than mutually exclusive, we get nothing but the whole parabola of perversion, as articulated by psychoanalysis. To be sure, perversion is far from immune or indifferent to the inexistence of the symbolic Other because it is actually presupposed in every perversion. The most distinctive feature of perversion is precisely that it turns the inexistence of the Other into a 'truth' or 'principle'. At this decisive point, Christianity and perversion actually share the same position. In fact, the three different versions of Christ's last words on the cross seem to be immediately translatable into psychoanalytic terminology:

1. 'My God, my God, why have you deserted me?' from Matthew 27:46 and Mark 15:34 fully acknowledges the inexistence of God as a supreme omnipotent being, which is why Žižek rightly argues that this sentence actually implies the death of the God from beyond.
2. 'Father, I put myself in your hands!' from Luke 23:46 already represents an attempt to fill up this hole in the big Other or in God with a pound of flesh, that is, with Christ's own body. Here we actually encounter a third option, which is somehow marginalised in Žižek's reading. If Christ is not just the son of God but His incarnation itself, and if he at the same time encounters the void in God as a void in himself alone, the void he tries to fill up with his own body, then we could say that in this case *Christ sacrifices himself for God*. Or, more precisely, because Christ as God is aware of his own inexistence, he performs his own death in the form of self-sacrifice in order to bring himself into being as God.
3. Finally, 'Everything is done!' from John 19:30 marks precisely the emergence of meaning out of the death on the cross because it implies the conclusion of a story which, from a structural point of view, corresponds precisely to Lacan's definition of the fantasy, conceived as the means for the imaginary unification of reality. The ontological catastrophe of the divine Being, the inexistence of God thus acquires a meaning *as* catastrophe, that is, the catastrophe or negation retroactively becomes the condition for some positive supreme end. In this way, the catastrophe becomes a transcendental principle; its truth is transcendental rather than immanent.

Reading the three versions of Christ's last words on the cross as a kind of three-step parable, we are thus able to see that Christianity acquires a perverse shift already in the Gospels themselves. In fact, there is no contradiction between the three versions in this respect: they represent a tripartite narrative in which the first stage functions as a precondition for the other two. The bare evocation of the inexistence of the big Other (the evocation of the absence of God in the moment of Christ's death) is thus insufficient. In the remainder of this chapter, I will thus try to argue that there are actually two different ways of thinking the truth of the inexistence of the big Other in psychoanalysis or the ontological catastrophe of the divine Being in Christianity: a Christian transcendental reading and a psychoanalytic immanent reading which—although psychoanalysis shares many of the same assumptions as Christianity—could be defined at this point as 'post-Christianity'.[19] In short, psychoanalysis thinks this truth of the inexistence of the big Other immanently, that is, as inherently attached to the real conceived in terms of the internal contradiction or impasse of the symbolic order and aims at splitting the symbolic from the imaginary, while Christianity redoubles this truth, thus making of it a transcendental 'truth *about* truth'.[20] As Chiesa has put it, the decisive question concerning psychoanalysis is if 'can we think onto-logically this truth in itself without turning incompleteness into another truth about the truth, i.e., into yet another figure of God as absolute being'.[21] This difference between these immanent and transcendent accounts of the in-existence of the sexual relationship becomes far most evident in Lacan's take on Christian Baroque art in the ninth lesson of his famous *Seminar XX*, titled 'On the Baroque', in which he sees this genre of art in terms of a perverse 'exhibition of the body evoking jouissance'.

III

To begin with, of course, Lacan's take on the relationship between Christianity and atheism is far more complex than first appears. After claiming in *Seminar XI* that the 'true formula of atheism is not *God is dead* . . . the true formula of atheism is *God is unconscious*',[22] for example, in *Seminar XVII* he argues that 'the pinnacle of psychoanalysis is well and truly atheism'.[23] In the ninth lecture of *Seminar XX*, titled 'On the Baroque', Lacan further complicates this picture by putting forwards some of his most controversial claims, such as Christianity is the 'true religion'[24] and, correspondingly, 'atheism is tenable only to clerics'.[25] So in order to introduce more clarity into these apparently misleading formulae, which seemingly imply an overlap between Christianity and atheism, a closer inspection of Lacan's take on the Baroque is needed.

There are two aspects of Christianity that Lacan constantly refers to and oscillates between in his discussion of the Baroque. The first aspect concerns the constitution of discourse on the basis of the desubstantialisation of God, while the second involves the constitution of fantasy by means of exhibiting partial, lost objects in Baroque painting. As far as the first aspect is concerned, Lacan notably associates the Christian God with the fact that truth can only be said halfway (*dit-mension*).[26] In fact, the way Christianity deals with truth acquires a completely different status than in the ancient cosmic world of the Romans and the Greeks. As mentioned earlier, truth can only be said halfway because there is a fundamental fault or negativity at work in the symbolic order, the fundamental lack of the first signifier which enables the emergence of language. This negativity is inherent and inextricably connected with language as such. Lacan locates the Christian God at this very same point: the well-known God's answer to Moses, who asked God about his name, 'I am, who I am' (from Exodus 3:14) indicates precisely the lack of the first signifier, the impossibility of saying the first name, which is then supplemented by the plurality of God's names.[27] This lack of the first signifier, which indicates the fundamental negativity upon which the symbolic order of language is constituted, ultimately corresponds to the ontological incompleteness which is epitomised in the theorem 'there is no sexual relationship'. By bringing the world back to its 'filthy truth' (*vérité d'immondice*), by exposing the fact that the truth can only be said halfway—which corresponds to the inexistence of sexual relationship and is then reflected by the absence of copulation in Baroque art, as we will soon see—Christianity rejects the cosmic balance of the ancient world, which was based upon the assumption of the supreme substance of the fully constituted divine Being. With the theorem of the inexistence of the sexual relationship, Lacan, in fact, aims at the fundamental absence of any measure or *ratio* according to which a harmonic relationship between the two sexes could be established. In other words, the sexual relationship does not exist because there is no signifier which would signify such a relationship.

By speaking the truth halfway, the Christian God is thus desubstantialised and becomes a discursive entity without relying on any substance. This is the moment of atheism within Christianity that psychoanalysis also shares. Moreover, this is ultimately the reason for Lacan's controversial claims, which we already mentioned earlier, that the true formula of atheism is not 'God is dead' but rather 'God is unconscious' and that 'atheism is tenable only to clerics'. These formulae aim precisely at the fact that God in Christianity, unlike the gods in ancient paganisms, is not the positive supreme substance but rather the 'Other qua locus',[28] an empty structural place that not only makes possible but even necessitates the appearance of language as a system of linguistic differences or binary oppositions. The consequences of the fact that the Other as *locus* corresponds to the hole of primal repression (the repression of the first signifier) is not only the inexistence of the sexual relationship but also the fact that the truth can only be said halfway. And according to Lacan, no one half-speaks the truth better than the authors of the Gospels: 'In this vein, you can't say it any better than the Gospels. You can't speak any better of the truth. This is why they are Gospels. You can't even bring the dimension of truth into play any better, in other words, push away reality and fantasy'.[29]

In this context, the Baroque returns to these origins of Christianity, yet it 'still disavows its filthy truth'.[30] It disavows the truth by an additional shift which ultimately corresponds to a perverse 'transcendentalisation' of the fundamental negativity or half-saying of the truth. More specifically, the Baroque replaces the symbolic dimension (half-saying the truth) with the imaginary one (where the truth becomes an object of identification)—while psychoanalysis, in contrast, insists on the separation between the imaginary and the symbolic. To put it differently, in the Baroque, Christianity replaces the truth conceived as a *locus* with the truth conceived as an object—half-saying the truth is replaced with an exposition of truth *about* the inexistence of sexual relationship or the ontological incompleteness of this world.[31]

Let us focus now on Lacan's consideration of Baroque painting more in detail. In his essay 'Exalted Obscenity and the Lawyer of God: Lacan, Deleuze and the Baroque', Lorenzo Chiesa points out Lacan's basic insight regarding the constitution of the so-called field of 'geometral vision'. Taking the example of Holbein's famous painting *The Ambassadors* (1533) which is featured on the front cover of the French edition of Lacan's *Seminar XI,* Chiesa focuses on the famous blurred image or stain which appears at the feet of the two men in the portrait (a stain which, if observed from a different angle, appears as the human skull). Chiesa argues that, for Lacan, the constitutive presupposition of the field of geometral (conscious) vision is the exclusion of such a stain. As soon as one changes the angle and deciphers the stain as a skull, one loses the rest of the picture. This is what Lacan calls 'anamorphosis' which is one of the main characteristics of Baroque paintings. As Chiesa stresses,

> Importantly, as soon as the skull appears, the other figures of the painting—those supported by geometral vision—disappear because of the convergence of the lines of perspective. Lacan carefully distinguishes these two moments of anamorphosis, and by extension of the baroque: that of the emergence of the undecipherable stain within geometral vision, which he understands as an encounter with the void; and that of the satisfying experience of extracting a form from this very void, which nonetheless evokes death, 'the subject as annihilated', and is made possible only at the cost of temporarily losing one's geometral, conscious bearings.[32]

Moving from these premises, Lacan argues that Baroque art in general and particularly paintings of St. Agatha and St. Lucia—the former exhibiting her amputated breasts on a tray before her and the latter exhibiting her gouged-out eyes—integrates the 'stain' (the organ related to a partial drive) into the field of vision. To be precise, the partial object is always already included in the picture, yet it is included as constitutively lacking. By moving beyond castration on the side of the organ, Baroque painting makes present the partial object as an organ in the field of vision—it literally 'exhibits' the castrated object. Simultaneously, this integration of a partial object into the field of vision is accompanied with the exclusion of copulation so that the former actually replaces the latter.[33] Lacan clearly stresses this point:

> In everything that followed from the effects of Christianity, particularly in art—and it's in this respect that I coincide with the 'baroquism' with which I accept to be clothed—everything is exhibition of the body evoking jouissance—and you can lend credence to the testimony of someone who has just come back from an orgy of churches in Italy—but without copulation. If copulation isn't present, it's no accident. It's just as much out of place there as it is in human reality, to which it nevertheless provides sustenance with the fantasies by which that reality is constructed.[34]

As we can see, the Baroque, on the one hand, reflects the inexistence of the sexual relationship by excluding copulation from the field of vision, while, on the other hand, it also replaces this exclusion with the 'exhibition of the body evoking jouissance', that is, with a series of partial objects related to partial drives which, according to Lacan's basic definition, *partially* represent sexuality.[35] However, this replacement, or the fact that images of partial objects in Christian Baroque art appear *at the place* or *instead* of the act of copulation which is excluded from the field of vision, is precisely what constitutes the perverse core of Christianity. As Zupančič points out, what is repressed in such paintings of St. Agatha or St. Lucia is not 'pure enjoyment, "enjoyment for the sake of enjoyment" . . . what is banned, or repressed, is *its link to sexuality*'.[36] The exposure of cut-off breasts or gouged-out eyes separated from the body suggests precisely the idea that the partial drives related to such objects are not shaped with the symbolic function (the barred Other conceived as a symbolic order revolving around the ontological gap which corresponds to the inexistence of sexual relationship). Such images instead suggest that the partial drives are detached from the very function that frames them as partial. The replacement of the Other as barred with the assumption that there is no Other at all (in this world) is the way in which Christianity nonetheless 'disavows its filthy truth', as Chiesa puts it. Yet what is at stake here is not just the disavowal of such truth; instead, as Chiesa argues, this disavowal paves the way to the very 'transcendentalisation' of the inexistence of the sexual relationship precisely by way of giving an 'unprecedented *meaning*'[37] to its filthy truth. In so doing, Lacan argues that Christianity turns the acknowledgement of the inexistence of sexual relationship into the reason for rejecting this world of ontological incompleteness (or catastrophe) while at the same time replacing it with the affirmation of an other-worldly domain of the divine. As Chiesa argues,

> Christ has become one of us to spread the good news that the love of God can eventually save us, but, as Lacan does not fail to add, he can save us only if we concomitantly save *him* from *his* filthy truth. Salvation is preserved by replacing the classical illusion of *jouissance* with the 'abjection' of *this* world, while opposing the latter to *another* world of eternal life. Christianity thus recuperates meaning (salvation and eternal life) precisely thanks to the disclosure of truth as meaninglessness (the abjection of this world). It turns incompleteness into the definitive reason to believe in completeness.[38]

We could complete Chiesa's argument by adding another formulation: what Christianity accomplishes is precisely the transformation of the assumption that there is (immanently) no Other into the idea of an absolute (transcendental) Other. Lacan, in his own way, seems to stress the significance of this perverse reversal or 'transcendentalisation' of the *meaning-*

less truth of the inexistence of the sexual relationship by drawing a far-reaching set of consequences from it. If it is true that Christ's death on the cross does not represent a sacrifice by which God would save humanity (this world), then this does not preclude the possibility that Christ's death may actually represent an attempt at saving God Himself. Lacan is sufficiently clear on this point: 'It is true that the little story of Christ is presented, not as the enterprise of saving man, but as that of saving God. We must recognise that he who took on this enterprise, namely Christ, paid the price—that's the least we can say about it'.[39] In other words, Christ's death on the cross is actually an attempt at saving God *qua* the inexistent Other who is thus brought to life. Lacan does not fail to add that it is thus the appearance of Christianity that confirms the existence of Christ, conceived as a sacrificial victim for God's own salvation: 'The proof of Christ's existence is obvious: it's Christianity'.[40]

Turning back from these arguments to the three versions of Christ's last words on the cross that we discussed in the first part, we should thus stress the interconnectedness between the three moments which constitute the perverse structure of Christianity: the first version of Christ's last words 'My God, my God, why have you deserted me', which are apparently indicating the inexistence of God as a supreme Being, cannot be separated from the other two versions by saying, for instance, that Luke 23:46 ('Father, I put myself in your hands') and John 19:30 ('Everything is done!') represent a kind of 'betrayal' of the originary atheistic moment contained in Matthew 27:46 and in Mark 15:34. The inexistence of the divine Being, its precarious status, does not necessarily contradict the perverse reversal that occurs in Luke and John, where Christ introduces himself in the form of the lost, separated object, a pound of flesh that is about to fill the hole in the Other, thus bringing God into being. On the contrary, the incorporation of the inexistent God into Christ's body, that is, Christ's taking the form of the pound of flesh, is actually the way Christianity and especially the Church sustain themselves through history: 'Christ, even when resurrected from the dead, is valued for his body, and his body is the means by which communion in his presence is incorporation—oral drive—with which Christ's wife, the Church as it is called, contents itself very well, having nothing to expect from copulation'.[41]

IV

Having shown, firstly, how the originary atheistic moment in Christianity (God's death on the cross) actually paves the way for its own perverse reversal enacted already in the Bible (in the three versions of Christ's last words on the cross) and, secondly, how Lacan's account of the Baroque highlights precisely this perverse core of Christianity (its fetishisation and disavowal of the gap in the big Other), it is now time to conclude by briefly explaining how psychoanalysis ultimately differs from the perverse evocation of the inexistence of the big Other. As I already hinted in the previous sections, psychoanalysis thinks this ontological negativity, which takes the form of a constitutive gap inscribed in the Other, immanently, that is, as the impasse or contradiction inherent to symbolic order. But what does it actually mean to think this impasse immanently? In my view, the best way to properly comprehend this decisive thesis is to point out how Lacan himself thought the encounter with this impasse in the moment of traversing the fundamental fantasy at the end of his analytic process.

As already observed, the gap in the big Other corresponds to Freud's hypothesis of primal repression. The latter encompasses the repression of the primal signifier, which was never actual and never conscious. In turn, this primally repressed signifier fixes the drive which thus circulates around the hole of the primally repressed. In so doing, this hole shapes the drive. The symbolic Other conceived in terms of a signifying chain appears at the place of the primally repressed signifier or rather *instead* of it. At the very end of *Seminar XI*, Lacan defines the end of analysis precisely in terms of the subject's encounter with this constitutive primally repressed signifier, which he calls the 'absolute difference': 'The analyst's desire is not a pure desire. It is a desire to obtain absolute difference, a desire which intervenes when, confronted with the primally repressed signifier, the subject is, for the first time, in a position to subject himself to it'.[42] In *Seminar XX*, he fully confirms and further reinforces this thesis by associating the obtainment of absolute difference *qua* the subject's encounter with the primally repressed signifier with the separation between the imaginary and the symbolic. To recall again the crucial passage from *Seminar XX*:

> The aim of my teaching . . . is to dissociate *a* and A by reducing the first to what is related to the imaginary and the other to what is related to the symbolic. It is indubitable that the symbolic is the basis of what was made into God. It is certain that the imaginary is based on the reflection of one semblable in another. And yet, *a* has lent itself to be confused with S(Ⱥ). . . . It is here that the scission or detachment remains to be effectuated.[43]

There are two main points from the last two passages which can be summarised as follows. The subject's encounter with the primally repressed *qua* obtaining absolute difference is articulated as the encounter with the barred Other (S[Ⱥ]), which emerges in the separation between the symbolic (A) and the imaginary (*a*). This detachment of *a* from A can be comprehended also in terms of the de-Oedipisation of the drive. However, and this is of the utmost importance, this detachment does not imply that the subject, once he had passed the moment of subjective destitution, achieves the status of pure drive which would *totally* represent sexuality; rather, the separation from the Other results in the experience of the real *qua* absolute difference, that is, in the experience that the de-Oedipised drive is not unshaped or 'raw', but shaped or 'cooked', as Miller puts it. So when he argues that the 'pre-Oedipal drive is not pre-linguistic or raw' and that 'what Lacan called Other is already there in the drive',[44] we should not misread this formulation to conclude that the drive was shaped with A. Instead, and this would constitute the immanent reading of the Lacanian mantra 'the big Other doesn't exist' (the fact that there is no Other of the Other or no meta-language which would totalise or make One of the symbolic order of language), the experience correlative to the separation from the Other at the end of analysis is precisely the experience that the drive is shaped by the hole of the real, that is, by S(Ⱥ) or the primally repressed signifier. It is only here, we may add, that Christian *a*theism (God as *a*; the substitution of S[Ⱥ] with *a*) truly becomes *a*-theism (the immanent separation between the signifier and the object *a*).

NOTES

1. To the best of my knowledge, Dominiek Hoens is the most radical advocate for the connection between psychoanalysis and its clinical scopes and the invention of the 'new perversion' which Lacan openly searched for but did not find: 'You have heard me more than once saying that psychoanalysis did not even succeed in inventing a new perversion. That is sad' (Lacan cited in Dominiek Hoens, 'Toward a New Perversion: Psychoanalysis', in *Jacques Lacan and the Other Side of Psychoanalysis: Reflections on Seminar XVII*, ed. Justin Clemens and Russell Grigg [Durham, NC, and London: Duke University Press, 2006], 98).
2. Lorenzo Chiesa, 'Exalted Obscenity and the Lawyer of God: Lacan, Deleuze and the Baroque', in *Lacan and Deleuze: A Disjunctive Synthesis*, ed. Boštjan Nedoh and Andreja Zevnik (Edinburgh: Edinburgh University Press, 2017), 152.
3. To be sure, Žižek conceives the 'perverse core of Christianity' in a similar yet slightly different way in his *The Puppet and the Dwarf*. He uses this expression to refer to the vicious circle of Law (prohibition) and its transgression, induced by the 'obscene superego supplement' (Slavoj Žižek, *The Puppet and the Dwarf: The Perverse Core of Christianity* [Cambridge, MA: MIT Press, 2003], 127). For the further reading of this point, also important in the context of Žižek's reading of Paul insofar as it differs from Badiou and Agamben's, see Adam Kotsko's 'Politics and Perversion: Situating Žižek's Paul', *Journal for Cultural and Religious Theory* 9, no. 2 (2008): 43–52. However, Žižek thinks Christian atheism as the revelation of the 'impotence of the big Other' (its ontological incompleteness), and thus precisely as breaking with this vicious circle of superego injunction (Žižek, *The Puppet and the Dwarf*, 127). As I will try to show, this revelation alone does not necessarily imply the break with the perverse superego injunction 'to enjoy!' On the contrary, as Lacan's take on Christian Baroque art confirms, this revelation of the inexistence of the big Other/the transcendent God may itself appear to be the condition of the 'perverse core of Christianity'.
4. Alenka Zupančič, *What Is Sex?* (Cambridge, MA: MIT Press, 2017), 48.
5. To recall the discussion from the beginning of this book, Deleuze was convinced not only that perversion is a structure *without the Other* but also that such an articulation of perversion actually comes from the Lacanian school itself: 'Lacan and his school insist profoundly . . . on the way in which the *difference of sexes* is disavowed by the pervert, in the interest of an androgynous world of *doubles*; on the annulment of the Other inside perversion, on the position of a "beyond the Other" (*un au-delà de*

l'Autre) or of an "otherwise Other" (*un Autre qu'autrui*)' (Gilles Deleuze, *The Logic of Sense*, trans. Mark Lester with Charles Stivale [London: The Athlone Press, 1990], 358).

6. This point has already become a commonplace in Žižek's writing. To list just some of the most important works where he discusses this position: besides *The Puppet and the Dwarf*, see also his *The Parallax View* (Cambridge, MA: MIT Press, 2006); 'From Job to Christ: A Paulinian Reading of Chesterton', in *St. Paul among the Philosophers*, ed. John D. Caputo and Linda Martín Alcoff (Bloomington and Indianapolis: Indiana University Press, 2009), 39–58; and 'The Fear of Four Words: A Modest Plea for the Hegelian Reading of Christianity', in *Monstrosity of Christ: Paradox or Dialectics?*, ed. Creston Davis (Cambridge, MA: MIT Press, 2009), 24–108.

7. Žižek, *The Puppet and the Dwarf*, 125.

8. Ibid.

9. Ibid.; my emphasis.

10. Žižek, 'From Job to Christ', 54.

11. Ibid., 44.

12. Ibid., 55.

13. Literally: 'The distance of man from God is thus the distance of God from Himself' (ibid.).

14. Ibid., 53.

15. See especially chapter 8 in this book.

16. See, again, Zupančič, *What Is Sex?*, 48.

17. Jacques Lacan, *The Seminar of Jacques Lacan, Book XI: The Four Fundamental Concepts of Psychoanalysis* (hereafter abbreviated as *Seminar XI*), trans. Alan Sheridan (London and New York: W. W. Norton and Co., 1998), 29–30.

18. 'The aim of my teaching (. . .) is to dissociate *a* and A by reducing the first to what is related to the imaginary and the other to what is related to the symbolic. It is indubitable that the symbolic is the basis of what was made into God. It is certain that the imaginary is based on the reflection of one semblable in another. And yet, *a* has lent itself to be confused with S(Ⱥ) (. . .). It is here that the scission or detachment remains to be effectuated' (Jacques Lacan, *The Seminar of Jacques Lacan, Book XX: Encore, On Feminine Sexuality, the Limits of Love and Knowledge* [hereafter abbreviated as *Seminar XX*], trans. Bruce Fink [London and New York: W. W. Norton and Co., 1999], 83).

19. Chiesa, 'Exalted Obscenity', 142.

20. Lorenzo Chiesa, *The Not-Two: Logic and God in Lacan* (Cambridge, MA: MIT Press, 2016), xii; my emphasis.

21. Ibid.

22. Lacan, *Seminar XI*, 59.

23. Jacques Lacan, *The Seminar of Jacques Lacan, Book XVII: The Other Side of Psychoanalysis*, trans. Russell Grigg (London and New York: W. W. Norton and Co., 2007), 119.

24. Lacan, *Seminar XX*, 107.

25. Ibid., 108.

26. Just to recall the famous first passage from Lacan's *Television*: 'I always speak the truth. Not the whole truth, because there's no way, to say it all. Saying it all is literally impossible: words fail. Yet it's through this very impossibility that the truth holds onto the real' (Jacques Lacan, *Television*, trans. Dennis Hollier et al. [London and New York: W. W. Norton and Co., 1990], 3).

27. Lacan unfolds this articulation in his failed Seminar on the 'Names-of-the-Father' (see Jacques Lacan, 'Introduction to the Names-of-the-Father Seminar', trans. Jeffrey Mehlman, *October* 40 [1987]: 81–95).

28. Lacan, *Seminar XX*, 114. Insofar as God is conceived here as the *locus* of the speech as such, this is why Lacan can insist that 'as long as the things are said, the God hypothesis will persist' (ibid., 45).

29. Ibid., 107.

30. Chiesa, 'Exalted Obscenity', 152.

31. And correspondingly, for Lacan, 'what analytic discourse dislodges *puts truth in its place*' (Lacan, *Seminar XX*, 108; my emphasis).
32. Chiesa, 'Exalted Obscenity', 146.
33. As Zupančič has noted, this point is surprisingly close to Foucault's position on the link between sexuality and pleasure because Foucault himself, like the Christian tradition, insisted very much on the necessity of disassociating pleasure from sexuality, accusing psychoanalysis of making, in his view, an unjustified connection between the two. See Zupančič, 'Biopolitics, Sexuality and the Unconscious', *Paragraph* 39, no. 1 (2016): 49–64, and *What* Is *Sex?*, 14–15.
34. Lacan, *Seminar XX*, 113.
35. To recall again: 'If all is confusion in the discussion of the sexual drives it is because one does not see that the drive represents no doubt, but *merely* represents, and partially at that, the curve of fulfilment of sexuality in the living being' (Lacan, *Seminar XI*, 177).
36. Zupančič, *What* Is *Sex?*, 14.
37. Chiesa, 'Exalted Obscenity', 152.
38. Ibid.
39. Lacan, *Seminar XX*, 108.
40. Ibid., 112.
41. Ibid., 113.
42. Lacan, *Seminar XI*, 276.
43. Lacan, *Seminar XX*, 83.
44. Jacques-Alain Miller, 'On Perversion', in *Reading Seminars I and II: Lacan's Return to Freud*, ed. Richard Feldstein, Bruce Fink, and Maire Jaanus (New York: State University of New York Press, 1996), 315.

TEN

The Sadistic Superego

From the Prohibition to the Imperative of Jouissance

I

In psychoanalytic theory, Lacan's inversion of Freud's view on the superego is well known.[1] It is usually generalised and reduced as follows: Freud interprets the superego as the agency prohibiting *jouissance*, while Lacan defines the superego as an imperative imposing *jouissance* ('Nothing forces anyone to enjoy (*jouir*) except the superego. The superego is the imperative of jouissance—Enjoy!'[2]). In this chapter, I will primarily focus on the conditions of possibility of such an inversion and, more precisely, on the conceptual shifts that enabled Lacan to define the superego as the agency that imposes the imperative of *jouissance* on the subject. I will argue that such a definition of the superego was not present in Lacan's theory from the very beginning of his seminar work, and that Lacan was able to formulate it only after a very specific set of conceptual rearticulations and inventions. Specifically, the formulation at stake became possible only when Lacan essentially redefined the concept of the object as the object *a* proper. This redefinition occurred only at a very precise point in Lacan's theory—from *Seminar X* on *Anxiety* onwards. In summary, I will argue that it is only by way of a closer inspection of the rearticulation of the object *a* in *Seminar X* that it becomes clear where the so-called sadistic nature of the superego comes from and, secondly, whether such a redefinition of the superego also actually involves Lacan's 'inversion' of Freud—or to what extent Lacan took credit, or at least part of the credit, for a gesture which is already in Freud himself.

We should therefore start directly with Freud's—anything but simple—conceptualisation of the superego. If we say that his conceptualisation is not simple, it is first and foremost because, in Freud, the superego can by no means be univocally reduced to the agency of prohibition. In his 1914 essay 'On Narcissism: An Introduction', he defines the agency of conscience, which, at this level, is a partial synonym for the superego and from which the superego—in combination with the ego ideal—is later derived, as a middle term between the ego and the ego ideal. The latter represents the point of imaginary identification at which, in the process of its formation, the ego has to be alienated: 'It would not surprise us if we were to find a special psychical agency which performs the task of seeing that narcissistic satisfaction from the ego ideal is ensured and which, with this end in view, constantly watches the actual ego and measures it by that ideal'.[3]

Freud names the moment of alienation or identification with the ego ideal 'secondary narcissism'. The state of primary narcissism is the state when the ego is not yet alienated by any external agency and the satisfaction of narcissistic drives takes place within the ego itself. At a certain point, however, this process runs into its limit or, better yet, to the limit of the ego. Due to the accumulation of the libido, the ego is forced to pass beyond its limits and direct the drive-cathexis towards some external agency, which, however, is not yet an object agency proper at the level of which we can talk about object libido. On the contrary, as Freud stresses in the above quote, the ego ideal, which is the first point of identification, is the continuation, as it were, of (primary) narcissism with different means. The ego is here alienated into an external image precisely in order to continue to satisfy its narcissistic drives.[4]

But as Freud's discussion implies, this identification is not autonomous; it needs its reality to be verified. What guarantees to the ego that the image of the ideal in which it recognises itself is truly the ego itself? The point here is not only that the agency of the ideal is formed on the basis of 'the critical influence of his parents (conveyed to him by the medium of the *voice*)',[5] but that the double-pole system of the ego and the ideal needs a third agency that is also introduced from the outside. For this purpose, an agency that Freud first names 'conscience' and defines as the moment of assessing the compromise between the ego and its ideal emerges in the psychical apparatus.

II

In his 1923 essay 'The Ego and the Id', Freud presents a more complex picture of this division. He foregrounds two seemingly contradictory theses in section III of this essay. On the one hand, Freud is aware that the condition of possibility of dividing the undifferentiated category of the 'parents' into the 'father' and the 'mother'—and thereby the condition of the Oedipus complex of course—is the experience of the difference between the sexes, that is, the detection of the missing (male) sex organ in the woman.[6] Before this subjective experience, it is thus impossible to distinguish between object-cathexis (for the mother) and identification (with the father). In fact, Freud himself admits this when he says that, in this phase of the child's development, that is, 'at the very beginning, in the individual's primitive oral phase, object-cathexis and identification are no doubt indistinguishable from each other'.[7] This is why at this level Freud also suggests that we should understand primary identification, which is the 'individual's first and most important identification, his identification with the father in his own personal prehistory',[8] ultimately as the identification with the 'parents' as a sexually undifferentiated other that gives the child the first support or the first external image through which it can experience itself as an imaginary whole.

But it is precisely this thesis that Freud will revise a few paragraphs later. When he gives a simplified reconstruction of the development of the Oedipus complex in a male child, he says that object-cathexis and identification nevertheless need to be distinguished already at the pre-Oedipal level. Identification and object-cathexis are here defined as two independent processes that run into each other only at a certain point of development, and this short circuit causes the emergence of the Oedipus complex. Despite the fact that, in this second step, Freud moves the mentioned difference to the level of 'prehistory', that is, to the pre-Oedipal phase, it is quite clear that it gains its true value only when both processes enter into a contradiction, a contradiction that is not contingent of course but is triggered by a precisely determined move, namely, the prohibition of the object-cathexis for the mother. This gesture of prohibition is correlative both to the experience of the difference between the mother and the father and to the difference between identification and object-cathexis. It is only through such a prohibition that a child can experience the mother as an external object of satisfaction and the father as an agency imposing the prohibition.

It is here that Freud notes a difference, albeit a minimal one, between the ego ideal and the superego, which were completely indistinguishable at the beginning. We could say that the superego is constituted as a prohibition that limits the reach of the ego ideal. The narcissistic identification/object-cathexis/alienation of the ego into the ego ideal (the undifferentiated image of the parents) is here split so that the place of the ego ideal is filled by the identification with the father, which the superego limits by prohibiting the object-cathexis for the mother, thereby also imposing its repression. In other words, the superego differentiates itself from the ego ideal by establishing itself not only as an imperative which imposes the identification of the ego with the ego ideal but also as a singular prohibition limiting the domain of this identification by imposing the repression of the mother's desire—and this is the point where the figure of the father is established as the figure of exception.[9]

What is obvious in Freud's modification of his own starting point is that the superego is differentiated from the ego ideal only in the Oedipal phase, at the level of the subject's history and not the subject's 'prehistory' (that is, in the pre-Oedipal phase). So what does Freud's evident oscillation between inscribing the genesis of the superego in the pre-Oedipal phase of the development of the human psyche and inscribing it in the (post-)Oedipal phase tell us? What, relatedly, is the meaning of Freud's evident inability to unambiguously either differentiate or equate the ego ideal and the superego—which would imply a forced choice between conceiving the superego as a prohibition that limits identification or as an imperative that imposes the identification with the father without limitations, a choice that would obviously exclude the synthesis of both moments as a third option?

Perhaps the seeming oscillation itself is already part of the answer to the quandary of the superego, an answer that can be found precisely in Freud's decision to locate the origin or condition of the superego's post-Oedipal manifestation in the pre-Oedipal phase. At this point, it is worth repeating Freud's emphasis from 'On Narcissism: An Introduction', which despite its seeming randomness and lesser significance, already anticipates all the key elements that will play a crucial role in Lacan's articulation of the superego. To recall Freud's argument, 'what prompted the subject to form an ego ideal, on whose behalf his conscience acts as watchman, arose from the critical influence of his parents (conveyed to him by the medium of the *voice*)'.[10] If we take into account the above presentation of Freud's points from 'The Ego and the Id' and recall that conscience, which is here a 'watchman' of the ego ideal, is actually a synonym for what later appears as the superego, then we see that Freud here adds a third element: the 'voice'. The latter is, in temporal terms, placed in the subject's pre-Oedipal phase or prehistory—a period when there is no experience of sexual difference and of the differentiation of the nondifferentiated image of the 'parents' into the father and mother. The first imaginary formative function of the 'parents' actually appears here in the form of an image into which the ego (formatively) alienates itself, while the alienation itself is conveyed through their 'critical influence', that is, 'the voice' as a material bearer which is irreducible to the 'image' of the parents.

III

To return to where we began in this chapter, what is at the core of Lacan's thesis that the superego as the imperative of *jouissance* is precisely Freud's conception of the direct relation, not between the superego and the image but between the superego and the 'voice of the Other', that is, the fragment of the real in the form of object *a*, to which the imperative evidently and directly refers. And the privileged example of object *a* at this level is precisely the 'voice of the Other', so the parental agency:

> The voice of the Other should be considered an essential object. Every analyst is solicited to accord it its place. Its various incarnations should be followed, as much in the realm of psychosis as at that extremity of normal functioning in the formation of the superego. Through seeing the *petit a* source of the superego, it is possible that many things will become more clear.[11]

So we can see that the superego and the ego ideal differ in at least one essential degree: the superego does not originate in the imaginary specular image of the Other but in the voice of the Other. To be clear, Lacan does not say that object *a* is already the superego (if this were the case, one could hardly argue for the difference between the drive and the superego, which is crucial for Lacan's ethics)[12] but that it is rather its 'source'. This is where we come across the core of the problem: the difference between the imaginary image and the voice as object *a*. And as we have already hinted, this is precisely a difference that is not evident in Lacan from the very beginning but is introduced only at a later point. It is no coincidence that we find the quote in his failed seminar 'Names-of-the-Father', which immediately follows and continues the conceptual break that Lacan introduced a year before in *Seminar X* on *Anxiety*.[13] This break concerns Lacan's rearticulation of the object as object *a*, that is, not as an image but as an unsymbolisable remainder, a fragment of the real irreducible to any dialectic (of desire) and the construction of the imaginary, as Lacan had proposed in the previous phase of his seminar.

This new claim can perhaps best be illustrated by Lacan's modification of his own theory of the mirror stage in *Seminar X*. To illustrate the formative function of imaginary identification, he famously argues that the child's ego as such is formed at the point of alienation into, and identification with, its imaginary image—the specular image.[14] Lacan defines this primary identification as the 'ideal ego', which is also the 'rootstock of secondary identifications'.[15] According to Lacan, this means that the child—aged between six and eighteen months—assumes its specular image 'prior to being objectified in the dialectic of identification with the other [secondary identification], and before language restores to it, in the universal, its function as subject'.[16] In short, this stage becomes the prototype of identification and will enable every subsequent identification of the child with its doubles. But towards the end of the same essay, Lacan somewhat loosens this categorical division between primary identification and all the other copies which are modelled on it or derived from it. The final moment of the mirror stage and thereby the moment of primary identification, the moment in which 'the mirror stage comes to an end', is already the moment of (secondary) 'identification with the imago of one's *semblable* and the drama of primordial jealousy', with which the mirror stage introduces 'the dialectic that will henceforth link the *I* to socially elaborated situations'.[17] The point here is of course the following: however primitive or raw the image with which the ego identifies itself may be, like the reflection of one's own face on the surface of water, it is always the image of the other. The ego's constitution is thus contaminated by the paradox of alienation: the ego can be formed only through the nonego, that is, through the *other*—hence, after all, Lacan's continuous recourse to Rimbaud's modernistic formula *I is another* ('Je est un autre').[18] In short, the imaginary identification is, on the one hand, formative for the ego, yet, on the other hand, precisely because the ego is formed through the *other*, it generates the ego's frustration: How can it be an ego at all if it is formed through the other? In short, the *place* of the ego is thus assumed by the other.

However, what is crucial is that, in both cases, the primary identification of the mirror stage also represents the function of 'libidinal normalisation'.[19] With this term, Lacan refers to the fact that the *entire* quantity of the libido flowing from the id is invested *without remainder* into this specular image, with which the child's ego is formed.

As I have mentioned, Lacan, in his *Seminar X* on *Anxiety*, adds to this familiar set-up a detail that entirely shifts emphasis:

> Already, just in the exemplary little image with which the demonstration of the mirror stage begins, the moment that is said to be *jubilatory* when the child, grasping himself in the inaugural experience of recognition in the mirror, comes to terms with himself as a totality functioning as such in his specular image, haven't I always insisted on the movement that the infant makes? This movement is so frequent, constant I'd say, that each and every one of you may have some recollection of it. Namely, he turns round, I noted, to the one supporting him who's there behind him. If we force ourselves to assume the content of the infant's experience and to reconstruct the sense of this movement, we shall say that, with this mutating movement of the head, which turns toward the adult as if to call upon his assent, and then back to the image, he seems to be asking the one supporting him, and who here represents the big Other, to ratify the value of this image.[20]

Unlike his initial conception of the mirror stage, in which the identification with the specular image precedes both the secondary imaginary identifications and the constitution of the subject by way of entering into language, Lacan here says that not only does the abstract presence of the Other precede, or is simultaneous with, the mirror stage, but that this presence *in concreto* supports or ratifies the value of primary identification in the mirror stage. This need for ratification opens a wholly new field. To put it simply, what does the child find in turning round to the parent behind him? He finds precisely the signifier, the signifying gesture ratifying the value of primary identification. This leads to consequences that completely change the emphasis of Lacan's original reading: the child's gesture of 'turning to the Other', which is precisely the *locus* where the child finds the signifier awaiting for him, is the price that the subject has to pay. In Lacan's words, 'not all of the libidinal investment passes by way of the specular image. There's a remainder'.[21]

It is precisely because of the fact that the imaginary ego is confirmed by the signifier which comes from the Other, which is also why not all of the libidinal investment of the id passes by way of the specular image ('there's a remainder'), that Lacan is able to extrapolate the theory of an absolute and nondialecticisable remainder, the remainder that is excluded from symbolisation and the dialectic of desire, the remainder named object *a*. Here, the object *a* no longer appears as an image (*i'*[*a*]) but as the remainder of the libido, which does not pass by way of the specular image but is rather satisfied on one's own body or on the topological holes of the body that, due to their particular anatomical structure, are predisposed to function as zones of *jouissance*. The narcissistic gaze at one's own image is thus contaminated by the signifier that comes from the Other but at the same time defies the dialectic of symbolisation. The pleasure of seeing one's own body totalised in the specular image is thus immediately replaced by the pleasure of being seen by the Other. However, this pleasure of 'being seen' should not be conceived in terms of the dialectic of recognition or desire. Instead this gaze as object is what falls out from the dialectics of desire and, due to this exclusion, it functions as that dialectic's driver—after all, Lacan insists that the object *a* is the object-cause of desire, which is to say, that it generates the dialectic of desire only insofar as it is internally excluded from symbolisation. This remainder is what Lacan explains not only later in the same seminar by referring to the 'detumescence' of the phallic organ during orgasm, which means a real separation or independence of the organ from the body, its 'evanescence' from the field of the imaginary whole, but also in *Seminar XI* by referring to the myth of the lamella as the unreal, undead organ of *jouissance*.

Crucial in this articulation of the nondialecticisable remainder is Lacan's reference to the anatomy of bodily orifices we have already discussed. To recall, Lacan wants to point out the separate presence of a 'pound of flesh', of the libido as the real, which precedes and is basically independent of the moment of symbolic castration and the emergence of any agency of castration. Hence Lacan's thesis that real anxiety is not castration anxiety, which presupposes the 'agent of castration': anxiety emerges precisely upon the appearance of the real remainder of the libido in the form of *jouissance* before the intervention of any (Oedipal) agent of castration. The reminder of the libido thus relates to castration in a linguistic sense, that is, to the primal repression or the barred Other, which is from a structural point of view prior to the emergence of any 'agent of castration'. The separation in question here is the separation of bodily orifices, in which we find the remainder of the libido that had been left over from the investment in the specular image. It is due to this anatomic particularity (with the surface of the body passing from the outside to the inside) that bodily orifices can function as a topology of the erogenous zones whose surface is the 'source' of the drive's *konstante Kraft*, constant force.

IV

At this point, it is worth returning to Lacan's initial thesis that the object *a* is the source of the superego. As we can see, the superego emerges when the object *a* is bound not with the hole in the Other, but with the signifier. If the superego is the materialisation, the embodiment of the 'voice of the Other', this means that the agency of symbolic castration has already intervened in the psychic economy. Yet this moment marks nothing else but the (postgenital) displacement of the original (pre-genital) object/*jouissance*. So in other words, if the circulation of the drive is the materialisation of that ontological negativity set up by primal repression, then the superego, by bounding together the object with the signifier, attaches the subject to this circulation itself, so that along the bare repetition of ontological negativity performed by the drive, the subject is forced to enjoy. In consequence, the repetition of that negativity is displaced onto the side of the subject, as that subject's very impossibility of catching the object in the field of the Other.

Freud's oscillation between conceiving the superego as the instance which imposes the identification with the father, on the one hand, and conceiving it as the instance of prohibition or limitation of such identification, on the other, here achieves its full significance. Namely, the superego as the 'voice of the Other' imposes identification with the father, yet this identification is impossible to fulfil insofar as the figure of the father is by definition exceptional: the repressed desire of the mother is allowed to him only. The superego is thus, as Žižek and Zupančič have argued many times, the obscene supplement of the symbolic figure of the father, which sustains this very figure in a sadistic manner: it invites the subject to transgress the limit or boundary set up by symbolic prohibition, yet it does not say what awaits the subject on the other side of the boundary, so to speak. It does not admit that even the Other does not know what is on the other side of symbolic prohibition insofar as there is only an ontological lack of knowledge, which amounts to the inexistence of sexual relationship for speaking beings. In this way, the superego replaces the *structural impossibility* of total *jouissance* (Freudian *ganze Sexualstrebung*) with the *subjective impossibility of* enjoying 'like the father'. The subject is guilty not because he does not enjoy at all but precisely because he does enjoy but *only partially*. The superego's injunction of *jouissance* is thus inextricably bound with the imposition of a guilt which derives from the fact that the subject always misperceives his enjoyment, as if it were his fault for failing to achieve the total *jouissance* which is imposed on him via the ideal of the father. In this respect, Andreja Zevnik was right to point out that 'the perversion of law is complete only in the face of the superego'.[22]

This is precisely where we run into the problem of squaring the circle of the psychic economy of the superego. If the drive circulates around the point of the primal repressed or ontological negativity (the primary repression of the first signifier) and thus only partially represents sexuality (the primal repression establishes the sexual relationship conceived as One as essentially absent or impossible), then we have to say that the prohibition imposed by the symbolic law refers precisely to the prohibition of something impossible that is constitutively absent from the very beginning—the enigma of the desire of the Other, that is, the mother's desire as repressed, is also an enigma for the mother herself. It is only at this point that the superego as the 'voice of the Other' can function as a real imperative of *jouissance*, a command that imposes on the subject the transgression of the prohibition, the transgression of the limit established by the symbolic law. Put somewhat more schematically, the superego imposes on the subject the imperative of satisfaction in the form of transgression of the prohibition, but what is promised as the result or the 'award' for this transgression simply does not exist. Such is the sadistic nature of the superego: what it demands from the subject is the transgression of the limit posited by the symbolic law, but because what is prohibited is impossible and not actually existent, the transgression by definition always fails. The subject's guilt thus originates in the fact that the subject never finds full satisfaction in any satisfaction. Satisfaction, however, is also never completely absent; rather, it is always partial, so there is never enough *jouissance* that would be at the level of the fantasy about the father's *jouissance* of the mother's body. The reason for this is that the 'measure' with which *jouissance* is measured is a negative measure.

The essential trait of the superego (as the obscene other side of symbolic law) thus lies, as Joan Copjec has remarked, in prohibiting something (and in inviting the transgression of this prohibition) but also in never saying what the prohibited object is: 'The prohibition proper to the superego renders something unsayable and undoable, to be sure, but it does not say *what* we should not say or do; it merely imposes a limit that makes everything we do and say seem as nought compared to what we cannot'.[23] However, the superego does not say what lies beyond the prohibition because the prohibited constitutively defies symbolisation and exists only by being permanently (fantasmatically) displaced into infinity. As Lacan does not fail to add in this regard, 'That is why the superego, which I qualified earlier as based on the (imperative) "Enjoy!", is a correlative of castration, the latter being the sign with which an avowal dresses itself up (*se pare*), the avowal that jouissance of the Other, of the body of the Other, is promoted only on the basis of infinity (*de l'infinitude*)'.[24] The fantasy that supports this displacement into infinity is the fantasy of the chimeric body of total *jouissance* or, as Lacan says—and we have to take him literally here—the fantasy of the *jouissance* of the 'body of the Other', so no longer the partial satisfactions related to the anatomy of bodily orifices but the total *jouissance* of the body without organs in its imaginary (noncastrated) whole from which nothing would be excluded.

This is why one of the possible subjective reactions to the superego's sadistic pressure is to disavow castration by way of direct identification with the object *a*, in other words, by way of perversion in a more narrow clinical sense. Such a self-objectivation of the subject[25] represents the attempt to escape guilt by way of instrumentalising oneself as the object-instrument of the Other's *jouissance*. In this sense, we could say that the pervert actually reverses the famous Freudian motto *Wo Es War, Soll Ich Verden* (Where id is, there shall ego be) which epitomises the clinical scope of Freudian psychoanalysis. In the perverse self-objectivation of the subject, we are not dealing with the separation between the imaginary object and the hole in the Other which accounts to the gap of the unconscious. On the contrary, the pervert disavows this gap precisely by bringing the object to the place of the ego, that is, by way of directly identifying with the object of (Other's) *jouissance* itself.

V

Let us focus in more detail in this last section on the relation between the so-conceived superego and the so-called formulae of sexuation as developed by Lacan in his *Seminar XX*. To do so, we will be able to draw a more precise contrast between Lacan's and Deleuze's position with respect to perversion, which is conceived by Deleuze, but not by Lacan, as 'beyond the Other'. In fact, it seems quite straightforward to argue here that the logic of repression and prohibition characteristic of the superego is also the logic that governs the male side of formulae of sexuation—it is thus no wonder that Lacan explicitly assigns 'polymorphous perversion' exclusively to the male position.[26] As Joan Copjec states, Lacan, by drawing upon Kant's antinomies of pure reason, presents the male side of sexuation with two contradictory logical propositions, both of which are true:

> $\exists x{-}\Phi x$ (there is at least one *x* that is not submitted to the phallic function)
> $\forall x \Phi x$ (all *x*s are [every x is] submitted to the phallic function)[27]

Both formulas, taken together, show nothing other than the construction of universality on the foundation of an excluded exception. All men are submitted to the phallic function—that is, in order to symbolically exist in the realm of the Other, they must lose a part of (their own) being (the subject as a 'lack of being')—on the condition that one (the fantasmatic

Primal father of the horde—*Urvater*) is not. If the figure of the Primal father is associated with the realm of freedom from the realm of prohibition, this is because he has, albeit fantasmatically, access to the desire for the mother, which is precisely what must be repressed and prohibited by all other symbolically existing men.

At this point, fetishistic disavowal is the mechanism to indirectly satisfy—by way of displacement onto a supplemental object—this repressed desire for the mother *as phallic*. More precisely, it is the construction of the fetish that constitutes the phallic or fantasmatic 'beyond' of the image of mother, as 'beyond' sustains the illusion of her phallic status. As we can see, fetishistic disavowal is here far from avoiding or even dismissing repression and prohibition; rather, it is inextricably connected with and conditioned by it. Thus, what Deleuze misreads in Lacan's theory of perversion in general and that of masochism in particular is the fact that the transgression of prohibition (or disavowing castration by way of fully assuming it, as in the case of masochism) doesn't result in the realisation of the sexual relationship in the sense of the *total* satisfaction of drives (Freudian *ganze Sexualstrebung*), which would at this point be freed from the fixation on the primal repressed signifier or inexistence of the sexual relationship. In other words, a man in an incestuous relation with his mother still doesn't reach the point of relating to her as *The* Woman (*La* femme), that is, as woman existing symbolically in the same way man does. To explain this, it seems worthwhile to unpack the logic that governs the feminine side of the formulae of sexuation. As was the case with man's formula, Lacan here, too, presents the feminine side in two logical propositions:

- $\exists x{-}\Phi x$ (there is not one *x* that is not submitted to the phallic function)
- $\forall x \Phi x$ (not all [not every] *x* is submitted to the phallic function)

Taken together, these two propositions logically restate Lacan's clear emphasis on the problem of woman's position with respect to the phallic function. Contrary to the dominant reading, which regards woman as simply excluded from the phallic function, Lacan insists that woman *is* submitted to the phallic function ('there is no woman [no *x*] which is not submitted to the phallic function'): the point is only that she is 'not-all' within it, that something (feminine *jouissance*) is added to her being in the phallic function.[28] In the last instance, this is the point of Lacan's expression 'beyond the phallus'[29] in relation to feminine *jouissance*: something more (*en plus*) is added to the fantasmatic (and therefore failed) totality of phallic *jouissance* supported by fantasy. In this respect, the *en plus* of feminine *jouissance* clearly indicates the infinity that is characteristic of the feminine position: contrary to the male side, which is based upon the exception that allows its symbolic existence in the realm of the Other, the female side is determined by the inexistent Other S(Ⱥ), that is, by the inexistence of the exception that would guarantee the symbolic existence of woman. Consequently, this is why woman does not exist as universal but only ex-sists as singular and can be counted only as singular, as one-by-one. However, this counting one-by-one never achieves totality, which would in the last instance only allow the finality of woman's existence (in the symbolic, that is, as universal). In short, Lacan argues that, where the logic of the male side is the logic of prohibition, the logic of the female side is the logic of impossibility: it is impossible to reach the totality (universality) of Woman.

This conclusion above all indicates that in Lacan's formulae of sexuation, 'man' and 'woman' indicate two different ways, rather than one single way, of expressing the failure of the sexual relationship—and, most importantly, as Joan Copjec stresses, their sum does not form any 'totality'. As she puts it, 'The sexual relation fails for two reasons: it is impossible and it is prohibited. Put these two failures together; you will never come up with a whole'.[30] It is precisely this that constitutes the very core of the problem in Deleuze's misreading of Lacan's theory of perversion which, according to Deleuze, points to the structure of perversion as the structure without or beyond the Other as symbolic order. For Lacan, however, there is no such thing as the univocity of being precisely because being, insofar as it is sexuated, implies not simply two different ontological positions but two failures of ontology. Put differently, in the (a-)topos of the 'absolute Outside' as 'beyond the Other', there doesn't appear a fully constituted sexual relationship in which Man could relate himself to Woman without any lack. On the contrary, the shift from the male to the female side of sexuation does not imply the abolishment of the phallic function as the common denominator that determines both sides. Rather, the 'beyond the phallus' of the feminine position implies the *nontotalisation* of *jouissance* as such, or as Lorenzo Chiesa has put it, a '*non*totalisation' whose condition of possibility—that is, the condition of its failure—*is* the phallic function and therefore has castration as its correlative.[31] If the male position is governed by the repressed and prohibited desire for the mother as correlative to the figure of the father, then the pervert, by transgressing this prohibition, does not achieve a relation to *The* Woman. Or, rather, he relates to Woman only at the price of turning perversion into 'père-version'—literally, 'Father-version' (which is in French a homophone for perversion).[32] This is the ultimate meaning of Lacan's theorem that Woman is one of the Names-of-the-Father, or God: the transgression of the paternal prohibition leads the subject not to ultimate and final *jouissance* but rather to the topological position where *jouissance* itself becomes infinite or nontotalisable precisely because of the *en plus* of feminine *jouissance*.

NOTES

1. See, for example, Alenka Zupančič, *Ethics of the Real: Kant and Lacan* (London and New York: Verso, 2000), 140–70; Slavoj Žižek, *In Defence of Lost Causes* (London and New York: Verso, 2008), 89–90; 242–43.

2. Jacques Lacan, *The Seminar of Jacques Lacan, Book XX: Encore*, trans. Bruce Fink (London and New York: W. W. Norton & Co., 1999) (hereafter abbreviated as *Seminar XX*), 3.

3. Sigmund Freud, 'On Narcissism: An Introduction', in *The Standard Edition of the Complete Psychological Works of Sigmund Freud, Vol. XIV*, ed. James Strachey (London: Vintage, 2001), 95.

4. For the sake of clarity, we should add at this point that Freud's concept of 'primary narcissism' is a theoretical extrapolation for analytic purpose which is constructed on the basis of his observation of an empirically present 'secondary narcissism'. In fact, Freud is not at all concerned with the question of whether 'primary narcissism' really exists or not but much more on the role this construction can play in setting up of the metapsychological theory of the drive. This thesis becomes unequivocal in the essay 'The Ego and the Id' (1923), where Freud defines the moment of the division between the ego and the id—with the former playing the role of the psychic representative of the external world (through its identifications with external images) in the latter—in terms of 'secondary narcissism'. Following this account, one can assume that primary narcissism, if it would have existed, should be prior to the emergence of the ego: 'Now that we have distinguished between the ego and the id, we must recognise the id as the great reservoir of libido indicated in my paper on narcissism. The libido which flows into the ego owing to the identifications described above brings about its "secondary narcissism"' (Sigmund Freud, 'The Ego and the Id', in *The Standard Edition of the Complete Psychological Works of Sigmund Freud, Vol. XIX*, ed. James Strachey [London: Vintage, 2001], 30, note).

5. Freud, 'On Narcissism', 96; my emphasis. Here Freud immediately adds that to the parental agency 'were added, as time went on, those who trained and taught him and the innumerable and indefinable host of all the other people in his environment—his fellow-man—and public opinion' (ibid.).

6. 'Perhaps it would be safer to say "with the parents"; for before a child has arrived at definite knowledge of the difference between the sexes, the lack of a penis, it does not distinguish in value between its father and its mother' (Freud, 'The Ego and the Id', 31, note). Thus, as Freud continues, the discussion is limited on the 'the identification with the father' only for the sake of simplicity, that is, 'in order to simplify my presentation' (ibid.).

7. Ibid., 29.

8. Ibid., 31.

9. This duality of the superego, which simultaneously imposes on the ego an identification with the father and constrains/prohibits this very same identification, is epitomised in Freud's brilliant formulation: 'Its [superego's] relation to the ego is not exhausted by the precept: "You *ought to be* like this (like your father)". It also comprises the prohibition: "You *may not be* like this (like your father)—that is, you may not do all that he does; some things are his prerogative"' (ibid., 34). Setting up a limit to identification obviously makes possible the prohibition of the mother as the object of libidinal satisfaction (the prohibition of incest).

10. Freud, 'On Narcissism', 96.

11. Jacques Lacan, 'Introduction to the Names-of-the-Father Seminar' (henceforward abbreviated as 'Names-of-the-Father'), trans. Jeffrey Mehlman, *October* 40 (1987): 87.

12. To be sure, it is precisely because of the fact that the voice and the superego are not ontologically bound together but become synthesised, so to speak, only in a post-Oedipal stage that Mladen Dolar can argue for a crucial distinction between the 'ethics of the voice' and the 'voice of the superego'—the ethical voice is thus the voice which

is not of the superego. See Mladen Dolar, *A Voice and Nothing More* (Cambridge, MA: MIT Press, 2006), 88–103.

13. Jacques-Alain Miller, 'Jacques Lacan's Seminar on *Anxiety*', trans. Barbara P. Fulks, *Lacanian Ink* 26 (2005): 21–28.

14. In this brief overview of Lacan's 'mirror stage' and the formative function of the imaginary identification, I rely also on Lorenzo Chiesa's reading in his *Subjectivity and Otherness* (Cambridge, MA: MIT Press, 2007), 12–32, and his 'The World of Desire: Lacan between Evolutionary Biology and Psychoanalytic Theory', *Filozofski vestnik* 30, no. 2 (2009): 83–112.

15. Jacques Lacan, 'The Mirror Stage as Formative of the *I* Function as Revealed in Psychoanalytic Experience', in *Écrits: The First Complete Edition in English*, trans. Bruce Fink (London and New York: W. W. Norton and Co., 2006), 76.

16. Ibid.

17. Ibid., 79.

18. Lacan discusses Rimbaud's formula in relation to imaginary identification in detail in his essay 'Aggressiveness in Psychoanalysis' (in *Écrits*, 82–101), which was written in 1948, that is, a year before the presentation of 'The Mirror Stage' (1949). In this respect, 'Aggressiveness in Psychoanalysis' features as a more in-depth anticipation of 'The Mirror Stage' intervention.

19. Lacan, 'The Mirror Stage', 76.

20. Jacques Lacan, *The Seminar of Jacques Lacan, Book X: Anxiety* (hereafter abbreviated as *Seminar X*), trans. A. R. Price (Cambridge and Malden, MA: Polity Press, 2014), 32; translation modified.

21. Ibid., 38.

22. Andreja Zevnik, 'Kant avec Sade: Ethics Entrapped in Perversions of Law and Politics', in *Jacques Lacan between Psychoanalysis and Politics*, ed. Samo Tomšič and Andreja Zevnik (London and New York: Routledge, 2016), 222.

23. Joan Copjec, *Read My Desire: Lacan Against the Historicists*, second edition (London and New York: Verso, 2015 [1994]), 236.

24. Lacan, *Seminar XX*, 7–8.

25. As Lacan puts it in *Seminar XI*, 'Next time, I shall come back to what I have called the structure of perversion. Strictly speaking, it is an inverted effect of the phantasy. It is the subject who determines himself as object, in his encounter with the division of subjectivity' (Jacques Lacan, *The Seminar of Jacques Lacan, Book XI: The Four Fundamental Concepts of Psychoanalysis*, trans. Alan Sheridan [London and New York: W. W. Norton and Company, 1998], 185).

26. This claim is made on the basis of the connection between the 'act of love' and perversion as it appears on the male side: 'The act of love is the male's polymorphous perversion, in the case of speaking beings' (Lacan, *Seminar XX*, 72).

27. Ibid., 78; see also, Copjec, *Read My Desire*, 214.

28. Most explicitly: 'But, and this is the whole point, she has different ways of approaching the phallus and of keeping it for herself. It's not because she is not-wholly in the phallic function that she is not there at all. She is *not* not at all there. She is there in full (*à plein*). But there is something more (*en plus*)' (Lacan, *Seminar XX*, 74). On the topic of feminine *jouissance* in Lacan's *Seminar XX*, I strongly rely on Lorenzo Chiesa's reading, which fits that of Copjec's but also makes some crucial steps further (see Lorenzo Chiesa, *The Not-Two: Logic and God in Lacan* [Cambridge, MA: MIT Press, 2016], 1–21).

29. Lacan, *Seminar XX*, 74.

30. Copjec, *Read My Desire*, 235.

31. For the sake of clarity, it is necessary to cite the whole categorisation of *jouissance* in *Seminar XX* as developed by Chiesa (note the homophony between Lacan's terms *étrange* [strange] and *être-ange* [being-an-angel]): '(a) masculine phallic *jouissance*, which in attempting to totalise enjoyment uncovers its very nontotalisability; (b) feminine phallic *jouissance*, or *jouissance étrange*, which is nontotalisation *inherent and immanent to* the thwarted process of totalising enjoyment, as well as mutually dependent on

it; (c) *a*sexual and mythical *jouissance être-ange*, which is the fantasy of masculine phallic jouissance as totalised (projected onto woman or adopted by her, as we shall see); (d) *non*sexual but really existing feminine *jouissance stricto sensu*, which is a mystical supplement of phallic *jouissance*. In order to refrain from locating it on a transcendent level, we could call it "*non*totalisability"; feminine *jouissance stricto sensu* is, for Lacan, beyond the phallus (and its inherent nontotalisation), but this beyond does not ex-sist without referring to the phallus' (Chiesa, *The Not-Two*, 4).

32. Lacan formulates this point in a marginal remark in his 'Preface' to the French translation of Frank Wedekind's play *Spring Awakening*: 'Woman [*La* femme] as the version of the Father couldn't configure herself otherwise than as *Father-version* [*Père-version*]' (Jacques Lacan, 'Préface à *L'éveil du printemps*', *Ornicar?* 39 [1986]: 7).

Conclusion

This book has not simply been about perversion but about the implications perversion has for the critique of ontology in the works of Gilles Deleuze, Giorgio Agamben, and Jacques Lacan. Already the very fact that we centred our discussion on these three theoretical enterprises implies an unconventional view on perversion, which has been analysed in this book not simply as a social critique but rather as an ambiguous structure which is read differently by the aforementioned thinkers and has different implications for their respective critiques of classical ontology. To begin with, we saw that Deleuze's discovery of Masoch's literature and his peculiar articulation of masochism enabled the former to argue for an 'irreducible dissymmetry' between sadism and masochism, that is, for a diverging difference between two 'basic perversions'. Such a differentiating reading of masochism with regard to sadism fully corresponds to Deleuze's own concept of difference as developed, for instance, in his masterpiece *Difference and Repetition*. The masochistic theatre described in Masoch's novels is also in accordance with the Deleuzian theatre of simulacrum—an essential figure in the task of 'overturning Platonism' that Nietzsche appointed to philosophy. No wonder that Foucault, in his review of Deleuze's *The Logic of Sense* and *Difference and Repetition*, praised the former's philosophy as a 'theatre'. If Deleuze in his collective works with Guattari tries to radicalise his initial view on perversion—via the rejection of pleasure and the invention of the body without organs, which consists of the immanentisation of desire within the 'plane of consistency'—this radicalisation still maintains his original view on perversion as a structure 'without the Other'.

Surprisingly or not, Agamben's own critique of classical metaphysics, which he constantly argues is structured as biopolitics, also owes much to Deleuze's take on perversion. As we tried to show, Agamben employs fetishistic disavowal as a privileged weapon against the metaphysics of signification and modern semiology—associating disavowal with the ancient speech of the Sphinx and semiology with the Oedipal deciphering of the riddle of the Sphinx. In a very Deleuzian, anti-Freudian move, he also positions psychoanalysis on the side of such an Oedipal operation insofar as he maintains that psychoanalysis translates the enigmatic message into the manifest word without ever thinking the bar that separates the signifier from the signified. What is more, the very Deleuzean distinction between sadism and masochism is actually mirrored in Agamben's distinction between the sovereign virtual state of exception and the Benjaminian state of exception of the messianic event. Beyond Agamben's problematic discussion of sadomasochism as a position in which the torturer and the bare life of *homo sacer* are bound together in a relation of 'complicity', the masochistic position (as anti-dialectically opposed to the logic of sadistic biopolitical anarchic institution) reappears metonymically precisely in Agamben's figure of the Messiah. No wonder, again, that in defining the messianic event, Agamben has recourse to the seventeenth-century messianic movement led by Sabbatai Zevi who also serves as a political inspiration of Masoch's own writings.

So what Deleuze and Agamben share on a very general level is precisely an animus against the sadistic position, which they both associate with the figure of the father and with the logic of sovereignty, and which can be counteracted precisely via the figure of the masochist and the operation of fetishistic disavowal. Moreover, both Deleuze and Agamben think such an anti-sovereign and anti-paternal position in the vitalist terms of the form-of-life, which is regarded as radically antithetical to the symbolic forms of human existence. Translating this into more Freudian terms, we argued that such a vitalist position corresponds precisely to the idea of 'polymorphous perversion' which (fantasmatically) posits the drives at the pre-Oedipal level. In summary, this position ultimately consists of an attempt to, as Alenka Zupančič points out, cleanly separate enjoyment from sexuality (that is, from the phallus and castration): recall again here Deleuze's idea of the masochist as a 'new man devoid of sexual love'.

Following Freud's discovery of the unconscious, which amounts not simply to unconscious content, but rather to the gap set up by primal repression (the repression of the primal signifier which implies the lack in the symbolic Other), I have finally argued that Lacanian psychoanalysis provides an alternative thinking of perversion with respect to the vitalism of Deleuze and Agamben. As we saw, such an articulation of the unconscious introduces a third dimension into being. Lacan articulated this point in terms of the 'unrealised', which goes beyond the being/nonbeing opposition. Perhaps most importantly, the Freudian-Lacanian drives are fixed by the point of primal repression and circulate around it, which implies that they are not free floating. Such an invention of the unconscious, and of the fundamental role the Freudian hypothesis of primal repression has in its constitution, enables us to (a) distinguish between the pre-Oedipal and pre-linguistic levels in the human psyche in the way Miller proposes and, relatedly, (b) to distinguish between the structure of the drive and that of perversion. To argue, as Lacan does, that the drive is irreducible to the structure of perversion also implies the dissociation between the drive and the superego. The latter distinction is also a cornerstone of Lacanian ethics of psychoanalysis. However, this in turn also comprises a radically denaturalised (nonbiological) view of the drive itself. If the task of psychoanalysis is to detach the symbolic in the form of the barred Other from the imaginary (object *a*) in the act of traversing the fundamental fantasy, it is thus clear that this act does not result in the complete abolition of the Other or in the untying of the drive. The pre-Oedipal drives are, to recall Miller's wonderful formulation, not pre-linguistic drives or 'raw' but 'cooked', that is, they are shaped by the primally repressed signifier (ontological negativity). For Lacan, what comes to name the final attempt to disavow the gap in the Other, thus keeping the bond between imaginary and the symbolic together, is precisely perversion as *père-version*, as an emergency 'call to the father'.

***

What, to conclude, might be the ontological future of perversion? To be sure, I think the very least a return to perversion requires is a rethinking of the differences within and between the vast bodies of work signed in the names Deleuze, Agamben, and Lacan. It is clear, for instance, that the vast field of Deleuze studies still tends to artificially distinguish between Deleuze's treatise on masochism and his early ontological project of *Difference and Repetition* and *The Logic of Sense*—notwithstanding the fact that he wrote these three masterpieces in exactly the same period between 1967 and 1969. Perhaps more astonishing is the way in which Agamben's early account of perversion in the book *Stanzas* is—with few exceptions—almost entirely unthematised in the body of secondary literature, even though Agamben himself clearly refers to perversion throughout his *Homo Sacer* project.

To the contrary, Lacanian psychoanalysis and especially contemporary philosophical readings of Lacan have thematised perversion in a more systematic way, although rarely in direct relation to Lacan's criticism of ontology. A more 'ontologically oriented' reading of Lacan has only started to emerge in the past ten years or so, not only in the works of Alain Badiou and Slavoj Žižek but of Alenka Zupančič, Lorenzo Chiesa, Adrian Johnston, and some others. In this spirit, this book has thus tried to cut through the aforementioned philosophical fields by introducing perversion as a question which is inextricably connected and immanent to critical ontological projects of Deleuze, Agamben, and Lacan.

By moving from considering perversion barely as a social critique or cultural (sexual) phenomenon to considering it as the central question of ontology, this book has not only shown how Lacan's theory of perversion moves beyond the residual vitalism of Deleuze and Agamben but also sought to demonstrate how perversion and especially the distinction between sadism and masochism underpin the critical renewal of social ontology for which Agamben and Deleuze powerfully argue. In this way, this book will—hopefully—remind future scholarship that, just as social ontology is in some sense perverse, every perverse theatre should be seen also as a fundamentally ontological phenomenon.

Bibliography

Agamben, Giorgio. *Stanzas: Word and Phantasm in Western Culture*. Translated by Ronald L. Martinez. Minneapolis and London: University of Minnesota Press, 1993.
———. *The Coming Community*. Translated by Michael Hardt. Minneapolis and London: University of Minnesota Press, 1993.
———. *Homo Sacer: Sovereign Power and Bare Life*. Translated by Daniel Heller-Roazen. Stanford, CA: Stanford University Press, 1998.
———. *Remnants of Auschwitz: The Witness and the Archive*. Translated by Daniel Heller-Roazen. New York: Zone Books, 1999.
———. 'The Messiah and the Sovereign: The Problem of Law in Walter Benjamin'. In *Potentialities: Collected Essays in Philosophy*, translated by Daniel Heller-Roazen, 160–74. Stanford, CA: Stanford University Press, 2000.
———. 'Bartleby, or On Contingency'. In *Potentialities: Collected Essays in Philosophy*, translated by Daniel Heller-Roazen, 243–71. Stanford, CA: Stanford University Press, 2000.
———. 'Absolute Immanence'. In *Potentialities: Collected Essays in Philosophy*, translated by Daniel Heller-Roazen, 220–39. Stanford, CA: Stanford University Press, 2000.
———. *State of Exception*. Translated by Kevin Attell. Chicago: University of Chicago Press, 2005.
———. *The Time That Remains: A Commentary on the Letter to the Romans*. Translated by Patricia Dailey. Stanford, CA: Stanford University Press, 2005.
———. *Profanations*. Translated by Jeff Fort. New York: Zone Books, 2007.
———. 'K'. In *The Work of Giorgio Agamben: Law, Literature, Life*, edited by Justin Clemens, Nicholas Heron, and Alex Murray, 13–27. Edinburgh: Edinburgh University Press, 2008.
———. *'What Is an Apparatus?' and Other Essays*. Translated by David Kishik and Stefan Pedatella. Stanford, CA: Stanford University Press, 2009.
———. 'La potenza del pensiero'. In *La potenza del pensiero—saggi e conferenze*, 281–96. Vicenza: Neri Pozza, 2010.
———. *The Kingdom and the Glory: For a Theological Genealogy of Economy and Government*. Translated by Lorenzo Chiesa (with Matteo Mandarini). Stanford, CA: Stanford University Press, 2011.
———. *The Use of Bodies*. Translated by Adam Kotsko. Stanford, CA: Stanford University Press, 2016.
Alliez, Éric. 'Deleuze with Masoch'. Translated by Alberto Toscano. In *Deleuze and Psychoanalysis: Philosophical Essays on Deleuze's Debate with Psychoanalysis*, edited by Leen de Bolle, 117–30. Leuven: Leuven University Press, 2010.
Attell, Kevin. 'An Esoteric Dossier: Agamben and Derrida Read Saussure'. *ELH* 76, no. 4 (2009): 821–46.
———. *Giorgio Agamben: Beyond the Threshold of Deconstruction*. New York: Fordham University Press, 2015.
Badiou, Alain. *Deleuze: The Clamour of Being*. Translated by Louise Burchill. Minneapolis and London: University of Minnesota Press, 2000.
Balmès, François. *Dieu, le sexe et la vérité*. Paris: Erès, 2007.
Benjamin, Walter. 'Theses on the Philosophy of History'. In *Illuminations*, translated by Harry Zohn, edited by Hannah Arendt, 253–64. New York: Schocken Books, 1968.
Bradley, Arthur. *Derrida's* Of Grammatology. Bloomington and Indianapolis: Indiana University Press, 2008.

———. 'In the Sovereign Machine: Sovereignty, Governmentality, Automaticity'. *Journal for Cultural Research* (2018): online first, 1–19.

Bryant, Levi R. *Difference and Givenness: Deleuze's Transcendental Empiricism and the Ontology of Immanence*. Evanston, IL: Northwestern University Press, 2008.

Chiesa, Lorenzo. *Subjectivity and Otherness*. Cambridge, MA: MIT Press, 2007.

———. 'Giorgio Agamben's Franciscan Ontology'. *Cosmos and History: The Journal of Natural and Social Philosophy* 5, no. 1 (2009): 105–16.

———. 'The World of Desire: Lacan between Evolutionary Biology and Psychoanalytic Theory'. *Filozofski vestnik* 30, no. 2 (2009): 83–112.

———. '*Jouissance* in Lacan's Seminar XX: Prolegomena to a New Reading'. In *The Care of Life: Transdisciplinary Perspectives in Bioethics and Biopolitics*, edited by Miguel de Beistegui, Giuseppe Bianco, and Marjorie Gracieuse, 295–308. London and New York: Rowman & Littlefield International, 2014.

———. *The Not-Two: Logic and God in Lacan*. Cambridge, MA: MIT Press, 2016.

———. 'Exalted Obscenity and the Lawyer of God: Lacan, Deleuze and the Baroque'. In *Lacan and Deleuze: A Disjunctive Synthesis*, edited by Boštjan Nedoh and Andreja Zevnik, 141–62. Edinburgh: Edinburgh University Press, 2017.

Chiesa, Lorenzo, and Frank Ruda. 'The Event of Language as Force of Life: Agamben's Linguistic Vitalism'. *Angelaki* 16, no. 3 (2011): 163–80.

Collett, Guillaume. *The Psychoanalysis of Sense: Deleuze and the Lacanian School*. Edinburgh: Edinburgh University Press, 2016.

Copjec, Joan. *Read My Desire: Lacan Against the Historicists*. Second edition. London and New York: Verso, 2015 [1994].

Crockett, Clayton. *Deleuze Beyond Badiou: Ontology, Multiplicity, and Event*. New York: Columbia University Press, 2013.

Deleuze, Gilles. *The Logic of Sense*. Translated by Mark Lester with Charles Stivale. London: The Athlone Press, 1990.

———. 'Coldness and Cruelty'. In *Masochism: Coldness and Cruelty and Venus in Furs*, translated by Jean McNeil, edited by Gilles Deleuze and Leopold von Sacher-Masoch, 9–138. New York: Zone Books, 1991.

———. *Difference and Repetition*. Translated by Paul Patton. New York: Columbia University Press, 1994.

———. *Essays Critical and Clinical*. Translated by Daniel W. Smith and Michael A. Greco. Minneapolis and London: University of Minnesota Press, 1997.

———. 'Postscript on Control Societies'. In *Negotiations 1972–1990*, translated by Martin Joughin, 178–82. New York: Columbia University Press, 1997.

Deleuze, Gilles, and Félix Guattari. *Kafka: Toward a Minor Literature*. Translated by Dana Polan. Minneapolis and London: University of Minnesota Press, 1986.

———. *A Thousand Plateaus: Capitalism and Schizophrenia*. Translated by Brian Massumi. Minneapolis and London: University of Minnesota Press, 1987.

———. *What Is Philosophy?* Translated by Graham Burchell and Hugh Tomlinson. London: Verso, 1994.

Derrida, Jacques. 'Before the Law'. In *Acts of Literature*, translated by Avital Ronell, edited by Derek Attridge. London and New York: Routledge, 1991.

de Saussure, Ferdinand. *Course in General Linguistics*. Translated by Wade Baskin. New York: McGraw-Hill, 1966.

Dolar, Mladen. *A Voice and Nothing More*. Cambridge, MA: MIT Press, 2006.

Elden, Stuart. 'Land, Terrain, Territory'. *Progress in Human Geography* 34, no. 6 (2010): 799–817.

Esposito, Roberto. *Immunitas. Protection and Negation of Life*. Translated by Zakiya Hanafi. Cambridge, MA, and Malden: Polity Press, 2011.

Foucault, Michel. 'Theatrum Philosophicum'. In *Aesthetics, Method, and Epistemology* (Essential Works of Foucault 1954–1984, Volume Two), translated by Robert Hurely and others, edited by James D. Faubion, 343–68. New York: The New Press, 1998.

Freud, Sigmund. 'Three Essays on the Theory of Sexuality'. In *The Standard Edition of the Complete Psychological Works of Sigmund Freud, Vol. VII*, edited by James Strachey, 123–245. London: Vintage, 2001.

———. 'On Narcissism: An Introduction'. In *The Standard Edition of the Complete Psychological Works of Sigmund Freud, Vol. XIV*, edited by James Strachey, 67–102. London: Vintage, 2001.

———. 'Instincts and Their Vicissitudes'. In *The Standard Edition of the Complete Psychological Works of Sigmund Freud, Vol. XIV*, edited by James Strachey, 109–40. London: Vintage, 2001.

———. 'Repression'. In *The Standard Edition of the Complete Psychological Works of Sigmund Freud, Vol. XIV*, edited by James Strachey, 141–58. London: Vintage, 2001.

———. 'Beyond the Pleasure Principle'. In *The Standard Edition of the Complete Psychological Works of Sigmund Freud, Vol. XVIII*, edited by James Strachey, 7–64. London: Vintage, 2001.

———. 'The Ego and the Id'. In *The Standard Edition of the Complete Psychological Works of Sigmund Freud, Vol. XIX*, edited by James Strachey, 1–66. London: Vintage, 2001.

———. 'Inhibitions, Symptoms and Anxiety'. In *The Standard Edition of the Complete Psychological Works of Sigmund Freud, Vol. XX*, edited by James Strachey, 75–175. London: Vintage, 2001.

———. 'Fetishism'. In *The Standard Edition of the Complete Psychological Works of Sigmund Freud, Vol. XXI*, edited by James Strachey, 147–57. London: Vintage, 2001.

Girard, René. *Violence and the Sacred*. Translated by Patrick Gregory. Baltimore, MD: Johns Hopkins University Press, 1979.

Goodchild, Philip. 'Why Is Philosophy So Compromised with God?' In *Deleuze and Religion*, edited by Mary Bryden, 156–66. London and New York: Routledge, 2000.

Grosz, Elizabeth. *Space, Time and Perversion*. London and New York: Routledge, 1995.

Heidegger, Martin. 'The End of Philosophy and the Task of Thinking'. In *Basic Writings*. San Francisco, CA: Harper, 1977.

Hoens, Dominiek. 'Toward a New Perversion: Psychoanalysis'. In *Jacques Lacan and the Other Side of Psychoanalysis: Reflections on Seminar XVII*, edited by Justin Clemens and Russell Grigg, 88–102. Durham, NC, and London: Duke University Press, 2006.

Holland, Eugene. *Nomad Citizenship: Free-Market Communism and the Slow-Motion General Strike*. Minneapolis and London: University of Minnesota Press, 2011.

Johnston, Adrian. *Time Driven: Metapsychology and the Splitting of the Drive*. Evanston, IL: Northwestern University Press, 2005.

———. 'Repetition and Difference: Žižek, Deleuze and Lacanian Drives'. In *Lacan and Deleuze: A Disjunctive Synthesis*, edited by Boštjan Nedoh and Andreja Zevnik, 180–202. Edinburgh: Edinburgh University Press, 2017.

Jöttkandt, Sigi. *First Love: A Phenomenology of the One*. Melbourne: re.press, 2010.

Kafka, Franz. *The Trail*. Translated by Mike Mitchell. Oxford: Oxford University Press, 2009.

Kant, Immanuel. *Critique of Pure Reason*. Translated by Paul Guyer and Allen W. Wood. Cambridge: Cambridge University Press, 1998.

———. *Critique of the Power of Judgment*. Translated by Paul Guyer and Eric Matthews. Cambridge: Cambridge University Press, 2000.

Klepec, Peter. *Vznik subjekta* [The Emergence of the Subject]. Ljubljana: ZRC Publisher, 2004.

———. *Dobičkonosne strasti: Kapitalizem in perverzija 1* [Profitable Passions: Capitalism and Perversion 1]. Ljubljana: Society for Theoretical Psychoanalysis, 2008.

———. 'For Another Lacan–Deleuze Encounter'. In *Lacan and Deleuze: A Disjunctive Synthesis*, edited by Boštjan Nedoh and Andreja Zevnik, 13–31. Edinburgh: Edinburgh University Press, 2017.

Kotsko, Adam. 'Politics and Perversion: Situating Žižek's Paul'. *Journal for Cultural and Religious Theory* 9, no. 2 (2008): 43–52.

Lacan, Jacques. *The Logic of Phantasy, 1966–67*. Unpublished seminar, translated by Cormac Gallagher from unedited French manuscripts. Available at http://www.lacaninireland.com.
———. 'Seminar of 21 January 1975'. In *Feminine Sexuality: Jacques Lacan and the* école freudienne, translated by Jacqueline Rose, edited by Juliet Mitchell and Jacqueline Rose, 162–71. London and New York: W. W. Norton and Co., 1985.
———. 'Préface à *L'éveil du printemps*'. *Ornicar?* 39 (1986): 7–9.
———. 'Introduction to the Names-of-the-Father Seminar'. Translated by Jeffrey Mehlman. *October* 40 (1987): 81–95.
———. *Television*. Translated by Dennis Hollier et al. London and New York: W. W. Norton and Co., 1990.
———. *Le Seminair, livre IV: La relation d'objet*. Paris: Seuil, 1994.
———. *The Seminar of Jacques Lacan, Book XI: The Four Fundamental Concepts of Psychoanalysis*. Translated by Alan Sheridan. London and New York: W. W. Norton and Co., 1998.
———. *The Seminar of Jacques Lacan, Book XX: Encore, On Feminine Sexuality, the Limits of Love and Knowledge*. Translated by Bruce Fink. London and New York: W. W. Norton and Co., 1999.
———. *Le séminaire, livre XVIII: D'un discours qui ne serait pas du semblant*. Paris: Seuil, 2006.
———. 'The Mirror Stage as Formative of the *I* Function as Revealed in Psychoanalytic Experience'. In *Écrits: The First Complete Edition in English*, translated by Bruce Fink, 75–81. London and New York: W. W. Norton and Co., 2006.
———. 'Aggressiveness in Psychoanalysis'. In *Écrits: The First Complete Edition in English*, translated by Bruce Fink, 82–101. London and New York: W. W. Norton and Co., 2006.
———. 'The Instance of the Letter in the Unconscious, or Reason Since Freud'. In *Écrits: The First Complete Edition in English*, translated by Bruce Fink, 412–41. London and New York: W. W. Norton and Co., 2006.
———. 'Kant with Sade'. In *Écrits: The First Complete Edition in English*, translated by Bruce Fink, 645–68. London and New York: W. W. Norton and Co., 2006.
———. 'The Subversion of the Subject and the Dialectic of Desire in the Freudian Unconscious'. In *Écrits: The First Complete Edition in English*, translated by Bruce Fink, 671–702. London and New York: W. W. Norton and Co., 2006.
———. *The Seminar of Jacques Lacan, Book XVII: The Other Side of Psychoanalysis*. Translated by Russell Grigg. London and New York: W. W. Norton and Co., 2007.
———. *The Seminar of Jacques Lacan, Book X: Anxiety*. Translated by A. R. Price. Cambridge, MA, and Malden: Polity Press, 2014.
Miller, Jacques-Alain. 'On Perversion'. In *Reading Seminars I and II: Lacan's Return to Freud*, edited by Richard Feldstein, Bruce Fink, and Maire Jaanus, 306–20. New York: State University of New York Press, 1996.
———. 'Paradigms of *Jouissance*'. *Lacanian Ink* 17 (2000): 8–47.
———. 'Jacques Lacan's Seminar on *Anxiety*'. Translated by Barbara P. Fulks. *Lacanian Ink* 26 (2005): 8–72.
Nancy, Jean-Luc. *L'imperativo categorico*. Torino: Besa Editrice, 2007.
Nedoh, Boštjan. 'Kafka's Land-Surveyor K.: Agamben's Anti-Muselmann'. *Angelaki* 16, no. 3 (2011): 149–61.
———. 'When the Tiger Leaps into the Past: Holocaust, History and Messianic Materialism in Giorgio Agamben, Walter Benjamin and László Nemes' *Son of Saul*'. *Angelaki* 24, no. 5 (forthcoming).
Prozorov, Sergei. 'Why Giorgio Agamben Is an Optimist'. *Philosophy and Social Criticism* 36, no. 9 (2010): 1053–73.
———. 'Living *à la Mode*: Form-of-life and Democratic Biopolitics in Giorgio Agamben's *The Use of Bodies*'. *Philosophy and Social Criticism* 43, no. 2 (2017): 144–63.
Riha, Rado. *Kant in drugi kopernikanski obrat v filozofiji* [Kant and the Second Copernican Turn in Philosophy]. Ljubljana: ZRC Publisher, 2012.

Sacher-Masoch, Leopold von. *Jewish Life: Tales from Nineteenth-Century Europe*. Translated by Virginia L. Lewis. Riverside, CA: Ariadne Press, 2002.

Santner, Eric L. *The Royal Remains: The People's Two Bodies and the Endgames of Sovereignty*. Chicago: University of Chicago Press, 2011.

———. *The Weight of All Flesh: On the Subject-Matter of Political Economy* (The Berkeley Tanner Lectures). Oxford and New York: Oxford University Press, 2016.

———. 'The Rebranding of Sovereignty in the Age of Trump: Toward a Critique of Manatheism'. In *Sovereignty, Inc.*, edited by Eric L. Santner, Aaron Schuster, and William Mazzarella. Chicago: University of Chicago Press, forthcoming.

Schuster, Aaron. *The Trouble with Pleasure: Deleuze and Psychoanalysis*. Cambridge, MA: MIT Press, 2016.

Smith, Daniel W. 'The Concept of the Simulacrum: Deleuze and the Overturning of Platonism'. *Continental Philosophy Review* 38, no. 1–2 (2005): 89–123.

Tomšič, Samo. *The Capitalist Unconscious: Marx and Lacan*. London and New York: Verso, 2015.

Troha, Tadej. 'Kafka and the Irreversible'. *Critical Engagements: A Journal of Criticism and Theory* 8, no. 1–2 (2014): 157–79.

———. 'On Ambivalence'. *Problemi International* 1, no.1 (2017): 217–44.

Watkin, William. *Agamben and Indifference: A Critical Overview*. London and New York: Rowman & Littlefield International, 2014.

Widder, Nathan. 'The Rights of Simulacra: Deleuze and the Univocity of Being'. *Continental Philosophy Review* 34, no. 4 (2001): 437–53.

Zevnik, Andreja. *Lacan, Deleuze and World Politics: Rethinking the Ontology of the Political Subject*. London and New York: Routledge, 2016.

———. 'Kant avec Sade: Ethics Entrapped in Perversions of Law and Politics'. In *Jacques Lacan between Psychoanalysis and Politics*, edited by Samo Tomšič and Andreja Zevnik, 217–32. London and New York: Routledge, 2016.

Zupančič, Alenka. *Ethics of the Real: Kant and Lacan*. New York and London: Verso, 2000.

———. 'On Repetition'. *Sats—Nordic Journal of Philosophy* 8, no. 1 (2007): 27–44.

———. 'Biopolitics, Sexuality and the Unconscious'. *Paragraph* 39, no. 1 (2016): 49–64.

———. *What* Is *Sex?* Cambridge, MA: MIT Press, 2017.

Žižek, Slavoj. *The Puppet and the Dwarf: The Perverse Core of Christianity*. Cambridge, MA: MIT Press, 2003.

———. *The Parallax View*. Cambridge, MA: MIT Press, 2006.

———. *In Defence of Lost Causes*. London and New York: Verso, 2008.

———. 'From Job to Christ: A Paulinian Reading of Chesterton'. In *St. Paul among the Philosophers*, edited by John D. Caputo and Linda Martín Alcoff, 39–58. Bloomington and Indianapolis: Indiana University Press, 2009.

———. 'The Fear of Four Words: A Modest Plea for the Hegelian Reading of Christianity'. In *Monstrosity of Christ: Paradox or Dialectics?*, edited by Creston Davis, 24–108. Cambridge, MA: MIT Press, 2009.

Index

www.ingramcontent.com/pod-product-compliance
Ingram Content Group UK Ltd.
Pitfield, Milton Keynes, MK11 3LW, UK
UKHW040910190926
475560UK00008B/92

9 781786 605511